T0369653

The Primacy of Metaphysics

Christopher Peacocke worked for many years in Oxford and London. He was successively a Prize Fellow of All Souls College, a Tutorial Fellow of New College, Susan Stebbing Professor of Philosophy at Kings College London, and finally for twelve years Waynflete Professor of Metaphysical Philosophy at Magdalen College, Oxford. In 2000 he became Professor of Philosophy at New York University. He is currently Johnsonian Professor of Philosophy at Columbia University and Honorary Fellow at the Institute of Philosophy at the School of Advanced Study in the University of London.

also published by

OXFORD UNIVERSITY PRESS

The Mirror of the World
Subjects, Consciousness, and
Self-Consciousness
Christopher Peacocke

Truly Understood
Christopher Peacocke

The Realm of Reason
Christopher Peacocke

Being Known
Christopher Peacocke

Praise for *The Primacy of Metaphysics*

'*The Primacy of Metaphysics* is a rich work, handsomely repaying multiple readings. It testifies to Peacocke's creativity and philosophical seriousness.'

Mark Johnston, *Philosophical Studies*

'this book is just as remarkable for its breadth...Most philosophers of mind, language, epistemology, and metaphysics are likely to find insights that bear on their research.'

Jacob Beck, *European Journal of Philosophy*

'the book develops a distinctive and novel position, which is often plausible and always interesting.'

Øystein Linnebo, *Philosophical Studies*

Jacket image acquired through the Lillie P. Bliss Bequest, and the Henry Ittleson, A. Conger Goodyear, Mr. and Mrs. Robert Sinclair Funds, and the Anna Erickson Levene Bequest given in memory of her husband, Dr. Phoebus Aaron Theodor Levene.

The Primacy
of Metaphysics

Christopher Peacocke

OXFORD
UNIVERSITY PRESS

OXFORD
UNIVERSITY PRESS

Great Clarendon Street, Oxford, OX2 6DP,
United Kingdom

Oxford University Press is a department of the University of Oxford.
It furthers the University's objective of excellence in research, scholarship,
and education by publishing worldwide. Oxford is a registered trade mark of
Oxford University Press in the UK and in certain other countries

© Christopher Peacocke 2019

The moral rights of the author have been asserted

First published 2019
Published in paperback 2021

All rights reserved. No part of this publication may be reproduced, stored in
a retrieval system, or transmitted, in any form or by any means, without the
prior permission in writing of Oxford University Press, or as expressly permitted
by law, by licence or under terms agreed with the appropriate reprographics
rights organization. Enquiries concerning reproduction outside the scope of the
above should be sent to the Rights Department, Oxford University Press, at the
address above

You must not circulate this work in any other form
and you must impose this same condition on any acquirer

Published in the United States of America by Oxford University Press
198 Madison Avenue, New York, NY 10016, United States of America

British Library Cataloguing in Publication Data
Data available

Library of Congress Cataloging in Publication Data
Data available

ISBN 978-0-19-883557-8 (Hbk.)
ISBN 978-0-19-289716-9 (Pbk.)

Links to third party websites are provided by Oxford in good faith and
for information only. Oxford disclaims any responsibility for the materials
contained in any third party website referenced in this work.

For Terry, Alexander, and Antonia

Preface

The broad outline of the ideas in this book occurred to me early in 2008, and was first presented, in exploratory form, at my summer seminar in University College London that year. These ideas were developed in my seminars at Columbia University and UCL, and in lectures and seminars elsewhere, in the following decade. I make my many personal acknowledgements in a separate section below, but I take the opportunity here to thank both of these institutions and those who run them at both departmental and decanal level not just for support, but for their dedication to promoting the integration of research with teaching.

The production of a book presenting this material has taken rather longer than I might have expected, for two reasons. First, the treatment of the self and the first person, which I had originally intended to handle as a special case of the general approach, developed a life of its own. It was too hard to put aside a longer discussion of that always fascinating special case, to which I devoted *The Mirror of the World* (2014). Second, for five years (2011–16) I was successively chair of Columbia's Tenure and Promotion Committee, and the Columbia Philosophy Department. I do not entirely regret the resultant delay in producing the book. Both the central claim of the general material and the treatment of the self and the first person have been modified following second and third thoughts since I was able to return a few years ago to devote undivided attention to the issues.

The claims of this book are highly general, and whether they are true or false, in either case there are wide ramifications. There are ramifications not just for many areas of philosophy, but also for domains in which the considerations of philosophy and the sciences intersect. I touch on some of these in the concluding remarks. A very long book could be written discussing these ramifications. It is a real question whether that would be either a feasible or even a desirable task for one person alone. In any case, and perhaps out of necessity as well as prudence, I have kept the discussion concise.

It is now eighteen years since I left Oxford, departing from a position with 'Metaphysical Philosophy' in its title. Perhaps I can at last offer this material, both to those in the new world and the old, as an attempt at Metaphysical Philosophy.

Contents

Acknowledgements and Sources

In addition to my regular seminars at Columbia and UCL, I presented two series of lectures based on the material presented here, one in the 'Master-Seminar' series at Fribourg University in June 2015, the other at the Institute of Philosophy at the School of Advanced Study in London University in the autumn of 2016. At the Fribourg events, I learned from the comments of Martine Nida-Rümelin, Laura Schroeter, and Gianfranco Soldati, whom I also thank warmly for the invitation to speak there. In London, I had the benefit of many exchanges, and extensive discussion of earlier versions of some of these chapters, with Bill Brewer and Nick Shea.

Chapter 1 was presented at the Mind and Language Seminar at NYU in the spring of 2013. It was only later that I fully appreciated the change in position needed to address the highly perceptive comments of the seminar organizers, Stephen Neale and Stephen Schiffer. I hope the treatment of the no-priority cases in Chapter 1 meets the needs they discussed. This chapter, along with some material on magnitudes, was also presented in Salvador, Brazil, at the 2013 meeting of the Inter-American Congress of Philosophy. Comments there from David Chalmers, Michael Devitt, Paul Horwich, and Peter Railton were particularly helpful.

Chapters 2 and 3 grew out of some earlier work on magnitudes (Peacocke 2015), and I repeat my thanks to those acknowledged there: David Albert, Philip Kitcher, and Robert Stalnaker. Extended comments from Tyler Burge and Hartry Field greatly influenced that earlier material. I also learned from the comments and suggestions of David Chalmers, Geoff Lee, Tim Maudlin, and François Recanati at a joint NYU/ENS (Institut Jean Nicod) meeting in Paris in 2015. The expanded treatment here involving analogue computation and representation was presented in a seminar at CSMN in Oslo in October 2016, where Sebastian Watzl's suggestions influenced the present text. Most recently, some of the material was presented at Jacob Beck's workshop 'Perceptual Capacities and Magnitudes' at York University, Toronto, in May 2018. My commentators there were Geoff Lee and Corey Maley, from both of whom I learned more than I have been able to include here. Their developing work will complement what I offer here. Discussions with Jacob Beck, Casey O'Callaghan, and Diana Raffman at the Toronto meeting have also influenced me.

An earlier version of Chapter 3 appeared as 'Temporal perception, magnitudes, and phenomenal externalism' (Peacocke 2017a). My thanks to Ian Phillips for valuable comments on that earlier version, and to Susanna Schellenberg, and members of her seminar, for discussion at my presentation to her Marc Sanders Seminar at Rutgers in 2015.

Chapter 4 on the self and the first-person way of thinking has had a rather longer evolution. As I noted in the Preface, the initial material from which my book *The Mirror of the World* (2014a) developed was originally intended as just one part of a book on the primacy of metaphysics. In fact I came to think that the position in that book needed some further development. I undertook some of that development in 'Philosophical reflections on the first person, the body, and agency' (Peacocke 2017b), prepared for the workshop in Copenhagen organized by Frédérique de Vignemont and Adrian Alsmith. There I was greatly assisted by discussion with Frédérique de Vignemont, with my commentator José Bermúdez, and with Patrick Haggard. Further meetings in 2016 at Harvard and in London produced significant observations from Matthew Boyle, Michael Martin, Tony Marcel, Lucy O'Brien, Sebastian Rödl, Hong Yu Wong—and from Patrick Haggard for a second time. Issues very closely related to those addressed in this chapter are pursued in the Symposium on *The Mirror of the World* in *Analysis*, and I have been helped by reflecting on the contributions to that Symposium made by Naomi Eilan (2016), Karen Neander (2016), and Susanna Schellenberg (2016).

In a further sign either of the apparently inexhaustible interest of the topics of the self and the first person, or of my own inadequacy to that subject matter, or both, I came to think that a deeper and more general understanding of the relation between mental events and ownership ought to be given than I had developed in *The Mirror of the World*. A very welcome opportunity to present some further points on that *ur*-issue, and also to address his own radical views on the matter, arose from an invitation from Mark Johnston to speak at his seminar in Princeton in the spring of 2017. I find myself again thanking him for valuable extended discussion of these issues. The inductive evidence is overwhelming that much more will need to be said on the metaphysics of subjects and the first person.

Chapter 5 on numbers offers a way, very different from the models of the preceding chapters, in which a metaphysics-first view of a domain can be correct without causal interaction with elements of the domain. I came to the view outlined here by reflecting on Frege's views on number, on Crispin Wright's 1983 treatment of the issues, and by Kit Fine's 2002 discussion. Like the principle-based treatment of metaphysical necessity that I offered in *Being Known* (1999), the treatment of numbers in this chapter proposes a noncausal but nevertheless metaphysics-first model of understanding. I am especially grateful to Øystein Linnebo on three counts: for substantive discussions of these issues; for his thoughts on the range of conceivable positions; and also for his guidance and advice on the recent literature. Ian Rumfitt's detailed comments on an earlier draft of this chapter have helped me, on this as on other philosophical topics.

In Chapter 6 I return to the issue of the principles that explain why the limits of intelligibility lie where they do. I claim that we can find an answer to this question by reflecting on the constraints on the proper relations between genuine concepts and their subject matter. This has long been an interest of mine, as it probably is for anyone drawn to philosophy at all. I hope the argument of this chapter can contribute to an explanation of what is correct, if anything, in my earlier diagnosis of the issues about the limits of intelligibility (1988). In addition to the lecture series mentioned above, the material of this last chapter was presented in the years 2014–16 at the University of Barcelona, the University of California at Davis, the Philosophical Society at Oxford University, and Paris Sciences et Lettres (EHESS). My thanks for very extensive discussions of these problems to David Albert, Bill Brewer, and Shamik Dasgupta, each of whom have made me rethink my position at one point or another. I have also been influenced by the comments at the presentations in 2014–16 from Manuel Garcia-Carpintero, Pascal Engel, Uriah Kriegel, Robert May, Joelle Proust, François Recanati, and Timothy Williamson.

As the reader can infer, I have had significant advice from many quarters. This book would be much the worse without the contributions of our generous philosophical community. That community includes the two anonymous referees for Oxford University Press, whose exceptional critical acumen, evident knowledge of the field, and helpful expository suggestions have much improved the text. Finally, as with my previous four books, Peter Momtchiloff's patience, standards, and devotion to philosophy have provided a supportive background that I suspect is even more important than he or his many authors know.

Introduction

There can be few issues as fundamental as the relation between the metaphysics of some domain and our ways of thinking about it. The issue arises in every area of thought. If the metaphysics of a domain is explanatorily more fundamental than our ways of thinking about it, there should be features of our ways of thinking that are explained by that metaphysics. If the opposite is true, if our ways of thinking are explanatorily more fundamental, then what may seem to be a feature of the metaphysics of the domain in question will really just be projections of our ways of thinking. If neither is prior to the other, then there is some interdependence between the metaphysics and the ways of thinking that needs elucidation.

It is to these issues of explanatory priority that this book is devoted.

A methodology for investigating these issues has to operate both at a general level, and at the level of particular domains and ways of thinking of them.

At the general level, we can ask what individuates a way of thinking, and we can investigate domain-independent constraints on the relations between ways of thinking and what is thought about. That is the general investigation I attempt in Chapter 1 of this book. I reach the conclusion that, for reasons of principle, ways of thinking cannot be explanatorily prior to the metaphysics of the domain. If that conclusion is correct, we are left with two kinds of case: that in which the metaphysics is explanatorily prior (the metaphysics-first case); and that in which neither is explanatorily prior to the other (the no-priority case).

At the level of any particular domain, we need to provide a metaphysics for that domain, and a corresponding elaboration of the domain-specific explanatory relation between the metaphysics so conceived and certain ways of thinking of the domain. In Chapters 2 through 5, I attempt that domain-specific exercise for various subject matters. I consider the domains of perceptible extensive magnitudes; of time; of the self; and of numbers. In each of these cases, I argue for a metaphysics-first view, a view that is differently realized in each case, radically so in the noncausal case of our ways of thinking of numbers.

I should have arrived at the general idea of a metaphysics-first treatment of certain domains and ways of thinking much earlier than I actually did. In my book *Being Known* (1999), I aimed to say how we can integrate the metaphysics and epistemology of various domains of philosophical interest. The integration proposed in that book proceeded by elaborating the required relations between the metaphysics of the domain and the nature of the intentional contents of the states justifying beliefs about the domain. What I failed to notice back then was that in every case treated in that book, once the epistemology and the metaphysics are properly formulated and integrated along the lines suggested there, the result was to attribute to the metaphysics an explanatory priority. One of the factors that focused my mind on the issue of explanatory priority was the publication of Michael Dummett's book *The Logical Basis of Metaphysics* (1991), which gives an explicit rejection, on entirely general grounds, of metaphysics-first and no-priority views. Dummett's is a meaning or content-first view, according to which metaphysics can have no role in philosophical explanation. Crispin Wright (1987) had also earlier expressed doubts about the explanatory powers of metaphysics. The present book is in fundamental disagreement with the position of Dummett and Wright on these issues. In fact, the example with which Dummett introduces his own discussion in that book, the case of time, I myself regard as one of the strongest counterexamples to his general position (see Chapter 3). Nonetheless, one of the many ways in which I am deeply indebted to Dummett is for his crystallization and formulation of the issues in that book. Similarly, I have debts to Wright for discussions of some of these issues many decades ago in Oxford.

The first five chapters of the present book are devoted to saying what a good account of the relations between a domain and ways of thinking of it should look like. They set constraints on an adequate account, and try to show how those constraints are realized in different subject matters. In the final chapter of the book, I argue that reflection on these constraints can generate a positive account of the limits of intelligibility. Various spurious hypotheses and conceptions, widely recognized to be spurious, have that status as spurious because they make it impossible for there to be an account of the relations in which a thinker would have to stand to their proposed domains in order to be employing ways of thinking of the entities they propose.

Many paths lead off from the point reached by the end of the last chapter of the book, and I conclude with some thoughts on further possible directions of travel.

1

Metaphysics and the Theory of Content

1. The Primary Thesis

Some philosophy is concerned with the broad area of the nature of objects or properties of a given kind—material objects, or abstract entities, or mental properties. Some philosophy is concerned with the broad area of the nature of the meaning of sentences, or the content of thoughts and perceptions, and more generally ways of thinking about a given subject matter. The work I present here is concerned with the relation between these two broad areas. How should we conceive of the relation between the nature or metaphysics of a given domain on the one hand, and, on the other, the concepts and ways we represent elements of that domain in thought and language? Is this relation one of dependence? If so, in which direction, and why? Can we gain explanatory insight from reflecting upon the nature of this relation? These are not just familiar questions about how sense determines reference. They are rather questions about sense and its relations to the metaphysics of the references in question.

The questions I am aiming to address have, in one form or another, been in the landscape of the philosophy of language and thought for many decades. Sometimes they have been in sharp focus, sometimes in the background. My aim in this work is twofold: to consider some particular domains in which these issues are of special interest or significance; and to offer in response to these general questions some answers that are intended to apply to any particular domain, and to any particular family of meanings, concepts, or intentional contents. Plausible answers to questions about the relations between the metaphysics of a domain and the ways in which we think about it have ramifications through multiple areas of philosophy, from issues in metaphysics itself, through the theory of mental representation, perception, and epistemology, to principles determining the bounds of legitimate meanings.

We can take it that the task of formulating the metaphysics of any given domain is to characterize the nature of elements in that domain, to say what is constitutive of those entities. Then the general answer I offer to our initial question about the two broad areas I mentioned can be stated in this simple Primary Thesis:

> The metaphysics of a domain is involved in the philosophical explanation of the nature of the meanings of sentences about that domain; and the metaphysics of a domain is involved in the philosophical explanation of the nature of intentional contents (ways of representing) concerning that domain.

So this is a metaphysics-involving thesis.

There are stronger and weaker positions that are committed to the Primary Thesis. But first we had better clarify the Primary Thesis by explaining the many terms of art contained in its statement.

By a 'domain', I mean a range of objects, in the broadest sense, and properties and relations on those objects. By 'the metaphysics of a domain' I mean a theory that states truly what is constitutive of the objects, properties, and relations of that domain—a theory of what makes them the objects, properties, and relations they are. We are not concerned here with what may merely be folk-metaphysics, or a merely mentally represented metaphysics. Those are both genuine and philosophically interesting conceptions of metaphysics, but they are both to be distinguished from what I mean by metaphysics in stating the Primary Thesis. I mean what is really constitutive of the objects, properties, and relations in question. Some feature attributed in the metaphysics of a domain can be explanatory of facts about intentional contents concerning that domain only if the elements of the domain really do have that feature, whether or not ordinary thought represents it as having the feature.

The entities in the domain are at the level of reference, whereas the intentional contents and meanings are at the level of sense. So if, for instance, we are considering the domain of spatial entities and their properties and relations, then the relation between three events of forming an isosceles triangle would be in the relations included in that domain. That relation is to be distinguished from the several ways in which the relation may be given in language or in perception.

Similarly, properties are to be distinguished from concepts, which are ways in which properties are given in thought or language. This is the same conception of properties as outlined in Hilary Putnam's paper 'On Properties' (1975). Of course there exists the special case in which we take as the domain the domain of concepts, notions, or senses themselves, and their properties and relations. But then the intentional contents and meanings mentioned in the Primary Thesis for that special domain will be higher-level concepts of concepts, and concepts of their properties and relations. The Primary Thesis is always a claim about the level of sense, concepts, and notions, on the one hand, and the entities to which these senses, concepts, and notions refer. It is always a thesis to the effect that the metaphysics of entities at the level of reference is explanatory of the nature of entities at the level of sense.

So much by way of explanation of 'domains'; now for 'explanation'. By 'an explanation of the nature of the meaning of sentences' in the statement of the Primary Thesis I mean an explanation that does not merely specify the meanings of expressions in the relevant language, but rather a theory that says, substantively, what it is to understand those expressions. In Michael Dummett's terminology, my concern here is with the theory of meaning in general, rather than meaning-theories for particular languages or fragments of languages (1991: 22). In parallel fashion, by 'an explanation of the nature of intentional contents concerning a domain', I mean a theory that says what it is to be capable of mental states and events containing those intentional contents—to possess or to grasp them, if you will. The intentional contents with which we are concerned here are contents that specify the way some element of the domain is given. These intentional contents are broadly at the level of sense, at the level of ways in which things are given, rather than at the level of reference.

I have stated the Primary Thesis both for concepts and for language. If the theory of concepts is also prior in the order of philosophical explanation to the theory of linguistic meaning, it would suffice to state the thesis for the case of concepts. The thesis for linguistic meaning would then be a consequence of the Primary Thesis for the case of concepts.

The Primary Thesis states a relation of philosophical explanatory involvement of the metaphysics of a domain, in the above sense, in the theory of meaning for expressions of a language for that domain, and in the theory of intentional contents for that domain. By such explanatory involvement for a given domain, I mean that the corresponding theory of meaning and theory of intentional contents in one way or another presupposes that the metaphysics of the domain has certain features.

Such a presupposition can take various forms. One form is that the theory of meaning and intentional contents for the domain requires one who understands the language, or is in mental states with the relevant contents, to be in states whose very nature requires the metaphysics of the domain to have certain properties. For example, the account of understanding or grasp of contents may make essential mention of relations in which a thinker stands to elements of the domain, relations which can be instantiated only if a certain kind of metaphysics is correct for the domain. Another form the presupposition might take is that the theory of meaning or intentional content is correct in its general structure only if a certain metaphysics of the domain is correct. I will illustrate each of these cases later in this work. The kind of presupposition here is not anything to do with conversational presupposition, nor is it anything to do with speech acts more generally. Rather, a theory of understanding or of grasp of a concept presupposes a proposition about the metaphysics of the subject matter of the concept if the full account of understanding or grasp requires the one who understands or grasps to be in states whose nature implies a certain metaphysics of the subject matter. The full account of understanding and of the states implies the correctness of a certain metaphysics. There is absolutely no implication that this metaphysics needs to be known, either explicitly or tacitly, by the subject who understands the relevant expressions, or grasps the concept in question. It is the metaphysics that is involved in the understanding or grasp, not any representation of the metaphysics.

The Primary Thesis is intended to apply only to what is assessable as true or as false. On expressivist views of some region of discourse, sentences in that discourse are said not to be assessable as true or as false. To take a very clear example, simply for the purposes of illustration, Allan Gibbard presents an expressivist view of rationality in his claim, a "first sketch", that "to call something rational is to express one's acceptance of norms that permit it" (1990: 7). On Gibbard's view, "to call something rational is not to state a matter of fact, either truly or falsely" (1990: 8). In particular, to call something rational is not to state that it has the property of being permitted by accepted norms (1990: 8). If Gibbard's treatment of rationality is right, there cannot be such a thing as the metaphysics of rationality. There is no metaphysics for sentences for whose components we do not need a relation of reference. The conditions for applying the Primary Thesis are not met. The scope of the Primary Thesis concerns meanings and contents whose nature involves a relation of reference.

Conversely, whenever there is reference and correspondingly truth-conditions for some part of language or thought, there will be a corresponding metaphysics. Whatever entities and properties are referred to, there must be an account of what makes them the entities and properties they are, and that just is a metaphysics for that domain.

So the Primary Thesis is not committed to the view that for every significant fragment of language there is a corresponding metaphysics. It is committed rather to the view that whenever there is a fragment of language for which there is a relation of reference, and so a metaphysics, then a metaphysics-involving thesis, the Primary Thesis, holds for it.

There is a fundamental division between a stronger and a weaker way in which the Primary Thesis can hold for a given domain.

In *metaphysics-first* cases, the metaphysics of the domain is prior in the order of philosophical explanation of the nature of the meaning of sentences about that domain, and in the explanation of the nature of intentional contents concerning that domain. It seems to me that for a large range of domains, the metaphysics-first view is correct. There is a case to be made that the metaphysics-first examples include not only the domains of space and time, and the corresponding perceptual contents concerning them, but also a wide range of domains of conscious mental states, and mental contents and language concerning them.

In *no-priority* cases, by contrast, the metaphysics of the domain on the one hand, and intentional contents and the meanings of sentences about that domain on the other, are each involved in the philosophical explanation of the other. The metaphysics and the contents and meanings are constitutively coeval; neither is absolutely prior in the order of philosophical explanation. We might describe these as cases of entanglement of the metaphysics with the theory of concepts and of meaning.

The Primary Thesis of metaphysical involvement is then intended to cover all cases in which we have truth-assessable contents, and those cases subdivide into the metaphysics-first cases and the no-priority cases:

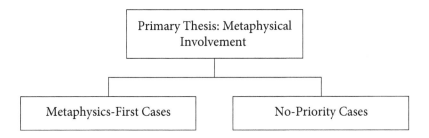

The Primary Thesis stands opposed what to we can call *meaning-first* views, which hold that theories of meaning and intentional content concerning a domain are always explanatory prior to the metaphysics of the domain. The meaning-first view is certainly no straw man. The meaning-first view is explicit, or is implied, in the positions of several manifestly important philosophers. The meaning-first view is clearly and explicitly endorsed by Michael Dummett in *The Logical Basis of Metaphysics* (1991). I will be addressing his views in the next section. The meaning-first view is also implied by the position developed in the writings of Robert Brandom, both in his first book, *Making It Explicit: Reasoning, Representing, and Discursive Commitment* (1994), and in his later expositions and development of his views (2000, 2009). Brandom's and Dummett's views differ in other important respects. Dummett (1981) expressed agreement with Frege that the sense of an expression is individuated by the condition for something to be its reference. Brandom, by contrast, holds that reference has no fundamental role to play in the philosophical elucidation of meaning and understanding. On Brandom's view, the metaphysics of what is referred to could hardly be expected to play any part in the philosophical elucidation of meaning and understanding.

We have here then, in summary, three large-scale positions in philosophy that can be assessed for any given domain: the metaphysics-first view, the no-priority view, and the meaning-first view. It is philosophically crucial which view is correct for any given subject matter. It is also of equally great interest to consider what general, domain-independent arguments can be given for or against each of these three major positions.

The issues raised by the Primary Thesis do not arise only on the supposition that senses are elements of some Third Realm of senses or meanings, utterly free of any anchors to the mental and physical realm. The issues raised by the Primary Thesis arise equally for anyone who very reasonably requires that talk of sense and meaning be anchored in complex properties of creatures in the spatiotemporal world. Suppose we aim to respect that requirement of anchoring, however it is spelled out, in an elucidation of grasp of sense in terms of properties of mental files (Perry 2002a; Recanati 2012; Peacocke 2014a). There are various ways of developing this idea, but under all of them, types of mental file correspond to senses or ways of representing something. We can then raise questions about the properties and relations of these mental files. What, constitutively, explains the fact that a mental file's type corresponds to a particular sense or meaning? Do we presuppose a prior metaphysics of the entity to which the file refers in explaining the relations in virtue of which the mental file corresponds to a particular sense or meaning? If so, that is a version of the metaphysics-first form of the Primary Thesis. Or is the metaphysics of the references not prior, but itself depends on relations to systems of mental files? That would be a version of the no-priority form of the Primary Thesis. These issues of priority and order of explanation remain real when we anchor sense and meaning in psychological reality. The issues are not artefacts of Frege's conception of the Third Realm.

My agenda for the remainder of this chapter is, first, to develop a general objection to meaning-first views, in a way that begins to outline what is involved in the correctness of the metaphysics-involving conception. According to the metaphysics-involving conception, a principle that McDowell (1994) has argued applies everywhere, what he calls 'the Unboundedness of the Conceptual', holds instead only for a distinctive proper subset of cases, the no-priority cases. It does not apply to the metaphysics-first cases. I then go on to consider the character of a variety of no-priority cases, and what makes them possible; to argue for the importance of applying the distinction between order of discovery and the order of explanation in these investigations; to say a little more about ways in which the metaphysics-first category can apply to a domain; and to elaborate some of the ramifications of the position as developed thus far.

2. Against Meaning-First Views

Those who believe in meaning-first views tend to hold them in entire generality for arbitrary domains of subject matters. They tend to do so because they think that there are domain-independent reasons for accepting the meaning-first view. We can begin a more detailed consideration of the issues by addressing the arguments in the early pages of Dummett's book *The Logical Basis of Metaphysics* (1991), which provides a particularly sharp and explicit formulation of an entirely general meaning-first view. Although for the most part Dummett does not write in terms of explanatory priority, he does endorse a series of claims that imply the falsity of the Primary Thesis.

Here are some of Dummett's claims:

(a) "The task of constructing a meaning-theory can, in principle, be approached without metaphysical presuppositions or *arrière-pensées*: success is to be estimated according as the theory does or does not provide a workable account of a practice that agrees with that which we in fact observe" (1991: 13–14).

(b) Of such a meaning-theory, Dummett asks, "Will it also settle the metaphysical controversies themselves?" He answers, "It is my contention that it will" (14).

(c) Further, "It will resolve these controversies without residue: there will be no further, properly metaphysical, question to be determined" (14).

(d) Dummett adds this comment on his hypothesized resolution of metaphysical disputes within the theory of meaning:

> Once resolved in favour of a particular doctrine, the picture of reality that goes with the doctrine and that gives it its metaphysical expression will automatically force itself upon us; but it has no additional content of its own. Its non-metaphorical content consists in the model of meaning which it suggests; however powerfully the picture impresses itself on us, we have to bear in mind that its content is a thesis in the theory of meaning, and, beyond that, it is no more than a picture. (15)

On Dummett's conception, then, the metaphysics of a domain is legitimate insofar, and only insofar, as it can be construed as making claims founded in the correct meaning-theory for a language about that domain. Metaphysics, on Dummett's view, simply could not have the kind of status it would need to have for the Primary Thesis to be correct.

The correctness of the position formulated in the Primary Thesis is a timeless, *ur*-issue in philosophy. The position has to be assessed in the light of two different kinds of evidence, both of which are essential for a full philosophical understanding.

The thesis can be assessed first at the level of a variety of particular domains and intentional contents concerning those domains. Does the Primary Thesis hold when we look at each of the cases of the domain material objects and their properties, or numbers and their properties, or reasons, or moral properties? It is a challenging and highly substantive matter to give a philosophical account of the metaphysics and of the theory of intentional content for any one domain. It is a further substantive task to give an explanatory philosophical account of the relations between these two theories.

The Primary Thesis obviously has to be rejected if it does not hold for some particular domain. But even if we examine a number of diverse domains, and the Thesis seems to hold in all of them, such progress, substantial though it would be, would not give us all of the philosophical understanding we ought to seek. For we should want to know *why* the Primary Thesis holds across all these domains. Are there general, domain-independent considerations for thinking that the Primary Thesis must hold? If so, what are they? Conversely, even if we have answers to questions at that very general level, we also need of course to understand how the Primary Thesis works out in detail in various particular domains.

There is a general, domain-independent consideration that tells against Dummett's equally general meaning-first view. I call it the argument from the nature of understanding.

The argument from the nature of understanding starts from the point that a concept is individuated by the fundamental condition for something to be its reference, or to fall under it. That is a classical Fregean thesis about sense, stated for complete truth-evaluable senses in his *Grundgesetze* (1967, 2013: §32). A plausible further elaboration of that core idea starts from the principle that to think of an entity under a given concept, the thinker has to stand in a particular relation to the entity. That is, for any given concept C, there is a corresponding relation R(C) in which the thinker has to stand to something to be thinking of it under that concept. This further elaboration is a generalization in the spirit of Evans (1985). The Frege-inspired claim is then that this relation R(C) is the relation that individuates the concept C, the relation that makes the concept the concept it is.

To illustrate this for the case of a singular concept and its corresponding relation, consider a singular demonstrative perceptual concept *that lamp* as employed by a thinker on a particular occasion. For an object to be the reference of this perceptual demonstrative on a particular occasion involves the object's being given in a certain way in perception on that occasion. An object is the reference of this singular concept, as employed by the thinker at a given time, if and only if the entity is the lamp that is perceived in that way by the thinker at that time. The way involves the lamp being perceived as at a certain distance and direction from the subject (and of course a lamp that is perceived in that way may not be where it seems to be).

For an example of the relation corresponding to a predicative concept, we can take the observational concept *oval*. Suppose we treat the references of concepts as extensions. Then something is in the extension of the thinker's observational concept *oval* if and only if it is the same shape as things are represented as being in the thinker's perceptual experiences of objects as oval, where this last occurrence of 'oval' alludes to the nonconceptual representational content of experience. It is in my view always a nontrivial matter to formulate the relation R(C) that corresponds to a given concept C. There is further discussion of this approach to sense and concepts in Evans (1985) and Peacocke (1981, 2008).

I myself would make the same claims about nonconceptual intentional contents. For each nonconceptual content c there is also a corresponding relation R(c). Similarly, it is this relation that is constitutive of that particular nonconceptual content that makes it the content it is.

The same points can be formulated for meanings. A fundamental component of the meaning of an expression, at the level of sense, is individuated by the fundamental condition for something to be its reference, or to fall under it. Other components of meaning include the nonreferential aspects needed to articulate the difference in meaning between 'and' and 'but'; we prescind from them here. To be referring, in a given language, to an entity in using an expression in that language, the user must similarly stand in a certain relation to the entity, the relation determined by the sense of the expression, possibly in a context-dependent fashion.

So, under these approaches, if a thinker is employing a certain concept to think about something, the thinker must stand in a certain relation to the reference, a relation specified by the fundamental reference rule for the concept. The argument against the meaning-first view can then be formulated as follows. Which relations a thinker can stand in to an entity depends on the correct metaphysics of that entity. It follows that the metaphysics of a domain constrains the theory of concepts of entities of that domain. The metaphysics similarly constrains the theory of meaning for language about that domain. The same argument applies to nonconceptual intentional contents.

The conclusion of this abstract, general argument from understanding directly contradicts Dummett's meaning-first view. I will be offering a substantive metaphysics for each of various particular domains later in this book. If this abstract, general argument is sound, it should be possible to say how features of the substantive metaphysics contribute to the explanation of the nature of concepts and meanings concerning entities in that domain.

This abstract general argument from understanding is consistent with both the stronger and the weaker forms of the Primary Thesis. It may be that while the metaphysics of some particular domain constrains the nature of meanings and intentional contents concerning that domain, the converse is also true: the meanings and the intentional contents equally constrain the metaphysics. Mutual constraint is not ruled out by anything in the above reasoning, and we will consider some examples of the phenomenon below. The argument from the nature of understanding does not decide between the metaphysics-first view of a domain and the no-priority view of that same domain.

The general argument from the nature of understanding seems to me to be sound. It is, however, formulated in highly abstract terms, and it can be illuminating and helpful to see it instantiated and at work in the case of various particular domains. We can start by considering a humble observational shape concept, such as *oval*, or *round* or *square*. In accordance with the approach outlined above, a subject thinks about a particular shape property using one of these concepts because it is the property represented as instantiated in certain perceptual experiences that the subject is capable of enjoying, or at least knows what it would be like to enjoy. The fundamental reference rule for such concepts requires that for an object to fall under it, the object must be of the same shape as things are represented as being in certain types of experiences, of things as oval, or as round or as square.

What is it, as a constitutive matter, for these experiences to have a particular representational content? I am in agreement with those who hold that the constitutive account of this matter must speak of causation of such experiences, when all is working properly, by and large by the properties these experiences represent as instantiated. This is the position argued in Burge (2003) and Peacocke (2004). There are significant further conditions for the presence of spatial representational content in perception: see Burge (2010, chapter 8) and some different further conditions for the presence of temporal representation content in perception (see Chapter 3). The crucial point for present purposes, however, is just that the causal requirement involves causation by mind-independent spatial properties and relations of objects, arrays, or events. That is, there is a commitment to mind-independence of these properties in the very account of what gives spatial experience its representational content. Any account of grasp of observational spatial concepts, or of understanding observational spatial vocabulary, that mentions the content of spatial experience thus presupposes a certain metaphysics of the properties so represented.

This argument does not turn on the details of the relation between an observational concept and the content of perceptual experience. The presupposition of a certain metaphysics of the properties represented in experience will be there, however that relation is understood. The present point is in itself consistent with the thesis, not held by me, that all perceptual content is conceptual, as McDowell (1994) holds. I will imminently be discussing McDowell's more general views in relation to metaphysics-first treatments. All that matters at this point in the argument is that the constitutive account of grasp of the observational concept mentions a link with perceptual experience, and what gives perceptual experience certain spatial contents is its complex relation to mind-independent properties.

How might Dummett as a meaning-first theorist respond to the argument from understanding? There is not much room for manoeuvre against it. Dummett might say that he has already insisted that metaphysical pictures are some kind of gloss on a more fundamental non-metaphysical characterization that, on his view, is to be found in the theory of meaning and content. This insistence, he might say in the case of spatial observational concepts, applies equally to the metaphysical claim of mind-independence of spatial properties and relations. What this more fundamental characterization might be in the case of mind-independence is far from clear on Dummett's own views. But in any case, this general response does not, in the case of spatial observational concepts, meet the need. The challenge for any opponent of the Primary Thesis is to provide an alternative positive account of what gives perceptual experience the content it has. By itself, this response does not offer an alternative. It would not be plausible to say that spatial observational concepts can be individuated without mentioning perceptual experience at all.

Moreover, the claim that it is mind-independent spatial properties that in central cases causally explain the spatial representational content of experience is confirmed by non-philosophical investigation of the world, and of perception's place therein. It is not a 'picture' or a metaphysical gloss on some underlying principles in the theory of meaning and content. The mind-independence of spatial properties of objects and events around us, and their causal influence on our perceptual states, is confirmed time and again in the relation between objects, events, and minds. There is no incompatibility in our confirming in empirical investigation something that, in further argument, we also propose as having constitutive significance.

Plausible examples of metaphysics-first domains and their concepts are not restricted to mind-independent entities and their properties and relations. The metaphysics-first category also contains some domains that consist of purely mental entities and their properties and relations. Thought and language about pain is constitutively dependent on its relations to pain itself. To possess the concept *pain* involves its possessor being willing to classify one of her own mental events as a pain when it is so, and for the reason that it is an experience of pain, in certain central cases. This conception needs to be elaborated, very likely by the apparatus of signal detection theory, to explain the full range of possibilities of errors of judgement, as Jorge Morales has suggested (forthcoming). But that is an elaboration, rather than a rejection, of the conception. Now pain is mind-dependent, if anything is. The metaphysics-first view plausibly holds for thought about pain. What is involved in having a concept of pain, as such, involves a suitable sensitivity of judgements involving that concept to the occurrence of pains themselves. But the nature of pain does not involve its conceptualization as pain. Human pain can be subjectively of exactly the same kind as pain occurring in animals that are not concept users at all. So if this is correct, a metaphysics-first view is not restricted to mind-independent subject matters. Pain has its own metaphysics. That metaphysics will, plausibly, be relevant to such matters as the connection between pain and apparent bodily location. At the conceptual level, it will be relevant to the explanation of a thinker's ability in normal circumstances to know the location of a pain.

McDowell presents a contrary view of pain, under which the concept of pain "is drawn into play as an awareness of the circumstance that the subject is in pain" (1994: 38). The challenge presented to this position by animal pain has been well discussed in the literature. Creatures can be in pain without possessing any concept or notion of pain. A particularly clear statement of the point is given by Crispin Wright (1996: 243). McDowell's position as just quoted also faces a further problem if there are or can be conscious subjects that represent the world around a location, but do not self-represent. These are the creatures that I described as being at Degree 0 in *The Mirror of the World* (2014a). These creatures can be in pain, but do not even possess a first-person concept or notion. They do not have the resources to represent the circumstance that they themselves are in pain, as McDowell's treatment would require.

We can further clarify the position in logical space occupied by the Primary Thesis by noting that endorsement of the primacy of metaphysics, the rejection of the meaning-first view, goes far beyond anti-individualism, or externalism, in the theory of meaning and intentional content, and is to be distinguished sharply from it. This is so for at least two reasons.

One reason is that meaning-first views can also be anti-individualist views. The assertibility-condition views of meaning found in Dummett and Wright can consistently be anti-individualist (Putnam 1973; Burge 1979). The contribution made by an expression to the assertibility-conditions of sentences containing the expression can mention the physical and social environment in which the asserter is embedded. An assertibility-condition theorist who is also a meaning-first theorist can thus consistently be an anti-individualist. In fact Dummett himself seems to be an instance of that combination. He is explicitly a meaning-first theorist, but in his discussion of Kripke on natural kinds, he strongly endorses theses best marshalled in support of anti-individualism (Dummett 1973: 143).

It is, however, very plausible that acceptance of the primacy of metaphysics for some empirical domain does imply anti-individualism about content and meaning for the corresponding contents. The force of the preceding points is simply that the primacy of metaphysics goes far beyond acceptance of anti-individualism.

A second reason for distinguishing the primacy of metaphysics from anti-individualism is that, as I will be arguing in detail in Chapter 5, the metaphysics-first view can be developed for abstract objects such as numbers. Grasp of ways of thinking of numbers does not involve any new environmental or social relations that are not already involved in whatever array of concepts are grasped by the thinker when we omit her concepts of numbers. If the conclusions of Chapter 5 are sound, then the metaphysics-first view can apply to domains and ways of thinking of them where it makes no sense to be an anti-individualist.

3. The Boundedness of the Conceptual

What is the relation between a metaphysics-first view of a domain and McDowell's thesis of "the Unboundedness of the Conceptual", as he states it in Lecture II of his book *Mind and World*? I am going to argue that they are incompatible. Where there are good reasons for holding the metaphysics-first view of a domain and a set of concepts about its elements, they are correspondingly reasons for disputing the thesis of the Unboundedness of the Conceptual. Here are three passages from McDowell's lecture on the topic that articulate his thesis of the Unboundedness of the Conceptual:

> *That things are thus and so* is the content of the experience, and it can also be the content of a judgement: it becomes the content of a judgement if the subject decides to take the experience at face value. So it is conceptual content. But *that things are thus and so* is also, if one is not misled, an aspect of the layout of the world: it is how things are. Thus the idea of conceptually structured operations of receptivity puts us in a position to speak of experience as openness to the layout of reality. Experience enables the layout of reality itself to exert a rational influence on what a subject thinks.   (1994: 26)

> Although reality is independent of our thinking, it is not to be pictured as outside an outer boundary that encloses the conceptual sphere. *That things are thus and so* is the conceptual content of an experience, but if the subject of the experience is not misled, that very same thing, *that things are thus and so*, is also a perceptible fact, an aspect of the perceptible world.   (1994: 26)

> When one thinks truly, what one thinks *is* what is the case. So since the world is everything that is the case (as he himself [viz. Wittgenstein—CP] once wrote), there is no gap between thought, as such, and the world.   (1994: 27)

Consider a development of the metaphysics-first view for a domain with this property: it treats causal sensitivity in some central cases to objects' having certain properties and standing in certain relations in that domain as partially constitutive of the nature of intentional contents and concepts concerning that domain. Such a metaphysics-first view will be in conflict with the thesis of the Unboundedness of the Conceptual as articulated in the above passages. The causal sensitivity cannot be to conceptual contents if we have here a genuinely metaphysics-first view. A causal sensitivity to the holding of conceptual contents would involve the explaining conditions already involving concepts. McDowell's thesis would allow at most a no-priority view of the matter.

That is the straightforward simple argument for the incompatibility of a metaphysics-first view of a domain with the thesis of the Unboundedness of the Conceptual. I will offer more detailed arguments in support of a metaphysics-first view of contents concerning various domains later in this book, including some spatial and temporal contents. Here I will argue that the considerations that McDowell advances for the thesis of the Unboundedness of the Conceptual do not support that view. I will also argue that we can avoid the unacceptable consequences he says follow from rejecting it. There are all sorts of insights that motivate McDowell's endorsement of the Unboundedness of the Conceptual, but I do not think that what is right in them carries us as far as that thesis.

First, and fundamentally, the causal explanation of a subject's perceptual states in basic metaphysics-first cases is *not* explanation by the holding of conceptual content. It is rather explanation by an object's having a property or certain objects' standing in a certain relation. This is a general fact about the nature of causal explanation in any domain. As I said earlier, we are throughout distinguishing properties and relations on the one hand from concepts, notions, or modes of presentation of them on the other. The explaining condition involves only the properties and relations of the objects, and not any mode of presentation of the properties and relations. To use a familiar example once again, being square and being regular-diamond shaped are the same property, given under different concepts or notions (Peacocke 1992: ch. 3). It does not make sense to say that some state of affairs or some event, including an event of a perception occurring, is explained by some object being square but not by its being regular-diamond shaped. They are one and the same shape property. Explanation is by the object's having the property itself, however picked out.

What is true is that the perception of something as regular-diamond shaped is explained by the perceived object's symmetry about the bisectors of its angles. That is a different property from that of being symmetrical about the bisectors of its sides. This is distinctness of properties, not of concepts or notions. These different symmetry properties could each be picked out by many different concepts.

This point about causal explanation is simply the application to properties of a point Elizabeth Anscombe made some years ago now (1969) against Donald Davidson's claim of the opaqueness of 'because...' contexts. Anscombe noted that we can simply apply Russell's theory of definite descriptions to disambiguate the sentence, "There was an international crisis because the man with the largest nose in France made a speech". (Anscombe was writing at a time when the large-nosed Charles de Gaulle had recently been President of France. Present-day students need the history explained to them to appreciate the case. There is a lesson here about the choice of examples if one wants one's examples to have a timeless accessibility.) The true reading of the sentence gives the definite description wide scope: concerning the man with the largest nose in France, there was an international crisis because he made a speech. By contrast, the narrow-scope reading is false. It is not the case that there was an international crisis because the largest-nosed man in France made a speech.

The same distinction applies to concepts of properties. The property of being symmetrical about the bisectors of its sides may be picked out by each of these descriptions: (a) the geometrical property mentioned on page 12 of a certain textbook; (b) the geometrical property characterized in such-and-such terms using Cartesian coordinates; (c) the geometrical property characterized in so-and-so way using a non-Cartesian geometrical descriptive apparatus. Of the single property picked out by each of the descriptions (a), (b), and (c), we can say in Anscombian fashion: concerning that property, the subject perceived the item as square because he was sensitive to the instantiation of that very property.

McDowell says that the world is everything that is the case. I suggest that if we are going to say that, then the statement should be understood to concern the level of objects, properties, and relations. The two conceptual contents *Object a is square* and *Object a is regular-diamond shaped* give the same partial specification of the world. To be more precise, we can distinguish unstructured from structured specifications of the "layout of reality", to use McDowell's phrase.

At the level of unstructured specifications, it is the same partial specification that is given by those two conceptual contents. They attribute the same shape to the reference of *a*.

At the level of structured specifications, we could speak of the different commitments of *is square* and of *is regular-diamond shaped* in respect of the finer-grained structure of the shape in question. Application of the first concept involves commitment to symmetry about the bisectors of the sides, while application of the second concept involves commitment to symmetry about the bisectors of the angles. But even on this structured version of the layout of reality, we are still speaking of properties and relations, rather than concepts thereof.

What of the various troubles that are said to follow if we reject the Unboundedness thesis? Under the metaphysics-first position for a given domain, when we are concerned with perceptual concepts and notions of the domain, *That a certain object is thus and so* can be a perceptible fact if a subject can perceive the presented object to have the property picked out by the *thus and so*. This will involve a certain perceptual sensitivity to property instantiations. A development along the lines indicated of a metaphysics-first view for a domain and its perceptual notions and concepts does not make reality perceptually inaccessible.

My own view is that nothing as a matter of principle prevents us from being in perceptual contact with the world itself if our perceptual experiences have nonconceptual representational content. Rational entitlement by experiences with nonconceptual but nevertheless genuinely representational content is in my view enough to avoid what McDowell rightly rejects in the Myth of the Given (Peacocke (2001); McDowell would disagree). But as far as I can see, it would even be possible to accept that all perceptual content is conceptual, consistently with the metaphysics-first view, if one accepts the model of explanation by objects, properties, and relations at the level of reference, rather than the level of sense. Whether the representational content of experience is treated as conceptual or nonconceptual, under the model of a perceptual metaphysics-first case outlined here, it will still be the case that "the world exerts a rational influence on our thinking" (McDowell 1994: 34). This can be so even though the position does endorse a boundary between the conceptual and the explaining world at the level of objects, properties, and relations. The position outlined here does not "delete the outer boundary from the picture" (McDowell 1994: 34). This is all entirely consistent with the existence of an external, environmental dimension to the individuation of concepts, senses, and notions.

Does a metaphysics-first view of a domain involve denying that 'When one thinks truly, what one thinks *is* what is the case'? What one thinks is a Fregean Thought. If the Thought is true, then it is the case. So the thing that one thinks, when one thinks truly, is also the case. It is hard to find an unacceptable gap between thought and world here. It seems to me that there is only the difference between sense and reference, which is obligatory, since thought always concerns the world as given in a certain way. We must indeed be able to show how senses, ways of thinking, notions, and the rest really are senses of objects, properties, and relations in the world. That is a genuine constraint, not always met by some extant theories. Theories that fail to meet it do suffer from a genuine thought/world gap. It is an important insight running through McDowell that we must avoid theories that leave such a gap. But nothing in the metaphysics-first view about a given domain implies that we cannot meet that genuine sense/reference constraint on acceptable theories. I will argue that the constraint is met in the case of domains of spatial and temporal magnitudes, and our perceptual notions of them, in Chapters 2 and 3.

4. No-Priority Cases

McDowell's position that implies that all cases are, in the terminology of Section 1 above, no-priority cases. I have just offered some reasons for disagreeing with that universal claim. I suggest instead that no-priority cases form a limited class of interesting special cases. They are cases in which there are domain-specific reasons for thinking that the reality to which a thinker must be sensitive in her judgements, if she is to possess a given concept or notion, is a reality that already in one way or another involves that concept or notion. Three kinds of case are salient.

One kind of case results from combining two views. The first of the views is the classical seventeenth-century view of secondary qualities, in the style of Galileo or Locke, that such properties as being red, and other perceptible properties not apparently mentioned in the physics of the time, consist in some complex relation to the property of looking red, or some corresponding experiential property, in specified circumstances. This first view in the combination is a view of the metaphysics of redness.

The second view in the combination is that in an account of the property of looking red, or any of the other perceptual or sensory states that would be mentioned in classical accounts of sensory qualities, there is no eliminating or explaining away the occurrence of the concept or notion *red* or its analogues within the intentional content of those mental states. This combination of views makes the concept *red* and its analogues ineliminably involved in the metaphysics of the property of redness. The general structure of the position is not intrinsically contrary to reason. It is indeed the view of secondary qualities advocated by McDowell (1994: 29–33).

Whether this structure is instantiated in any particular cases is always a substantive philosophical issue. In the case of the property of being funny, for instance, it is not so plausible that one can find something funny only if one has the concept *funny*. Amusement at something can be present even in those that lack any notion or concept of being funny. But not all such cases of seeming F, or looking F, or sounding F are such 'false friends', and this first kind of specific no-priority case seems to be a genuine phenomenon.

This first kind involves mental events other than just judgement—what is distinctive of this first kind is the involvement of perception rather than judgement. Maybe there are also cases of the first kind where emotion plays the role played by perception in the secondary quality case. One way of developing a no-priority treatment of moral properties and concepts would be to advocate the need, in an account of grasp of moral concepts, to mention the sensitivity of moral judgements to the moral emotions that themselves have irreducibly moral conceptual content.

A second kind of specific no-priority case differs from the first in that it does not make essential appeal to mental events or actions other than judgement. These are social cases in which the social reality embeds the concept. For instance, a case can be made that what it is for something to be a law in a community is that it is a consequence of something that is promulgated as a law in that community. The case would be developed by insisting that it is not sufficient for something to be a law that its violations are commonly known to lead to, or even to merit, unwanted consequences in the community. Comparable points about embedding might be argued for the property of being fashionable. These claims would have to be made out, case by case, for each of the specific domains in question.

A third, very different, kind of no-priority case is provided by ontologies such as those of fictional characters or the ancient Greek and Roman gods, considered as an ontology that a modern unbeliever can comfortably accept. The existence of Sherlock Holmes, Candide, and Zeus depends upon social practices that evidently and in the nature of the case involve some conceptualization of each of these entities. For those who hold that there is a good theoretical case that these entities cannot be analysed away, a no-priority view of the ontology of these domains is required. Grasp of the concept *Sherlock Holmes* involves a rational sensitivity in one's judgements containing the concept to what the fiction says about Holmes, and potentially to the way the character has been developed by more than one writer. That is a sensitivity to the properties possessed by the fictional character. But there is also a converse dependence of the nature of the ontology of fictional characters to what, in various complex ways, has been said about Sherlock Holmes, using the very concept *Sherlock Holmes*. If the ontology of fictional characters really is irreducible, then the no-priority position seems unavoidable for such domains.

No-priority cases need much further discussion than they have received hitherto in the philosophical literature. It seems to me that we (or certainly I) do not fully understand either their nature, or what makes them possible. There are constitutive questions about what it is to grasp the concepts for which a no-priority account is correct. If the generalization of Anscombe's point above is correct, viz. that explanation is always by the properties of objects and events, rather than by the holding of a conceptual content, we cannot say that mastery of the concepts in a no-priority case involves causal sensitivity to the holding of the conceptual contents of the no-priority case. Nor, it seems, do we give a fully explanatory account of grasp of a concept in a no-priority case by saying that the thinker who grasps the concept has tacit knowledge of the metaphysics of the property picked out by the concept. That model plausibly applies in some examples, but what is distinctive of a no-priority case is that the metaphysics of the property has itself to mention the very concept grasp of which is in question. There are correspondingly pressing questions about the acquisition of a concept in a no-priority case. If there are no-priority cases, there must be answers to these questions. We need more work on these issues, on which there are various theoretical options of interest.

The discussion of these most recent cases should not leave us with the impression that any account in which there is a social dimension to possession of a concept will also necessarily be a no-priority treatment. That would be a false impression. The distinction between the individualistic and social accounts cuts across the distinction between metaphysics-first cases and no-priority cases. A constitutive account of a particular kind of intentional content may involve social matters whilst still also being a metaphysics-first account. Though it is an account with which I will be disagreeing, Donald Davidson's 'triangulation' treatment of the content of perceptual beliefs in 'The Second Person' (2001a) and similar papers is an example of a non-individualistic but still metaphysics-first view.

Davidson's idea is that we attain a correct account of which object or kind of thing or event that a subject or person is representing in a perceptual belief only if we mention the classificatory dispositions of a second subject or person. Davidson is offering a non-individualistic constitutive account of the content of perceptual beliefs. It is a constitutive account of the reference-relation for a subject's representational states that makes essential mention of the properties and relations of the intentional contents of another person, a second subject's intentional states. Davidson asks what makes it the case that a creature is representing the ringing of a bell rather than the sound waves emanating from the striking of the bell, or is representing tables rather than properties of the light waves reflected by the table. He writes,

What explains the fact that it seems so natural to say the dog is responding to the bell, the child to tables? It seems natural to us because it *is* natural—to us. Just as the dog and the child respond in similar ways to certain stimuli, so do we. It is we who find it natural to group together the various salivations of the dog; and the events in the world that we effortlessly notice and group together that are causally linked to the dog's behavior are ringings of the bell. We find the child's mouthings of 'table' similar, and the objects in the world we naturally class together that accompany those mouthings is a class of tables.

(2001a: 118)

Given our view of child and world, we can pick out 'the' cause of the child's responses. It is the common cause of our response and the child's response.   (2001a: 119)

...the kind of triangulation I have described, while not sufficient to establish that a creature has a concept of a particular object or kind of object, is necessary if there is to be any answer at all to the question what its concepts are concepts of.   (2001a: 119)

The problem is not, I should stress, one of verifying what objects or events a creature is responding to: the point is that without a second creature responding to the first, there can be no answer to the question.   (2001a: 119)

This Davidsonian view does properly acknowledge a basic level of mind-independent objects and properties that are causally influential in the production of perceptions (or beliefs, he would insist for other reasons). The common causes of the perceptions of the first and second creatures are the possession by mind-independent objects and events of properties—being a ringing, being a table—that are independent of the occurrence of the perceptions of the two creatures. The concept *table* as a partially functional concept is of course not entirely mind-independent, but that is an avoidable feature of the example. Davidson could have chosen a shape concept such as *square*. But Davidson's theory is not a no-priority account. It is rather a metaphysics-first social account.

One way of making this clear is the fact that the account can be cast in what I called the A(C) form in *A Study of Concepts* (1992). For Davidson, what makes an arbitrary concept C the concept *square* is that it is that concept C such that in two different subjects, the basic applications in ordinary perceptual circumstances of the concept C are caused by square things. In this most recent occurrence the concept is used, not mentioned. The A(C) form can be used across multiple subjects, not just within a single subject. So the boundary between cases in which the metaphysics-first view applies and those in which it does not does not coincide with the individualistic/social distinction.

At least one major indicator of no-priority status is not the presence of a social dimension in the constitutive account, but rather use of the very concept, embedded in propositional attitudes, in the reality to which a thinker must be sensitive to possess the concept. That is what is present in the secondary quality and the legal examples. The case of the concept *square* as treated in a Davidsonian account is very different from this, in two respects. First, in the metaphysics of the property of being square, there is no need to mention experiences of things as square. Second, when the Davidsonian account is cast in the A(C) form, there does not need to be any mention of experiences of things as square, described as such with conceptual content. Those two features that ground the no-priority character of the secondary quality and the legal cases are not present in the Davidsonian treatment.

The Davidsonian account of the content of perceptual beliefs can be offered as an example of the consistency of a combination, but I do not in fact think it is a correct account. There are developed theories that give a philosophical account of what makes it the case that a creature is representing ringings of bells, or tables, rather than patterns of sound or light waves, that do not make any reference to a second subject and what is natural for a second subject. One such account is that of Burge (2010). Burge's account appeals to what is biologically important to the creature to represent. It is obviously biologically important, and adaptive, to represent objects and events in the world, rather than properties of light and sound waves. A second, apparently different account I have endorsed (1993, 2014b) appeals to the role of represented objects and events in explaining the creature's actions under their environmental descriptions. The explanations and counterfactuals involving mental events that represent external objects and events concern the relations of the creature to the represented items in its environment. Explanations that mention ringings and tables will explain relational properties of the creature's actions that concern ringings and tables, rather than relations to patterns of sound and light. If the creature is moving under the table to avoid something, it would have moved in a different direction if the table had been in a different direction, even though the pattern of light when the table is in that different direction would be rather different; and so forth. Neither Burge's account nor mine mentions the classificatory dispositions of a second person in its constitutive account of what makes it the case that the creature is perceptually representing one thing rather than another.

In discussing the relation between what makes something the object and properties represented in a perception or thought on the one hand, and the role of a second creature that Davidson invokes on the other, it is important to respect the distinction between the modal and the constitutive. Suppose one subject is related to an environmental object in a way R that makes available to the subject a certain way of representing the object in perception and thought. Then in a wide range of cases, it will be possible for a second person to stand in that same relation R to the object, and to display some of the same sensitivities to the object as the first person does. But this possibility for the second person is not what *makes* it the case that the first subject is representing the object in question. What makes that the case is rather that the first subject stands in the relation R to the object. The fact that there is a common cause of the first person's and the second person's perception of the object is a consequential feature of the situation, that each is perceiving that object. The common cause when there is a second subject suitably situated is not something constitutive of the first person's perceiving it, or constitutive of the second person's perceiving it, for that matter. The fact that it is always possible for there to be a second subject for which the first subject's reference is a common cause also of the second subject's representations in no way supports the claim that this possibility is what makes the first subject's reference what it is. In the perceptual case, and I would argue too in other cases, we can specify what the relation is that makes a subject be thinking about or representing one thing or property, without mentioning a second subject. The possibilities that must exist for a second subject are derivative from the possibility of the second subject's standing in the same relation to the object as the first subject.[1]

Though Davidson's position on the determination of perceptual content involves a second person, it does not fundamentally involve interpersonal relations between the two perceivers, at least as applied in an account of what determines perceptual content. In this respect it is not really an example of a

---

[1] The qualification 'in a wide range of cases' earlier in this paragraph is to take account of such cases as the first-person concept or notion. The relation in which one person x stands to x and which makes available to her the first-person way of thinking of herself is not a relation in which some other second person can stand to x. For the apparatus that can help to explain why this is unthreatening to the Primary Thesis, see Peacocke (1981, 2014a).

deeply intersubjective treatment, which would require such interpersonal inter-action. Davidson does endorse some further theses that would require a repre-senting subject to have knowledge of other subjects (see his 'Three Varieties of Knowledge', 2001b); but these further theses seem to me too strong. A subject can represent the nonmental world without having any conception at all of other subjects. The position developed above helps to explain how this can be so. I suspect Davidson wanted to arrive at a deeply intersubjective view of content. It would certainly be of great interest to see such a view fully developed. My point in these recent paragraphs has been that the triangulation argument is not a vehicle that will take one all the way to the destination of a deeply and entirely general intersubjective thesis about content.

5. An Argument from Rationality?

It may seem that there is a second general, domain-independent argument in support of the Primary Thesis. This second argument is an argument from rational sensitivity. The argument starts from the point that it is part of the nature of concepts and subsentential meanings that they can combine to form complete, truth-evaluable contents. Consider a predication Fa. Someone who grasps the concepts F and a can make a rational assessment, in various circum-stances, whether to judge that Fa. Whether it is rational to judge Fa in given circumstances depends on what it takes for it to be true that Fa. But what it takes for Fa to be true depends on the metaphysics of the object that is the reference of the singular concept a and on the metaphysics of the property that is the reference of the concept F. Does it not follow that there must already be a sensitivity to the metaphysics of the object and the property built into the condition for grasping the singular concept a and the predicative concept F?

While I think this argument from rational sensitivity is sound, it has two limitations. The first limitation is that, in applying considerations of rationality, the argument from rational sensitivity is applicable only to conceptual contents, and not to nonconceptual contents that feature in the content of states that subjects are not in for reasons at all, states whose individuation is below the level of rationality and judgement.

The second limitation is dialectical. The argument from rational sensitivity is question-begging when used against the meaning-first opponents of the Primary Thesis. Those opponents will object to the step that says that what it takes for Fa to be true depends substantively on the metaphysics of the references of a and F. They can take the view, explicitly endorsed by Dummett in the quota-tions above, that metaphysics rides entirely on the back of an allegedly metaphysics-independent theory of meaning. On their approach, there cannot be such a thing as a substantial dependence on a metaphysics of a domain, because metaphysics itself is epiphenomenal—it has no substance independently of the theory of meaning. To avoid question-begging against this meaning-first position, we need to invoke the main argument from the nature of understanding for the Primary Thesis. We need to raise the issue, as we did earlier, of what constrains the thinker's relations to elements of the domain that are involved in having concepts or notions of that domain, and this will be a substantive metaphysics of the domain. So the argument from rational sensitivity does not have any dialectical force on its own. The general case for the Primary Thesis rests upon the argument from the nature of understanding or possession of concepts or notions.

Nonetheless, once we have the argument for the Primary Thesis, the soundness of the argument from rational sensitivity does set various tasks for philosophy. One task is to elaborate and elucidate, in each domain, the rational sensitivity which the argument says must exist to the properties and relations discussed in a correct metaphysics for the domain in question. We will do this for some selected domains in Chapters 2 through 5.

The argument from the nature of understanding and the argument from rational sensitivity are closely intertwined. They are not utterly independent from one another. The argument from understanding starts from a more explicit theoretical conception of what understanding is than does the argument from rational sensitivity. But that theoretical conception, of understanding as consisting in a certain relation to the reference of the concept, is precisely what is needed to explain the considerations invoked by the argument from rational sensitivity. In explaining how possession of a concept or grasp of a notion can involve a sensitivity to the properties and relations identified in a constitutive account of what is involved in a content's holding, we need to invoke a conception of possession and grasp as involving the thinker's standing in a certain relation to the reference of the concept. The domain-independent argument from the nature of possession or grasp and the argument from rational sensitivity draw on the same philosophical resources, though in different ways.

6. Discovery, Explanation, and a Theory of Conditions

In developing the metaphysics-involving position stated in the Primary Thesis, it is essential at several points to apply a variant of Reichenbach's distinction between the context of discovery and the context of justification (1938). More specifically, we need to apply the distinction between the context of discovery and the context of explanation.

Earlier I quoted Dummett's comment that the success or otherwise of the enterprise of constructing a meaning-theory for a language "is to be estimated according as the theory does or does not provide a workable account of a practice that agrees with that which we in fact observe". That is a very reasonable position. No one should disagree with it, including the metaphysics-involving theorist, provided that 'practice' is allowed to include judgements as well as overt linguistic performances. However, Dummett's reasonable comment concerns the context of discovery, in Reichenbach's sense, rather than the order of constitutive philosophical explanation. It is entirely possible that a total theory provides a workable account of what we in fact observe precisely because it respects constraints on concepts and meaning that are drawn from the metaphysics of the domain in question—for instance, that the thinker has the right relations to mind-independent properties, in the case of spatial observational concepts.

This is analogous to a position about the relations between radical interpretation and a theory of concept possession. No one should disagree that an interpretation of a language has to make its speakers maximally intelligible. Maximizing intelligibility may involve respecting constraints on the possession of the concepts whose use is attributed to the speakers of the language (Peacocke 1989). The constraints on possession of concepts are, on that combination of views, more fundamental in the order of philosophical explanation. My point here is not to argue about whether the constraints on maximizing intelligibility are basic or not, but rather to note the danger of a structural non sequitur. From the fact that any acceptable theory will meet a certain condition, it does not follow that the condition on making the theory acceptable is fundamental in making the theory correct. The condition on acceptability may be derivative from something more fundamental that is involved in correctness.

The same point about respecting the distinction between the order of discovery and the order of philosophical explanation applies to the metaphysics of a domain. Our understanding of metaphysical modality provides an illustration. Consider David Lewis's modal realism, the thesis that other possible worlds are concrete entities of the same kind as the actual universe around us (1986). Our initial discomfort with this modal realism may well flow from doubts about how we could understand modal discourse, and from how we could really know modal propositions, if their subject matter were as David Lewis claimed it to be. That point, if correct, shows a priority in the order of discovery of the theory of understanding, and of epistemology, in the attainment of a more plausible modal metaphysics. It does not by itself show anything at all about the relative standing of the metaphysics and the theory of understanding in respect of explanatory priority. A more plausible metaphysics of modality than is given in Lewis's modal realism will likely involve modal truth being explained in terms of facts about consistent sets of propositions or Thoughts, where the consistency relation is not explained in modal-realist terms, and not in purely logical terms either.[2] Once we have that positive non-Lewisian metaphysics, then what is involved in understanding, and also in knowing, modal propositions will be described in terms of a thinker's relations to such consistent sets of propositions or Thoughts.

The temporally prior knowledge of what the theory of modal understanding and modal epistemology cannot be thus sets a task. The task is that of saying what the nature of modal reality is, and how modal understanding and epistemology is related to that reality. All of this is consistent with the explanatory priority, in the order of philosophical explanation, of modal metaphysics over modal understanding.

This application of the distinction between order of discovery and order of explanation in the modal case illustrates a more general methodological point that is applicable to any subject matter. All sorts of facts about the possibilities of understanding, or about the possibilities for the objects and properties picked out by the concepts in question, may potentially be evidentially relevant to assessing questions about the relative order of explanation of metaphysics and meaning or intentional content. Resourceful investigation of either sort of possibility may be necessary to determining this order of explanation. Sometimes the relevant possibilities are highly salient and very obvious. No one will be surprised by the relevance of the point that causal interaction with the numbers is not required for understanding and knowing propositions about the numbers. The challenge is then to give an adequate account of thought about numbers, as numbers, that respects both this point and our ordinary, and knowledgeable, procedures in thinking about numbers. That is a challenge I attempt to address later in Chapter 5.

In other cases, more creative thought may be necessary in the very formulation of possibilities concerning understanding. It is, for example, always potentially an issue whether our thought and language apparently concerning a given domain can be adequately described without using the distinctions that ordinarily trip off the tongue in describing that domain. Perhaps we are under an illusion that we can significantly draw certain distinctions, and the correct metaphysics of the

---

[2] For one way of explaining such a notion of consistency, see the chapter 'Necessity' in Peacocke (1999).

domain in question should be formulated without them. Many philosophers would say that this is precisely the type of situation instantiated by Newton's conception of absolute space and time. I discuss this and other cases that seem to have the same structure in Chapter 6.

The distinction between order of discovery and order of explanation also distinguishes the Primary Thesis from one of the claims of Michael Devitt's collection of essays, *Putting Metaphysics First*. Devitt writes, "We should approach epistemology and semantics from a metaphysical perspective rather than vice versa. We should do this because we know much more about the way the world is than we do about how we know about, or refer to, that world" (2010: 2). Devitt's advice here seems to concern the order of discovery, rather than the order of explanation, which is the concern of the Primary Thesis.

In fact my own general position on these issues is in several significant respects closer to Devitt's than to Dummett's. In trying to think through these issues, I have learned from reflecting on Devitt's arguments. Nonetheless, there is a further crucial difference between my position and Devitt's. For any given subject matter, I am concerned with the metaphysics that is implicated in the *conditions* for the correctness of various intentional contents and sentences concerning that subject matter, rather than whether they are actually correct. Devitt in the passage quoted above talks about "the way the world is", rather than the conditions required for it to be as we represent it to be. Devitt says it is one of the major themes of his book to emphasize "the distinction between metaphysical issues about what there is and what it's like as against semantic issues about meaning, truth, and reference" (2010: 2). The "as against" contrast in this formulation does not seem to me to exist when we are talking about conditions for correctness. Issues about meaning, truth, and reference can hardly fail to be relevant to the nature of the correctness conditions for contents of any given type.

There are certainly some types of example in which what is actually the case determines what intentional contents and meanings are available to subjects. A relatively uncontroversial example is that first-person *de se* way of thinking each subject has for thinking of herself. If she were not to exist, that way of thinking of her (as opposed to its indexical type) would not be available either. More controversial cases concern non-indexical concepts of objects or properties. But object- and property-dependent meanings and intentional contents are of interest precisely because they connect what is actually the case with the very conditions for correctness—and hence existence—of meanings and intentional contents. The significance of the examples turns on their bearing on correctness conditions.

The distinction between which contents are correct and a theory of correctness conditions bears also on Devitt's discussion of what he describes as various "aberrations" in discussions of realism over the past few decades, especially in chapter 2 of *Putting Metaphysics First*. He objects to identifying issues about realism with issues about truth (Dummett). He also objects to dismissing realism because of a rejection of a correspondence theory of truth (Rorty). These various discussions of which Devitt is critical are not aberrations on a view on which metaphysics, and a development of realism therein, is properly involved in a theory of conditions for correctness. In the case of Dummett, for instance, his discussions, whether or not we agree with them, are not off-topic if the possibility of truth that transcends verification is an unavoidable consequence of the involvement of the metaphysics of space and time in the individuation of spatial and temporal notions and concepts. In the case of Rorty, too, his discussions, again whether we agree with them or not, are not off-topic if a correspondence theory of truth is an unavoidable consequence of the involvement of metaphysics in the individuation of meaning and intentional content.

I agree with and applaud Devitt when he writes,

Putnam and Dummett wonder what I mean by 'independent' and see a choice between *logical* and *causal* independence. I am quite explicit about what I mean and it is neither of these. I mean *constitutive* independence: thus I say that the known world "is not *constituted by* our knowledge, by our epistemic values, by the synthesizing power of the mind, not by our imposition of concepts, theories, or languages; it is not limited by what we can believe or discover".   (2010: 54)

I am in agreement with Devitt on this characterization of mind-independence for certain central subject matters. But when we combine that mind-independence with a concern for the nature of correctness conditions for contents referring to elements of that mind-independent reality, this mind-independence does have a bearing on the nature of those intentional contents and meanings themselves. In the mind-independent domains Devitt is discussing, the Primary Thesis will hold in the form of a metaphysics-first treatment of the domain. The metaphysics-first character of the case will contribute to the very explanation of the nature of meanings and contents about the domain. I am wholly sympathetic to Devitt's forceful insistence that certain contents with entirely mind-independent correctness conditions are true. But we need also to explain, philosophically, how this mind-independence is involved in the individuation of the very contents that we grasp.

The constitutive involvement of metaphysics in the nature of intentional content and meaning is, on the views I am defending, also not restricted to wholly mind-independent subject matters. I noted that there is plausibly such a constitutive dependence even in the domain of pains and their properties and relations. This is another respect in which, although we have wide agreement on certain issues in metaphysics itself, my concerns are somewhat different from, and cut across, those of Devitt.

7. That and How

That the metaphysics of a domain is involved in the explanation of the nature of intentional contents and meanings about that domain is one thing. *How* it can be so is another. Explaining how it can be so is a major task.

For each of various general kinds of domain, there are different kinds of relation in virtue of which a subject is capable of representing elements of that domain. The involvement of the metaphysics in the theory of content is differently realized in different kinds of domain. When considering the relation between a domain and its mental representation, we should always ask the question: what is the nature of the relation in virtue of which a subject is capable of representing the domain in particular ways? Different answers to this question can illuminate not only the way in which the Primary Thesis is realized in different cases, but also much else that depends on the nature of the intentional contents for that domain.

Here is a spectrum of different relations in which a thinker or perceiver may stand to a subject matter. Each of the different kinds of case illuminates one variety of the involvement of the metaphysics in the individuation of content and meaning.

In the basic perceptual case that we have already mentioned, where there is causal interaction between mind-independent elements of a domain and thinkers' informational states, those causal relations contribute to the individuation of the intentional content of the informational states. An account of what it is for a perceptual state to have a certain mind-independent intentional content has to mention what causes it in certain canonical circumstances (and it has to mention other matters too). This causal model applies more widely than one might have thought. I will, for instance, be discussing the case of perceived magnitudes as a special case of it. It is always more than just causal influence that is involved, and what those additional elements are is often a substantive philosophical issue.

The Primary Thesis can also be realized in a multitude of different ways in other cases.

As a first departure from the central perceptual cases, the causal relation to thinkers of states with contents concerning a domain may be somewhat different. The states may share a common cause with what they represent as occurring. That is plausibly so for states of action awareness that represent the subject, given first personally, as doing something. The action and the awareness have a common cause in some neurophysiologically specifiable event that initiates the action. Perhaps the initiating event is the action, in which case we have a further variant of a non-perceptual causal model.

The interaction of mental states with a domain can also be causal and rational without being perceptual. That is the case for the concept of pain, and for concepts of conscious perceptual events themselves as perceptual events. A conscious perceptual event can also give a subject a reason for judging that he is seeing (or hearing, or touching, etc.), and that it does so is a consequence of the nature of the concept of the relevant concept of a conscious perceptual event. But the perceptual events are not themselves perceived (Peacocke 2008: ch. 6).

Some domains and their ontologies do not stand in the right kind of causal relations at all for the Primary Thesis to be realized in their cases by any causal structures. The point applies to domains of abstract objects in general. In these cases the Primary Thesis still applies because abstract objects are individuated by the fundamental principles governing them, and in some cases by their application conditions too. Subjects are thinking about those entities because their thinking fundamentally respects those principles. I argue for both of these points in the case of the natural numbers and the real numbers in Chapter 5. The involvement of the metaphysics in the individuation of content is given precisely by this: the concepts used by the subject who is representing abstract objects refer to the entities they do only because the principles the subject employs in making judgements using those concepts are the very principles that individuate the abstract objects the judgements are about. We need to draw on the metaphysics of the domain of abstract objects in question to explain why the concepts are concepts of those very abstract objects. This is not a causal relation of thinkers to the domain. Rather, as recommended, we ask once again the question about the relevant relation: 'What is the relation to the number 2 that makes it the case that the thinker is thinking of that number, and thinking of it as the number 2?' The answer to this question will advert to certain basic principles the thinker follows in making judgements about the number 2, as such. Conformity to these principles determines a way of thinking of the number 2, precisely because the number 2 is, as a matter of the metaphysics of numbers, individuated by these principles. This model, like the others, also raises a host of issues, discussed in Chapter 5.

The cases I just picked out on this spectrum are merely illustrative, and they are far from exhaustive. There are distinctive features of the way that the Primary Thesis is realized that we could cite for other distinctive kinds of case. These would include recognitional concepts; the first-person concept; concepts of action-types of which it is distinctive that they feature both in action awareness and perceptual awareness; and so forth. In all of these cases, and many others, there is much more to be said about the relation between a subject and the objects, events, or properties the concept or notion picks out that enable the subject to represent in these distinctive ways, and about how that relation realizes the Primary Thesis in its own distinctive way.

Different ways of realizing the Primary Thesis generate fundamental differences between the intentional contents for these various domains, and for the relations in which they stand. For example, the range of available perceptually based ways of thinking of particular magnitudes (distances, directions, areas) will depend, constitutively, on which types of magnitudes there are in the actual world, and on our perceptual capacities. Which magnitudes there are in the actual world is a contingent and empirical matter. The same applies to the scope of our perceptual capacities. By contrast, whenever there are individuating principles of an appropriate sort, the corresponding abstract objects will exist, however the actual world may be. The existence of the individuating principles for the abstract objects is a noncontingent, nonempirical matter. The available ways of thinking of abstract objects will be limited by our intellectual capacities, but not by empirical and contingent features of the nonmental world.

8. Ramifications

If it is correct, the Primary Thesis has many ramifications. It has ramifications for issues that themselves have connections with metaphysics and the theory of intentional content. In particular, it has ramifications for epistemology; for the integration of metaphysics with epistemology; and for the limits of intelligible intentional contents. I take these three in turn.

(a) *Epistemology*. It is widely accepted that many concepts have associated epistemic grounds and consequences that are constitutive of the concept, in the sense that possession of the concept involves some kind of appreciation of those grounds or consequences. For these constitutively associated grounds (and consequences, an addition I henceforth omit), we can identify an explanatory task:

> to explain why a concept's constitutively associated mental states or propositional grounds to which the concept possessor must be sensitive in making certain judgements containing the concept are also states or grounds that genuinely give good reasons for thinking the judged content is true.

We can call this the *possession-to-correctness explanandum*. I suggest that the Primary Thesis helps to explain the possession-to-correctness explanandum. As we consider, case by case, the involvement of the metaphysics of a domain in an account of possession of concepts of entities and properties in that domain, a certain pattern appears. The reason-giving states in the perceptual cases (or for example the principles in the case of abstract objects) are states (and principles) whose very nature will, if relied upon in certain standard circumstances, give correct information about the objects falling under the concepts. This pattern is instantiated in all the examples of concepts mentioned to date. It does not seem to be an accident, but rather itself also has an explanation. For if the pattern were not there, if there were not this connection between the metaphysics of a domain and possession of concepts of it, how could concepts allow us to think about the reality—the level of reference—that the concepts concern?

(b) *Integrating Metaphysics with Epistemology.* The Primary Thesis bears upon our understanding of the form of good responses to what, in earlier work, I called the Integration Challenge, the challenge of properly integrating the metaphysics and epistemology of a domain (Peacocke 1999). I ought to have noticed, in earlier work, that all that the various accounts, in several different areas, which plausibly achieve integration of the epistemology and the metaphysics of a subject matter are accounts that display an explanatory involvement of the metaphysics in the individuation of contents and concepts, precisely in accordance with the Primary Thesis. As I noted in earlier writing, to achieve integration, sometimes it is right to deflate a proposed metaphysics for a domain, and sometimes it is right to enrich our conception of entitling conditions for judgements about that domain. But in all cases, when integration is satisfactorily achieved, it is achieved by linking both metaphysics and epistemology to a substantive theory of grasp of contents and concepts that is itself in accord with the Primary Thesis.

(c) *The Limits of Intelligibility.* A good theory of concepts and intentional content should provide the resources for giving an explanatory account of the distinction between genuine concepts and various spurious notions that exceed the limits of intelligibility. In earlier work, I tried to explain this distinction in terms of the unavailability of acceptable possession-conditions or understanding-conditions for the alleged spurious concepts (Peacocke 1988). While there may indeed be no such possession-conditions or understanding-conditions, nevertheless, if the Primary Thesis is true, a more fundamental account of what is wrong with the spurious concepts is available. The more fundamental account will address the alleged metaphysics associated with the spurious concepts, and the impossibility of giving an account of possession of the alleged concepts that relates a thinker in the right way to that associated purported metaphysics. Defects in a proposed metaphysics, and corresponding defects in the relations in which items in that proposed metaphysics can stand to contents and concepts, will on this view be explanatory of the absence of an adequate possession-condition for the spurious concepts. I develop this position further to offer a new account of the limits of intelligibility in Chapter 6.

The Primary Thesis lies right at the centre of a nexus of general issues relating metaphysics and the nature of understanding. The Primary Thesis, and the argument I have offered for it, together take a stand either explicitly or implicitly on a range of issues in the recent literature on these topics. We can distinguish at least four general kinds of position in philosophy that are committed to disagreeing with the Primary Thesis, and committed thereby to disagreeing with the considerations I have offered in support of it.

Some of the opposing positions have to do with the nature of sense and concepts; some of them have to do with the nature of metaphysics; and some of them have to do with the relation between sense and concepts on the one hand, and metaphysics on the other.

(1) Pleonastic theories of sense and concepts, propounded and developed by Stephen Schiffer (2003), will say that no substantive account of what it is to grasp a sense or concept can be given. If this is correct, then the Primary Thesis involves a mistake in its very formulation. If Schiffer is right, there cannot be any such thing as a substantive theory of concepts and intentional content to which a metaphysics may or may not be explanatory prior.

(2) There are pure conceptual role theorists such as Brandom (1994) and Harman (1999) who agree that substantive accounts of concepts and grasp of concepts can be given, but deny that reference and relations to references have any fundamental role to play in the individuation of concepts and of grasp of concepts. This would certainly block the domain-independent argument I offered for the Primary Thesis, because the argument appeals to a conception of concepts as individuated by fundamental reference rules, rather than pure conceptual roles. Neither Brandom nor Harman would accept that a sense or meaning is individuated by the fundamental condition for something to be its reference. For them, a sense would be individuated by a certain kind of pure conceptual role, pure in the sense that it does not mention or presuppose a reference-relation for the sense or meaning.

I myself have argued elsewhere that there are many reasons we need to mention reference and truth in an account of sense, meaning, and understanding, and I will not repeat those arguments here (1992, 2008). I do note, however, that what may be presented as an apparently pure conceptual role theory of a certain sense or meaning may in less obvious ways presuppose a reference-relation and a certain metaphysics of what is referred to. Consider a seemingly pure conceptual role account of an observational shape concept. To be plausible, the account must link a thinker's application of the concept to perceptual experiences that represent the concept as instantiated by something given in perception. For those perceptual experiences to have such a content, they must be of a kind some instances of which are suitably caused by mind-independent instantiation of the property, or of closely related mind-independent properties, as mentioned earlier in this chapter. The apparently pure conceptual role account, by rightly mentioning a certain type of perceptual experience, would be presupposing a certain metaphysics of the observational property picked out by the observational shape concept.

In a rather different kind of case, an apparently pure conceptual role theory of a particular logical constant, such as conjunction, may not on its surface mention reference or truth. The account may nonetheless determine a genuine sense or meaning only because it meets certain constraints, such as fixing a truth-function for which principles mentioned in the pure account are truth-preserving (cp. Peacocke 1992, forthcoming). I mention this and the preceding perceptual example not as some decisive resolution of the dispute between pure conceptual role and truth-conditional theories of sense and meaning, but rather to emphasize that apparent purity of a conceptual role account may in one way or another involve a dependence or presupposition concerning reference and truth.

(3) A third type of position is committed to rejecting the Primary Thesis because positions of this type take a deflationary attitude to metaphysics. They regard metaphysical claims as intrinsically incapable of explaining in the way required by the Primary Thesis. Crispin Wright in his 'Reply to Strawson' regards metaphysical theses as no more than a reflection of various features of linguistic practice. So, for instance, what some theorists would regard as part of the nature, or the metaphysics, of mental states ought, according to Wright, be regarded as "platitudinous reflections of features of our mental language" (1987: 77). Wright's position in that essay arguably instantiates the conception of the relation between a theory of meaning and metaphysics that we saw Dummett endorsing in the Introduction to *The Logical Basis of Metaphysics*. Rudolf Carnap similarly stated, of a new part of language that apparently introduces a new ontology, "we take the position that the introduction of the new ways of speaking does not need any theoretical justification because it does not imply any assertion of reality" (1956: 214). Carnap thought it a mistake to hold that a metaphysics dealing in external questions could be genuinely explanatory at all.

The metaphysics-involving view is certainly committed to elaborating a much more substantial conception of metaphysics, in respect of both its nature and its explanatory powers, than in these views of Carnap and Wright. In fact, the relations between the position I will be developing and Carnap's own views is complex and interesting, and I will, in the case of abstract objects, by no means be rejecting everything he said or implied. But what I have to say necessarily comes along with a conception of metaphysics as substantive.

In his work *Postmetaphysical Thinking: Philosophical Essays*, Jürgen Habermas, if I have understood him correctly, suggests that "a new paradigm, that of mutual understanding" involved in communication in speaking a common language is a way to develop and engage in "postmetaphysical thinking" (1992: 43). It may be that Habermas writes into his conception of metaphysics more than I would. Nonetheless, since the conditions for understanding a common language will certainly mention the contents and concepts employed by language users, a full account of what that involves will involve a metaphysics, if the Primary Thesis is correct.

(4) The Primary Thesis and the way I have been developing it is incompatible with a generalized anthropocentrism about properties, relations, and magnitudes. This generalized anthropocentrism claims that insofar as we can make sense of an ontology of properties, relations, and magnitudes, they are all constitutively dependent upon human ways of going on in judgements and reactions. This view is not an anthropocentrism about sense, which may have its attractions in certain limited classes of cases, but is rather a generalized anthropocentrism about entities at the level of reference. Such a generalized anthropocentrism has sometimes been canvassed as a development of views allegedly found in the later writings of Wittgenstein. But if, for example, there are genuinely mind-independent spatial properties of objects that not only explain physical phenomena, but also contribute to the individuation of the content of our spatial perceptions, the mind-independence of those properties rules out a generalized anthropocentrism.

I am not going to attempt at this point to take on in more detail positions of these four types, even though the task of doing so is of philosophical interest in each case, and the writings I am contradicting are of enormous philosophical interest. If a critic in philosophy says that a certain kind of account—in the present instance, the Primary Thesis—is impossible, there are at least two ways of proceeding. One is to try to show that the critic's arguments are unsound. The other is to actually try to do what the critic claims is impossible. If it can be done, then the arguments that it cannot be done must be unsound. In Chapter 2, I am going to attempt to show that it can be done for one particular case, the ontology of physical magnitudes.

I conclude with a reflection on the nature of the project of expounding, arguing for, and illustrating the Primary Thesis. In such work, we are theorizing philosophically from a fully immersed location. We use spatial notions made available by perception, we enjoy perception with intentional contents concerning distances, directions, and so forth, and we employ concepts made available by our relation to the world to assess the very conditions for possessing various concepts and the conditions for grasping certain intentional contents concerning spatial magnitudes and properties. We could not do this unless we already possess the concepts and grasp the intentional contents ourselves. Our very ways of thinking (canonically) of the concepts we are theorizing about are made available by our own possession of those concepts.[3] When this kind of immersed investigation is successful, we learn of the relations in which we must already be standing in order to grasp the concepts or intentional contents in question. We are engaged in an immersed investigation into the very conditions of such immersion.

---

[3] On canonical concepts of concepts, made available by possession of those concepts themselves, see Peacocke (2009). There has finally been some convergence on the nature of concepts of concepts, even amongst theorists of very different stripes: see Burge (2005) and Chalmers (2011).

2

Magnitudes

In this and Chapters 3 to 6, I will consider various domains with a view to investigating in more detail the way in which the metaphysics-involving thesis, the Primary Thesis, about the relations between metaphysics and content holds for the various subject matters involved. In this chapter, I consider the domain of spatiotemporal magnitudes, and its relation to our capacity to perceive magnitudes as such.

The case of spatiotemporal magnitudes and our capacity to perceive some of them is plausibly an example falling under the metaphysics-first classification of Chapter 1. It seems highly plausible that the metaphysics of this domain is prior, in the order of philosophical explanation, to an explanation of the nature of the intentional contents of our perceptual states when we perceive magnitudes. This impression of plausibility does, however, need to be substantiated.

In accordance with the argument of Chapter 1, in order to make good the claim of the metaphysics-first classification, we need to draw on a substantive metaphysics of magnitudes. That is the first task of the present chapter. I will then draw on that substantive metaphysics in offering an explanation of various features of the perception of spatiotemporal magnitudes. I will also be arguing that the presented account of this metaphysics, and its relation to perception, allows us to address some further issues about analogue representation, analogue devices, and the analogue/digital distinction more generally. I will also argue that the treatment allows us to reply to at least one form of scepticism voiced by Thomas Kuhn about the powers of perception.

In spite of the immense and very welcome growth of philosophical writing about perception in the past forty years, there has been little philosophical material about the perception of magnitudes, and only somewhat more on the metaphysics of magnitudes. Quite independently of its intended role as contributing to an elaboration of the Primary Thesis, I hope the material on magnitudes in this chapter will be of interest in filling at least some of those gaps.

1. Seven Principles of the Metaphysics of Magnitudes

The metaphysics of magnitudes on which I propose to draw in advocating a metaphysics-first view of spatiotemporal perception can be formulated in Seven Principles. In discussing magnitudes, we need always to distinguish between magnitude-types, magnitudes, and magnitude-tropes. The magnitude that is measured by 10 inches and the magnitude that is measured by 10 miles are both instances of the same magnitude-type, distance. The magnitude that is measured by 10 minutes and the magnitude that is measured by 10 years are both instances of the magnitude-type duration. The magnitude that is measured by 10 inches is one and the same as the magnitude that is measured by 25.4 centimetres. That distance magnitude is the magnitude that is the distance between the mark '0' and the mark '10' on every good physical ruler employing the Imperial system. Every magnitude is of some magnitude-type, as Frege recognized when he wrote in the *Grundgesetze*, "Something is a magnitude not all by itself, but only insofar as it belongs with other objects of a class which is a domain of magnitudes" (2013: Vol. II §161: 159).

For some purposes, it can be advantageous to slice more finely than the magnitudes just described, down to magnitude-tropes. The magnitude-trope of distance between the '0' and '10' marks on your ruler, and the magnitude-trope of distance between the '0' and '10' marks on my ruler, are distinct. We may, for example, want to insist that the former magnitude-trope explains your perception of the distance between the marks on your ruler, and the latter magnitude-trope explains my perception of distance between the corresponding marks on my ruler. In this book, however, my primary concern will be with the middle level of this threefold distinction, the magnitudes, rather than with the types or tropes. Unless otherwise specified, 'magnitude' in what follows refers to magnitudes at this middle level.

The following discussion will also be limited to what in the literature are called extensive magnitudes. These are magnitudes for which an intuitive notion of addition of the magnitudes has application. Distances, durations, velocities, areas, and angles are all examples of extensive magnitudes. Temperatures, by contrast, are not extensive magnitudes. The non-extensive magnitudes—the intensive magnitudes—are interesting and important, both in physical theory and in psychology and the philosophy of mind. Temperature, for instance, features in the gas laws, and in laws about the expansion of solids with heat. Some subjective intensive magnitudes present in experience are also plausibly no-priority cases in the sense of Chapter 1. But we have to walk before we can run, so I set aside the intensive magnitudes for the purposes of this chapter. The main philosophical issues I want to discuss arise already in the more tractable case of the extensive magnitudes.

I now turn to a statement of the Seven Principles.

Principle I: Realism about magnitudes

Such magnitudes as distances, inertial masses, angles, and durations should all be regarded realistically, as elements of our ontology. We refer to magnitudes; we quantify over magnitudes; we apply comparative predicates to them; we treat them as entities to which such operations as addition, subtraction, and multiplication all apply, with limits. Under this realistic approach, the canonical form of attribution of a magnitude is, in the monadic case:

> object or event x has magnitude m of type T at time t (relative to frame R in the relativistic case).

Here it is important that 'm' is a variable ranging over magnitudes themselves, not over numbers. In the relational case, the canonical form is:

> objects or events $x_1 \ldots x_n$ have magnitude m of type T at time t (relative to frame R etc.).

Possession by any particular object of a magnitude is usually a heavily contingent matter. You could have had a different height now; you could have been a different distance from the equator; the lecture could have been shorter. The best way of expressing these contingencies formally involves an ontology of magnitudes. Consider Kripke's example of the true statement that the standard metre rod, which we can call *s*, could have had a different length (1980). *s* actually has a certain length m, and it could have had a different length. This is naturally regimented as:

> Has (s, m, length) & $\exists m'[\neg(m' = m)$ & $\lozenge$ Has (s, m', length)]

For a huge range of magnitude-types, magnitudes of those types are relative to a frame of reference. We know from the special theory of relativity that this applies to durations. Such relativity is entirely consistent with the fact that two events' being separated by a certain duration, in a given frame, is causally explanatory of other events and states of affairs. What we should be realistic about are magnitudes relative to a frame of reference. The frame to which a correct attribution of a magnitude is relative is not just a matter of coordinate labelling. It is relativity to a body in standard expositions of special relativity (and it could be formulated as relativity to a location with an identity over time). This relativity is hugely more consequential than relabelling of a coordinate system of a kind that would make sense even in a Newtonian universe. If spatiotemporal magnitudes were absolute, there would be no need for relativity to a body or to a location, for then identity of magnitudes would make sense without such relativization. A conception of magnitudes under which such relativization is unavoidably present in the specification of a magnitude is a conception that does not apparently involve any commitment to absolutism about magnitudes.

The present realism about magnitudes does not mean that they exist in splendid isolation from other magnitudes. Magnitudes of a given type can be real and irreducible, even if they have fundamental and even individuative connections with magnitudes of other types. Realism about something is consistent with its individuation being a partially relational matter. An attractive conception of realism about instances of a magnitude-type is that their possession by entities involves a nexus of causal powers. It would be possible to develop a treatment of magnitudes in terms of their causal powers that is a generalization of the spirit of Shoemaker's treatment of the individuation of properties in terms of their causal powers (Shoemaker 1984c).

For every magnitude m, there is a corresponding property P_m such that for an entity to have magnitude m involves its having the corresponding property P_m. A realistic treatment of magnitudes in terms of properties is given by Mundy (1987), and these claims of contingency of magnitudes could equally be formulated in terms of an ontology of magnitude-properties. I myself think the treatment of magnitudes as entities referred to by singular terms is closer to the surface semantics of English. We certainly seem to use definite descriptions to refer to the size of objects, and to the duration of events, and we seem to use first-level operators to describe functions from magnitudes to magnitudes. It is certainly possible, however, to formulate a realism about magnitudes at the level of properties. Where the first-level treatment would speak of a relation of being greater than, >, on a pair of magnitudes m1 and m2, the property theorist would speak of a corresponding higher-level relation $>_P$ on the corresponding properties P_{m1} and P_{m2}. The property theorist need not be committed, and given threats of paradox prima facie should not be committed, to any general comprehension axiom for the existence of magnitude-properties. The question of whether magnitudes are first-level entities, or are rather properties, or indeed whether it is a matter of indifference which of these approaches is adopted, is rather an issue internal to the best formulation of realism about magnitudes. There is further discussion of the issues in Mundy (1987) and Peacocke (2015). All the Seven Principles of realism about magnitudes I offer here could be formulated in terms of magnitude-properties, should that treatment be thought preferable.

Principle II: Irreducibility of magnitudes to extensions or to extensional entities

Statements about magnitudes cannot be reduced to statements about extensions, or anything purely extensional not involving magnitudes. Suppose you are 1.6 metres tall. Consider the extension of the property of being 1.6 metres tall—the set of things that are 1.6 metres tall. Concerning that very set: you could still be a member of that set without being 1.6 metres tall. In fact, it is necessary that, provided you exist and the other members of the set exist, you are an element of that very set. It is not necessary that if all those things exist, you are 1.6 metres tall. Conversely, you could still be 1.6 metres tall even if many of the elements of that set never had existed, as Hume might have put it.

There is of course some kind of necessary equivalence between being 1.6 metres tall and being in the set of things that are 1.6 metres tall, where the description of the set falls within the scope of the necessity operator. But that kind of equivalence simply uses the ontology of magnitudes in specifying the relevant set. It does not at all reduce statements about magnitudes to statements about sets.

All these points about sets apply equally to functions from objects to truth-values, and to more complex extensional entities. They apply also to any alleged equivalence of an attribution of magnitude with a statement specifying non-numerical comparative relations to some standard object taken as a unit. There is no particular relation in which it is necessary that you stand to the object that is the standard metre in Paris, nor indeed to any other object that is contingently one metre, if you are 1.6 metres tall. There is further discussion of the point in Peacocke (2015).

These points about the irreducibility of statements of magnitude to something purely extensional are parallel to points Putnam made long ago in his paper 'On Properties' about the irreducibility of properties to anything purely extensional (1975). For the special class of cases in which the property in question is that of having a certain magnitude, these points are in fact a special case of Putnam's point.

These points may seem to reopen the question of whether one can be a realist about magnitudes without being an absolutist. If we are relationalists rather than absolutists about space and time, it seems obligatory to be relationalists rather than absolutists about spatiotemporal magnitudes. But relationalist analyses of magnitudes do typically strive to analyse statements about magnitudes into statements about relations to other entities. In fact, the whole structure of the central arguments of this book arguably implies an endorsement of Leibnizian, rather than Newtonian, views of space and time. This is part of the argument developed in Chapter 6. So how are we to reconcile these points? I myself regard the relationalist's programme as in need of further development, in ways that can be reconciled with the evident modal facts emphasized in the case for this Principle II of the metaphysics of magnitudes. These modal points seem to be obvious and non-negotiable, and it is a task for a fully developed relationalism to offer treatments of statements of magnitude that explain how they can be so.

Principle III: No number is intrinsic to any particular magnitude in itself; there are no intrinsic units for any given magnitude

One single distance magnitude is measured both by 5.08 centimetres and 2 inches. Neither the number 2.54 nor the number 1 is intrinsic to that single magnitude. The numbers are used in characterizing the relation of the single magnitude to other magnitudes; that is, to the other magnitudes which are measured by one centimetre and by one inch, respectively, in this example. No units are intrinsic to any such magnitude. There may be reasons varying from theoretical consideration in the formulation of some particular science to practical convenience for selecting one particular magnitude rather than another as a unit. But metaphysically all the different units are on an equal footing, and no number associated with a magnitude under a choice of a particular unit has any special status.

Principle III needs a restriction, as Corey Maley pointed out to me. If numerosity is included as a magnitude, it is a magnitude with intrinsic units, viz. the cardinal numbers. Numerosity does in its very nature presuppose some individuation of objects other than the magnitudes themselves. Principle III should be restricted to magnitudes that do not presuppose some particular individuation of objects other than the magnitudes themselves.

Though there are no intrinsic units for magnitudes that do not presuppose some particular individuation of objects, the question of intrinsic status is very different for ratios of magnitudes, as the next Principle IV states.

Principle IV: For extensive magnitudes of any given type, the ratios in which those magnitudes stand to one another are intrinsic to them

Since extensive magnitudes support an operation of addition of magnitudes, it also makes sense, for any such magnitude x, to talk of the magnitude nx, where n is a positive integer. nx is just the magnitude obtained by adding x to itself $n-1$ times. These resources are enough by themselves to allow a characterization of identity of ratios between magnitudes. If we use the notation $x{:}y$ for the ratio of x to y, then we can characterize the identity of ratios thus:

$x{:}y = z{:}w$ iff for all m, n, $mx < ny$ iff $mz < nw$.

This is the concise formulation given by Dana Scott (1967). It is equivalent to the historic formulation in Definition 5 of Book V of Euclid's *Elements*.[1]

The network of ratio relations in which magnitudes of a given type stand to one another do seem to be essential to them. Unlike the choice of a unit, there is nothing arbitrary about these ratio relations, and they seem to have to do with the nature of the magnitudes themselves.

Principle V: Magnitudes themselves enter causal and scientific explanations

Light takes a duration of eight minutes to travel from the sun to the earth because the distance between the sun and the earth is 93 million miles. This statement is approximately true, and it is a statement about the duration itself, and about the distance itself. Just as statements of causal explanation are about objects, events and properties themselves, and not modes of presentation thereof, as we discussed in connection with Anscombe (1969) in Chapter 1, so the same applies to magnitudes as mentioned in statements of causal explanation. The above statement about the explanation of the duration it takes light to travel from the sun to the earth concerns the magnitude itself, not a mode of presentation of the magnitude. Concerning the distance that is 149.637 million kilometres, it is equally true (indeed it is the same truth) that light takes eight minutes to reach the earth because that distance is the distance of the sun from the earth.

Principle VI: Extensive magnitudes support an algebra of ratios on those magnitudes

Principle VI is, if we are strict, a mathematical rather than a metaphysical point, but it will be an important lemma in making the case for the later metaphysical Principle VII. We saw that it makes sense to talk of the identity of ratios of magnitudes. It also makes sense to talk of the same ratio across magnitudes of different types. The ratio of two lengths, for example, can be the same as the ratio of two durations. This point was already exploited in Euclidean geometry, when it is discussed whether the ratio of two angles is the same as the ratio of the lengths of two corresponding lines. Scott (1967: 29) gives the following definition of addition for ratios:

> The sum a + b of two ratios a and b is the unique ratio c for which there exist magnitudes x, y, and z such that
>
> a = x:z, b = y:z, and c = (x + y):z.

---

[1] "Magnitudes are said to be in the same ratio, the first to the second and the third to the fourth, when, if any equimultiples whatever be taken of the first and third, and any equimultiples whatever of the second and fourth, the former equimultiples alike exceed, are alike equal to, or alike fall short of, the latter equimultiples respectively taken in corresponding order." This is the translation given by Heath (Euclid 1956). The contents of Book V of the *Elements* are attributed to Eudoxus.

Similarly, there is the natural definition of multiplication of ratios, which will be important in what follows (Scott 1967: 31):

> The product a*b of two ratios a and b is the unique ratio c for which there exist magnitudes x, y, and z such that
>
> a = x:z, b = z:y, and c = x:y.

Principle VII: Magnitudes can feature in causal-explanatory laws

Principle VII may seem puzzling. Formulations of scientific laws characteristically involve quantification over the real numbers. In taking instances of the laws, we substitute terms for real numbers. This role of the real numbers may seem difficult to reconcile with the preceding principles—was not their point that numbers are not intrinsic to the magnitudes themselves? There is in fact no incompatibility or tension here. Scientific laws are already about ratios of magnitudes, because of our implicit reliance on units when we substitute numerical values in the numerically formulated law. Consider Newton's second law, that force is the product of mass and acceleration. We do indeed substitute numerical terms for the variables over mass and acceleration when we apply this law to particular instances. As noted, however, we implicitly assume some units—that is, unit magnitudes—for mass and acceleration when we make such substitutions. What Newton's second law really states, concerning the magnitudes involved, is this: the ratio of any two forces is the product of the ratios of the masses involved with the ratio of the accelerations involved. These are ratios of magnitudes; and we have seen that we can take the product of ratios. This is a simple model for the way in which magnitudes are really the subject matter of what look like numerically formulated laws (see further Peacocke 2015). The model can apply in other cases in which there are laws relating to extensive magnitudes.

The discussion so far has concerned physical magnitudes. There can also be realistic treatments of the magnitudes of higher-level and special sciences, such as psychology and economics. National income and rates of growth of national income are magnitudes that can be explanatory of social and economic states of affairs. It is certainly tempting to hold that genuine magnitudes stand in causal-explanatory relations to various states of affairs. By contrast, spurious magnitudes, such as Spearman's notorious 'g', alleged to stand for a magnitude that was labelled as 'general intelligence', have no explanatory power whatsoever, however good their nominal definitions (Spearman 1904).

2. Magnitudes as Perceived

Magnitudes seem to enter the content of almost every perceptual experience. This applies to intensive as well as extensive magnitudes. Kant was well aware of the point. He wrote, "All intuitions are extensive magnitudes" (B202); and "In all appearances the real, which is an object of the sensation, has intensive magnitude, i.e., a degree" (Kant 1998: B207). As Geoff Lee remarked to me, Kant likely had a more restricted notion of an extensive magnitude-type than the one I have been using. Kant likely required that an extensive magnitude-type not only possesses an addition operation on the magnitudes of the type, but also has a mereological structure. It is likely that for Kant, an extensive magnitude-type is one whose magnitudes have parts that are also magnitudes of the same type (Kant 1998: A162/B203). In the case of extensive magnitudes both in my sense and in Kant's stronger sense, any experience with what I called spatial scenario content (1992) will involve the experience of extensive magnitudes. The distances that objects and events are experienced as having from one another, and from oneself, are Kantian extensive magnitudes. The angles they are experienced as having in relation to one's body and their sizes are also magnitudes. Even those experiences that do not have spatial content at all will often have a content involving temporal magnitudes such as duration, which is also a Kantian extensive magnitude.

The domain of spatial magnitudes and the intentional contents of perception presenting those magnitudes are a paradigm example of a case to which the metaphysics-first view applies. There is no plausibility in the suggestion that the metaphysics of spatial magnitudes has to mention the contents of mental states and events. Spatial magnitudes are utterly mind-independent. A constitutive account of what it is for perceptual states to have intentional contents concerning spatial magnitudes will mention the causation of those states by mind-independent spatial magnitudes themselves in central cases. It will also mention the capacity of those states to explain actions of the subject of the perceptual states under descriptions that relate the actions to spatial magnitudes themselves.

Explanations of actions by the perception of spatial magnitudes will sustain counterfactuals that concern magnitudes in the subject's environment. If the target of the action had been at a different angle to the subject, then other things equal, the perceiving subject would have turned through that different angle; and so forth for myriad other possible examples.

Under the realistic ontology of magnitudes advocated above, it is not surprising that one and the same extensive magnitude can be perceived by more than one sense. One and the same angle or one and the same distance may be perceived both in sight and in touch, as when you both see and feel the angle at which the tongs are open. The angle itself is a mind-independent magnitude, available for perception in more than one modality, and capable of causally explaining perceptions of itself in more than one modality.

The perception of spatial and temporal magnitudes also has some more specific features, and the question arises of the relation of these features of perception to a metaphysics of magnitudes that endorses Principles I–VII. Let us consider two features of perception first.

(1) The perception of magnitudes is unit-free. We do not perceive distances in, say, inches as opposed to centimetres. Even when someone knows how long a centimetre is just by looking, that is substantive knowledge. That knowledge could also be lost even while things still look the same length. Maybe some subjects perceive certain distances as just over a forearm's length away, or as roughly twice the width of their hand. But these subjects also see how long their arms are, and see how wide their hands are, and again this is non-trivial knowledge. Modulo some fuzzy boundaries, there is some distance magnitude m such that the subject sees that her forearm has length magnitude m. When all in the perceptual system is working well, an experience as of an object having length m is causally explained by that object's having length m. Such facts contribute to giving the experience the content concerning magnitudes that it actually has.

In perceiving magnitudes as unit-free, a subject perceives the unit-free magnitudes as they really are, according to any metaphysics that endorses Principles I–VII. I am somewhat embarrassed to note that, although I noted the unit-free character of the perception of magnitudes more than thirty years ago (1986), for decades I failed to connect it properly with the metaphysics of magnitudes themselves, and their role in perception.

Perception of a magnitude, like the perception or representation of anything at all, is always under a mode of presentation. One and the same magnitude can be given in perception under different modes of presentation. A certain distance can be perceived between two objects on one's left, and what is in fact the same distance can at the same time be perceived as the distance between two objects on one's right. It does not follow that the distances are perceived as the same, even when there is no misperception. The canonical form of the attribution of magnitude perception, in the monadic case, is

object or event x as given under mode of presentation α is perceived as having magnitude m under mode of presentation μ relative to frame Rs.

(2) Subjects sometimes perceive the ratio of two magnitudes, and may on occasion perceive that two pairs of magnitudes are in the same ratio. You can

sometimes perceive that the ratio between the heights of two adjacent buildings is the same as the ratio between the lengths of two other objects perceived at the same time. Again, in accordance with any metaphysics of magnitudes that endorses Principles I–VII, in so seeing this identity of ratios, you can be seeing the ratios as they really are, independently of any classification or units for them.

Now, are such features of perception as (1) and (2) sufficiently explained by a metaphysics of magnitudes that endorses Principles I–VII? The metaphysics of magnitudes is certainly an essential component of the explanation. But it cannot be the full explanation, because the fact that a magnitude is extensive in reality does not by itself guarantee that it is perceptually extensive. This needs some clarification and examples.

A magnitude-type is *perceptually extensive* for a subject iff for magnitudes of that type, there is some operation of summing magnitudes such that a magnitude of that type can be perceived by the subject as the sum of two other magnitudes. This requires that the subject perceptually represent the summing operation—summing in this characterization of being perceptually extensive is not just an operation on reality. Perceptually extensive magnitudes for humans include length, duration, and, arguably, approximate numerosity. One length can be seen as the sum of the length of two other nearby lines; one duration can be experienced as about twice the length of another.

By contrast, some magnitude-types are extensive in reality, but are not perceptually extensive for human perceivers. Weight is one example. It does not feel as if an 8lb book supported on your hand is double the weight of a 4lb book supported on your hand. Another example is pitch in musical perception. Consider your experience of the note E, frequency 660 Hz, above the modern orchestral tuning note A, frequency 440 Hz. It does not seem perceptually as if that note E is the sum of the A one octave lower, 220 Hz, and the tuning note A, 440 Hz, even though 220 + 440 = 660, and even though it makes sense to add frequencies, as the number of peaks per unit time. We do not experience pitch as frequency at all—neither in Hz units, nor in any unit-free manner.

Similarly, the colour of light of one pure wavelength does not seem in perception to be the sum of light of two other wavelengths.

The fact that a magnitude-type can be extensive in reality without being perceptually extensive is an instance of a more general phenomenon, of structural features of the type being absent from the perception of that reality. To return to musical pitch for another example: in perceiving the relation between two notes in western tonally based music, what you are perceiving is in fact the ratio between the frequencies. An octave increase in pitch is a doubling of the frequency; a fifth is the ratio 3:2; a whole tone step up is 9:8; and so forth. But we do not hear these pitch relations as those ratios.

Similarly, in the case of temperature, the ratio between two differences in temperature is an objective, unit-independent matter. But equally we do not perceive the ratios between differences in temperature.

The distinction between objectively extensive and perceptually extensive prompts at least two questions. A first question: since it doesn't follow from a magnitude being perceived that it's perceived as extensive, what more is needed to explain it's being so perceived? The gap between the objectively extensive and the perceptually extensive shows that we must say more to explain the unit-free character of magnitude perception, since a magnitude-type being unit-free similarly doesn't imply it's perceived that way. A second question is this: what can we infer about the mental representations underlying the perceptions of instances of a magnitude when they are also perceived as extensive?

I suggest that the same resource can answer both questions. Suppose magnitudes of a given type T are perceived as extensive; suppose that m1, m2, and m3 are instances of T; and that magnitude m3 is the sum of m1 and m2, for the operation of summing under which T is an extensive magnitude-type. Then when these three magnitudes m1, m2, and m3 are perceived, and all is working properly, there are three underlying mental representations of them r1, r2, and r3, and these three representations are all magnitudes of a given type R. There is also some binary operation o on magnitudes of the type R such that r3 = o (r1, r2). It is a certain sensitivity within the subject's perceptual apparatus to r3 being the result of the operation of o on r1 and r2 that allows the subject to represent magnitudes of type T as extensive. That is the first condition met by representationally extensive systems. The second is that there is some mental representation in the perceptual system of one perceived magnitude being the sum of two others. This latter mental representation is triggered by the operation of o on r1 and r2 in the preceding condition. To formulate the significance of this condition loosely but intuitively: the representations of magnitudes of type T in such a system are such that it is determinable from the representations of any three magnitudes of that type whether one is the sum of the other two, and this instance of the summing relation is itself perceptually represented. We can call a system meeting this condition a *representationally extensive* perceptual system for magnitudes of type T.

For an example of an analogous representationally extensive system operating at the personal level, for our public representational systems, consider the duration of some event as represented by the length of a straight line. We can tell from this representation of duration whether it is the sum of two other durations also represented by length, simply by operation on the representing magnitudes, the lengths, themselves. Also in this example, no unit is represented by instances of the representing magnitude, because it too is unit-free. (One can conceive of mixed cases, but they would need to be mixed for any unit to be represented.)

By contrast, there's no magnitude-property of Arabic digits that allows one to work out that what's represented by '12' is the sum of what's represented by '7' together with what's represented by '5'. Musical pitch is also not represented by an extensive magnitude to which the perceptual system is sensitive.

I suggest that it is the fact that a perceptual system is representationally extensive for a magnitude-type T that we have to add to the objective extensive character of the magnitude T itself to explain the fact that the subject perceives the magnitude as extensive. The extensive character of the magnitude in reality contributes essentially to the explanation of features of the particular representations caused in the perceiver by the environmental magnitudes. So we still have a metaphysics-first view of the domain here. But the metaphysics-first treatment has to be combined with recognition of the representationally extensive character of a perceptual system if we are to explain such features as the unit-free character of spatial and temporal perception, and the perception of ratios of these magnitude-types. Citing the metaphysics alone is not enough. The metaphysics has to work hand-in-hand with the representationally extensive character of the system.

Of course, even with the addition of an outline of an account of perceptually extensive systems, we are still far from a full explanation of the experience of magnitudes as extensive. We lack an account of perceptual consciousness itself. The present proposal is simply that, if and when a satisfactory philosophical and psychological theory of perceptual consciousness is attained, it will be aided by drawing on an account of what is distinctive of representationally extensive systems for some objectively extensive magnitude.

We have already moved into the territory of mental representation, and to the question of what certain special kinds of representation can explain. This territory sets an agenda that we will pursue in the remainder of this chapter, and in part of Chapter 3. What is the bearing of the metaphysical treatment of magnitudes on the notion of analogue representation and analogue computation? And can we make sense of an analogue/digital distinction not just for mental representations, for the vehicles of content, but also for the intentional content of those representations, for the way in which they represent what they represent? These questions I take up in the remainder of this chapter. More generally, if we really do perceive magnitudes themselves, then part of the content of experience is fundamentally externalist, and not purely narrow. The view that magnitudes themselves can be perceived has both explanatory and epistemological ramifications, and is correspondingly controversial. I will address some of the resulting issues about this externalism in Chapter 3. First we turn to some analogue/digital distinctions, which can receive a different account when we acknowledge an ontology of magnitudes.

3. Analogue Computation and Representation

Analogue representation is representation of magnitudes, by magnitudes.

Analogue computation is the operation on representing magnitudes to generate further representing magnitudes.

In the remainder of this chapter, I will elaborate these claims. In doing so, I will draw on a metaphysics of magnitudes respecting Principles I–VII. Prima facie, this elaboration is in accord with a metaphysics-first view of the domains of magnitudes in question.

We can start with the notion of analogue computation and analogue computers. Familiar examples of analogue computers include the following:

astrolabes;

tide-predicting machines composed from arrangements of ropes, wheels, and pulleys;

electrical systems composed of capacitors, inductors, and resistors;

systems involving actual fluids and channels used to represent the flow of national income in an economy.

Each of these systems is governed by special science laws. As always, these special science laws have *ceteris paribus* clauses (Fodor 1974). For instance, the special science laws relate one physical magnitude present in an astrolabe—say, the angle between two wheels—to another. The laws may relate the current in one part of an electrical system to the current in other parts of the system, given in the intervening resistors and other inputs; and so forth.

These systems meet two necessary conditions for being analogue computers. First, their operation is governed by special science laws that state that instances of certain magnitude-types in the system are specific functions of other instances of magnitude-types in the system. More specifically, instances of those magnitude-types in the system are causally explained by corresponding instances of magnitude-types in the system, where the correspondence is fixed by the specific function mentioned in the law.

Second, the magnitudes mentioned in these special science laws represent, or are used to represent, magnitudes in the world. In a good analogue computer, the special science law relating the representing magnitudes determines, via the representational mapping, a principle about magnitudes in the represented domain, be it a principle about planetary motions, or a principle about national income.

We can diagram the situation thus, where the representing magnitudes in the antecedent of the special science law are of type K, and represent instances of magnitudes of the type R(K); and where the representing magnitudes in the consequent of the special science law are of type M, in turn representing magnitudes of the type R(M):

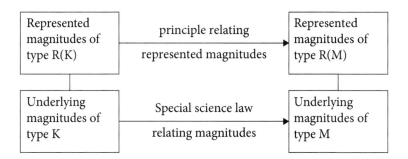

Many earlier characterizations in the literature state that analogue computation has to involve magnitude-types in the computing system that are continuous. In one standard text, A. S. Jackson wrote, "The most significant feature that distinguishes analog computation from numerical computation is continuity; analog computation implies continuous computation; that is the variables involved in a calculation appear as continuous or smooth functions" (Jackson 1960: 1–2). On the characterization that I just offered, all that is required for analogue computation is that the special science laws governing the computing device are laws of magnitudes themselves, whether those magnitudes are continuous or not, and whether they are dense or not. I suspect that there would now be widespread acceptance that the requirement for analogue computation of continuity or even of density is too strong (Piccinini 2015: 200). Analogue computation can be present in an entirely quantized, discrete universe. The hypothesis that the actual universe is fundamentally discrete is taken as a serious option in current physics (Dowker 2010).

In accordance with the preceding discussion of Principle VII of a metaphysics of magnitudes, the special science laws governing these analogue systems, though normally written to state that one magnitude given as a number is a certain function of several others, should be understood as making statements about ratios of magnitudes. Given a set of fixed electrical resistors and an arrangement of connecting wires in a system, we have a standardly written special science law that the current at one point in the system is a certain function of the current at another point. Under the metaphysics of magnitudes I have been advocating, this law should be understood as stating that the ratio of any two unit-free current magnitudes at the first location in the system is a constant function of the ratio of any corresponding two unit-free current magnitudes at the second location in the system.

Analogue mental processes are a special case of analogue computation in the sense just specified. Analogue mental processes in humans are the special case in which the representing states and events are mental, and in which the special science laws underlying the mental processes are laws concerning magnitudes in the human brain. The magnitudes need not at all be those of a basic physics, or of an almost-basic physics. Neurophysiological states and events are a long way from being almost primitive physical states that feature in David Lewis's discussion of related issues (1971). I want to focus particularly on the large subset of cases in which the analogue process involves a process of change of intentional content, rather than, say, a process of change in mood, or of the intensity of some other mental state. Processes involving a change of intentional content include that of mentally rotating a complex shape, as in Shepard's and Metzler's original experiments (1971). Such processes also include actual perception of a rotating shape, and perception of an object moving in the subject's environment, or changing shape, or changing its location egocentrically identified, if the subject is moving. They include too the process of scanning a mental image from one location in the image to another. These cases all involve a series of different demonstratives over time, demonstratives based either on perception or imagination, such as 'that angle', 'that distance', 'that location', 'that shape', and 'that direction', where the demonstratives themselves refer to magnitudes.

The crucial point is that in an analogue mental process, properties of the magnitudes that do the representing, the formats of the representations themselves, are explanatory of intentional properties of the mental process. To give a simplified example, let us consider the comparative time taken to scan mentally from one location A in a mental image to another location B, as compared with the time taken to scan from location A to a different location C, as in the famous map image, Figure 2.1 below, in Kosslyn, Ball, and Reiser (1978).

I will use upper-case letters for locations and distances in the mental image, and lower-case letters for locations and magnitudes at the level of brain representations, such as retinotopic locations and distances. Suppose, as some experiments suggest, the ratio of the time taken to scan mentally from A to B in the image as compared with scanning from A to C is proportional to the ratio of the

Figure 2.1 Illustration from Kosslyn, S., Ball, T., and Reiser, B. (1978) 'Visual Images Preserve Metric Spatial Information: Evidence from Studies of Image Scanning', *Journal of Experimental Psychology: Human Perception and Performance* 4(1): 47–60. Copyright © 1978 American Psychological Association. Reprinted by permission.

distances AB and AC in the image. In such an analogue mental process governed by special science laws relating to brain magnitudes, this proportionality is explained by, for instance, the ratio of the real distances in a retinotopic map between the brain magnitude, call it d_{AB}, representing the distance AB, and the brain magnitude d_{AC} representing the distance AC. The time taken to scan between two locations in the image is causally explained by magnitudes in the representation in the brain that represents the image; indeed, some form of distance magnitude if the representation is retinotopic.

There is also a dependence of the time taken on the nature of the scanning process. We can conceive of scanning processes that do not preserve proportionality of time to distance, but preserve only comparative relations, so that scanning greater distances in the image always results in longer scanning times. But in either case, the properties of the representing magnitudes, and the processes operating on it, would be explanatory of the temporal phenomena.

As is very familiar from other cases, a lawlike correlation between a representing magnitude-type and features of a mental process does not necessarily mean that properties of the magnitude-type causally explain those features of the mental process. The lawlike correlation may be the result of some other common cause. We must always distinguish pseudo-dependence from real causal explanation. The first condition for analogue computation requires real causal explanation, not just a lawful connection.

Here is an actual example from the imagery literature that illustrates at least the possibility of such a mere pseudo-dependence in the case of mental representations. Stephen Kosslyn discusses those image transformations that he describes as "motion-added" (Kosslyn 1994: chapter 10). Some mental images that we enjoy have motion already built into them. This is a case that very likely applies to your mental image of serving in tennis. But in other cases, characteristically images of objects rather than event-types, motion is not involved in the content of the original image. Transformation of these latter images Kosslyn classifies as "motion-added". Kosslyn hypothesizes that the motor system plays a role in motion-added transformations. He suggests that the motor system does so "by altering an object's representation in the spatiotopic mapping subsystem, and thereby guiding the transformation itself. My hypothesis is that *one actively anticipates what one will see when one makes a movement*, and this anticipation not only primes representations of object properties in the pattern activation subsystem... but also alters representations of spatial properties in the spatiotopic mapping subsystem... In imagery, the priming processes are so strong that a mental image is generated, and this image moves through the sequence one anticipates seeing" (1994: 351). If Kosslyn is right about this, then the distinction between mere lawlike correlation and real causal explanation by magnitudes applies straightforwardly to the original Shepard and Metzler experiments on mental rotation of 3D shapes. Mental rotation of those (constructed) 3D shapes would then be motion-added cases. There would be a lawlike correlation between some subpersonal magnitude that represents the imagined egocentric angle of the 3D shape. But that lawlike connection would not be causally explanatory of the time course of an imagined rotation, if Kosslyn's hypothesis is right. What would be causally explanatory would plausibly be a different range of subpersonal magnitudes, those involved in the motor system. This is a hypothetical illustration—the currently published literature does not, to the best of my knowledge, resolve the issue. The point is just that there is such an issue.

Here are three other applications of the conception of magnitude-involving analogue computation that I have been advocating.

(1) Where there is representation by magnitudes, we can expect there also to be what Shepard and Chipman call 'second-order isomorphism' between representations and what in the world they represent (1970). Shepard and Chipman write,

> the isomorphism should be sought…in the second-order relation between (a) the relations among alternative external objects, and (b) the relations among their corresponding internal representations. Thus, although the internal representation for a square need not itself be square, it should (whatever it is) at least have a closer functional relation to the internal representation for a rectangle than to that, say, for a green flash or the taste of persimmon.   (1970: 2)

'Second-order' is not quite an accurate characterization of the phenomenon they are identifying. The isomorphism they say is present in their example is still a first-order isomorphism, between objects (shapes, in their example) and mental representations, an isomorphism that preserves certain closeness relations that hold in each of these two domains. Shepard and Metzler draw a contrast between their position and that of the benighted theorist who thinks that mental representations of something square must themselves be square. The contrast is clear, but it is not a contrast between various kinds of isomorphism. Their contrast is rather a contrast with a theorist who is making a claim in support of an identity of property, viz. being square, allegedly instantiated both in the domain of objects and in the domain of their mental representations. This point noted, I will call the kind of isomorphism Shepard and Metzler do endorse 'Shepardian isomorphism'. It is a first-order isomorphism of a closeness relation in the domain of representations with a closeness relation in the domain of what is represented.

Shepardian isomorphism is to be expected when there is representation by instances of some magnitude-type. Different magnitudes of the given magnitude-type will represent instances of some given magnitude or property in the world. Different values of the representing magnitude will correspond systematically to variations in the represented magnitude or property. So comparative closeness relations between instances of the representing magnitude will map on to corresponding closeness relations between what is represented by the magnitude.

(2) What is the relation between analogue representation by magnitudes and iconic representation? Iconic representation is often characterized in a way that intrinsically restricts it to the spatial, both on the side of what is represented and on the side of the representations themselves. Thus Susan Carey writes, "In analog iconic symbols, such as a realistic picture of a dog representing a dog, parts of the symbol represent parts of the represented entity: the ears on the picture represent the ears of the dog, respecting spatial relations that hold in reality" (2009: 135).

An analogue representation by magnitudes need not be iconic in that spatial sense. Suppose that the duration of some perceived event is represented by the frequency of firing of some group of neurons. That would be representation by a magnitude, a frequency. A firing of fifty times per second does not have a firing of seventeen times per second as a part (not even as a temporal part). Insofar as special science causal laws about magnitudes at the level of representations contribute to explanations, that is something that extends beyond the special cases of iconic representations. It is true that the iconic character of certain representations can explain some features of mental phenomena, notably some of the phenomena of scanning of mental images of spatial layouts mentioned earlier. That is a special case of the more general phenomenon of explanation by properties of representing magnitudes.

If these points are correct, and the representation of duration, for instance, is included in core cognition, and if its representation is not iconic, then not all core cognition involves iconic representations. Susan Carey writes, "I have claimed that all of core cognition is likely to be represented in iconic format" (2009: 458). The recent points raise the question of how this could be so for the perception of duration. Nonetheless, this point still leaves in place two weaker important hypotheses about core cognition, wholly within the spirit of Carey's position. One is that core spatial cognition is iconic. The other is that all core cognition, whether spatial or not, involves analogue representation at some level.

These points also leave in the field the hypothesis that all core cognition involves a general-purpose analogue representation system, a hypothesis to which I now turn as the third of the applications of the above discussion of representation by magnitudes.

(3) Several writers, notably Vincent Walsh (2003), have proposed that the human brain employs a general-purpose analogue magnitude system. Walsh discusses the cases of time, space, and quantity. The present treatment of representation by magnitudes, considered as an ontology in its own right, provides for this possibility. A generalized analogue representation system will have at least two components.

(a) One component will be a range of magnitudes of events and states in the brain, together with operations on them in a system governed by special science laws that apply to those magnitudes. This first component is the system of general-purpose representations that can serve several different representational functions.

(b) The other component will be one that, from occasion to occasion, connects the representing magnitudes in the first system with various other states, which function to represent on that occasion the represented magnitudes (in some cases given at the personal level by analogue intentional contents; see below).

Features of the first component (a), for example its ability to generate representations of the ratios of the magnitudes it employs, could then provide an explanation of such phenomena as the ability to perceive ratios of magnitudes that apply across the various domains to which the general-purpose system is variously connected on particular occasions.

I have offered two necessary conditions for a computer to be analogue: that its operation is governed by special science laws relating magnitudes, and that the relevant magnitudes in states and events of the computer represent. These two conditions are, however, not jointly sufficient for the device to be an analogue computer. You can conceive of a computer that starts with analogue input; it then converts that analogue input into digital form; it then engages in digital computation on digital representations; and finally converts the last digital representation into analogue form (as a DAC does in some stereo setups). This device is not, or not wholly, an analogue computer, even though it meets the two necessary conditions I gave. We need also to require for a wholly analogue computer that no subpart of the computations involved be digital in form. For that to have any general explanatory force, we will need a characterization of the digital, a task to which I will return after applying what we have so far to the perception of magnitudes.

4. Analogue Content, Digital Content

The central and most fundamental examples of intentional contents of perception that we may intuitively want to classify as analogue are demonstrative perceptual modes of presentation of magnitudes. These modes of presentation are naturally expressed in language by such phrases as 'that length', 'that angle', 'that speed', 'that shade', and, in the auditory case, 'that pitch', each of them used in connection with a particular experience on any given occasion. These modes of presentation, as employed on a particular occasion in language or thought, present a particular magnitude, or narrow range of magnitudes, as an instance of a type—length, speed, shade, pitch—and, as always, present it under a certain mode of presentation. The magnitude may or may not be of an extensive magnitude-type, as the case of 'that shade' shows. The magnitude may be intensive, in the traditional terminology. Whether the magnitude is extensive or intensive, the ontology of magnitudes is here conceived along the lines of the Seven Principles above, under which magnitudes are real entities that are unit-free, and which enter into causal explanations both as components of various explaining conditions and as components of various explained conditions.

It is plausible that both conceptual and nonconceptual modes of presentation may be analogue in this sense. There is every reason to believe that organisms that represent the world around them, but which do so only in states with nonconceptual content, enjoy states with these central cases of analogue perceptual content. Though I will not discuss the matter here, it is plausible that the conceptual analogue contents concerning magnitudes, the conceptual contents expressed in language by 'that length', 'that angle', and the like, are themselves individuated in part by their relations to more primitive nonconceptual perceptual analogue contents.

All of these central, fundamental cases are intuitively classified as analogue because they present magnitudes in a way that does not involve any kind of intuitive digitization of the spectrum of magnitudes they present. But what does that mean? I aim to elucidate the content of this intuitive classification as we proceed.

There are analogue contents that do not present magnitudes in any obvious sense of the term, but whose status as analogue is grounded in the fact that these contents are defined, in part at least, by their relations to analogue contents that do present magnitudes. Consider perceptual demonstrative modes of presentation such as 'that shape' or 'that (musical) chord'. These will count as analogue in virtue of their relations, in the first case, of the perceived shape to analogue contents presenting lines and angles, and, in the second case, to perceived pitches. The analogue mode of presentation of the shape or the chord will also involve further representational matters—perceived spatial or tonal relations between the presented components in these two cases.

As I said, in almost all the literature on the analogue/digital distinction, the notions of the analogue and of the digital have been applied at the level of representations—characters, marks, inscriptions, events, utterances—rather than at the level of perceptual experience and its intentional content. We will need eventually to connect the two levels. I propose to lead up to doing this by considering certain features of the notion of the digital, as it has been applied at the level of representations.

We need psychologically realistic and psychologically constrained accounts of the distinction between analogue and digital representations. We can illustrate the point by considering a feature of Nelson Goodman's justly famous account that in my view has been insufficiently noted. For Goodman, analogue systems are syntactically and semantically dense. Goodman writes, "A symbol *scheme* is analog if syntactically dense; a *system* is analog if syntactically and semantically dense" (1968: 160). To say that a system is syntactically dense is to say that between any two of its characters, there is another character. As Goodman notes (136), syntactic density of a system means that its characters are not 'finitely differentiated'. A set of characters is finitely differentiated, for Goodman, if the set of characters meets this condition:

For every two characters K and K' and every mark m that does not actually belong to both, determination either that m does not belong to K or that m does not belong to K' is theoretically possible.   (1968: 135–6)

The presence of the phrase 'theoretically possible' in this condition means that Goodman's notion of finite differentiation prescinds from actual psychological capacities. Take Hilbert's stroke notation for natural numbers. Each symbol in the notation is a finite sequence of simple vertical strokes. This system is clearly digital by Goodman's criterion. It is theoretically possible for any characters K and K' in this notation and any inscription that is not of both types to determine that it does not belong to K or that it does not belong to K'. How would we in fact determine that? Consider a symbol like this one for the number 23:

We come to know which character this inscription belongs to, and which it does not, by counting the individual vertical strokes. We count in our everyday Arabic notation. By such counting, we can determine that the above displayed inscription belongs to a character with twenty-three strokes, and not to the same characters as this one, which in fact has twenty-four strokes:

But in fact we cannot tell that these are instances of different Hilbertian characters just by looking at the individual instances separately. Goodman's conception as defined in terms of what is theoretically possible is an entirely legitimate notion, but it cuts much less finely than the important psychological kind that requires perceptual recognizability of characters.

The reason this matters is the link between a notion of digital representation, and the reproducibility and recognizability of texts, scripts, and the like when written in a digital system. Goodman and, later, John Haugeland emphasized that when finite differentiation in his sense fails, we do not have the reliable and knowable reproducibility that we need for the reproduction of texts, scripts, and scores (Goodman 1968; Haugeland 1998). Now failure of Goodman's finite differentiation requirement, with its talk of what it is theoretically possible to determine, is certainly sufficient for failure of knowable reproduction of texts, scripts, and scores, as we normally use that notion of reproduction. If determination of distinctness of character is not even theoretically possible, it would not be possible to know that one text or score is a reproduction or copy of another. But failure of Goodman's condition of finite differentiation is not necessary for failure of normal reproducibility. Texts, scripts, and scores would not be reproducible by normal standards, in ordinary life, if we had to use an electron microscope to tell whether an inscription is of a given character, or to measure below what's perceptible in normal human vision. The use of the electron microscope may suffice to show that a certain determination is theoretically possible; but that sort of determination cannot be the foundation of the kind of reproducibility that is important to us in normal life.

The point applies in the most homely of examples. For the Hilbert notation for natural numbers, if we can recognize the same symbol again, and reproduce it, by counting up to 23 in Arabic notation, then it is the Arabic notation, and not Hilbert's, that is making possible the reproducibility and recognition of a given symbol. The theoretical possibility of determining what is the character of a long inscription in Hilbert's notation does not make it usable for normal transmission of facts about the size of your restaurant bill, for instance.

What then is a criterion of differentiation of characters that is tied more closely to recognition as the same again, a criterion properly founded in facts about perception and memory? Roughly this, intuitively: characters that are differentiated must be perceptible and recognizable again on the basis of a certain kind of intentional content in which the characters are given in normal human perception. The intentional content of the perception of the characters must be one that engages recognition of the kind of characters in question. When the subject has another experience presenting a given character, the subject can recognize that character simply on the basis of her perceptual recognitional capacities. Similarly, when the experience presents a different character, the subject can recognize simply on basis of her perceptual recognitional capacities that it is not that same character again. These conditions are not met by an experience of the first Hilbertian inscription above and a later experience of the second Hilbertian inscription above. We can summarize this requirement as *the recognizability condition*.

Recognizability is always recognizability in a given respect. You may be able to recognize instances of the lower-case letter 'a', but you may not be able to recognize just by looking whether an instance is in Helvetica font, as opposed to Calibri font. Recognition is recognition of an instance as of a given kind, or in a given respect. To be able to recognize one kind under which an instance falls is not necessarily to be able to recognize it as an instance of other kinds.

The fact that one cannot recognize just by looking which character a Hilbertian inscription instantiates is consistent with any two Hilbertian inscriptions being discriminably different if presented in the right kind of way in the same experience, for instance with one immediately above another:

That is, the recognizability condition for characters in a successful, reliable, and knowably reliable notational system can fail even when instances of the characters in the notation are discriminably different in perception. It follows that any notion of the digital that contrasts with the analogue by insisting on the recognizability of the digital cases should not be taken to imply perceptual non-discriminability of the characters it counts as analogue.[2]

For a system of digital representations to be suitable for ordinary reproduction with ordinary reliability, knowable transmission of texts, scores, and the like, the characters of that system must be perceptually recognizable. Since recognizability

---

[2] Here I diverge in letter but not in spirit from Matthew Katz's discussion (2008). One can readily determine that the most recently displayed two Hilbertian tokens above are not of the same type when they are juxtaposed. Katz writes, of two systems of representation C and D, "System D's representations appear continuous to the user. System C's representations appear discrete to the user. This then is the sense in which analog representations are continuous and digital representations are discrete. The former appear continuous—the user cannot readily distinguish them from each other. The latter appear discrete—the user can readily distinguish them from each other" (405). The symbols of Hilbert's notation do not appear continuous to the perceiver, and they can be perceptually distinguished if juxtaposed. But there remains an intuitive sense in which 'that array of vertical strokes' can express an analogue mode of presentation of the array. I say this is a divergence in letter but not in spirit because Katz is explicit that "whether a given representational system is analog or digital will sometimes turn on facts about the user of that system" (407), and Katz also connects this fact with the reliable and knowable reproducibility of inscriptions in the system.

is dependent on the psychological capacities of perception and memory, this characterization can be applied only relative to some background set of perceptual and memory capacities. It is really a relational requirement on a system of representations. A digital system of representations allows reliable and knowable transmission of texts, scores, and the like for creatures with given perceptual and memory capacities only if its characters are recognizable with those perceptual and memory capacities.

A notation that is usable by ordinary, finite perceivers over a certain range in ordinary perception and memory, and without the use of counting or other non-perceptual, non-recognitional procedures, must also be recognizable over that same range. The preceding example shows that this is an additional requirement over and above the notation being digital in Goodman's sense. Different notational systems may become non-recognizable over different semantic ranges. The Arabic numeral system is recognizable for us over a wider range than Hilbert's notation, but its recognizability still gives out over much larger integers. That is why we use notations like 10^{23} instead of 100000000000000000000000.

There are several analogue/digital distinctions, each legitimate in themselves, and appropriate for different purposes. Some make representation by primitive or almost primitive magnitudes crucial to the analogue, as in David Lewis's contribution (1971). Corey Maley by contrast says that what is crucial for the analogue is covariation of the represented quantity with some property of the representational medium (2011). Goodman, as we saw, requires density for analogue representation, which is independent of both Lewis's and Maley's treatments. But when, as in the discussion here, we are concerned with the non-recognizability of the representations as crucial to the analogue, we are concerned with something that cuts right across these various analyses. For example, representation by magnitudes can also be recognizable. Consider the hour hand of a traditional circular clock, where the hand is capable of clicking into only twelve positions, and where there are no markings on the clock face. This can be a recognizable and entirely reproducible representation of the hour of the day, but it is representation by a magnitude, the angle of the hour hand. This case is an example of what David Lewis in his elegant discussion would call analogue but differentiated representation (1971: 325). Though we cannot perceive absolutely precise angles, we do not need to in order to read the hour hand of the clock without markings. We do not need to, because what does the representing is what Lewis describes as magnitudes rounded to the nearest unit of a certain kind. In the clock face example, we are concerned with magnitudes rounded to the nearest thirty-degree unit, in thirty-degree steps from the top of the circular clock face. Angles rounded to the nearest such thirty-degree unit are perceptible by humans; which is why stylish watch faces that do not have markings still allow us to tell the hour of day.

Conversely, representation by something that is not a magnitude (not even a rounded magnitude) may not be recognizable in perception itself, as is illustrated by the very long Arabic notation (without power superscripts) for the number 10^{23}.

The distinction between what is perceptually recognizable and what is not equally cuts across Maley's criterion too. Maley writes, "analog representation is representation in which the represented quantity covaries with the representational medium, regardless of whether the representational medium is continuous or discrete" (2011: 122). Hilbert's stroke notation for natural numbers would be counted as analogue by Maley's criterion, since the natural number represented varies with the length of the sequence of individual vertical strokes. We can specify that there must be a uniform separation of the strokes in the notation; or we could count the numerosity of the strokes as a magnitude if that is allowed (as Maley himself does in other cases). Yet up to sequences of six or seven in length, these symbols are perceptually recognizable by humans without counting. Representations in the Hilbert notation would be widely classified as digital, not least because they are of the kind of representation of natural numbers used in Turing machines, the paradigm of digital computation. Maley's distinction is clearly a good and significant one in itself, but the distinction between what is recognizable in human perception and what is not cuts across it.

These considerations suggest that if we want to characterize the analogue/digital distinction for the content of perceptual experience in a way that captures the role of the digital in reliable reproduction and transmission of content, then we should endorse these points:

(a) a mode of presentation in perceptual content is digital if it involves perceptual recognition of its reference;
(b) perceptual demonstrative modes of presentation of magnitudes, such as 'that height' and 'that shade', are therefore never digital, since they do not involve recognition.

The explanation of point (b) relies on the Seven Principles of a metaphysics of magnitudes. Magnitudes themselves are perceived; particular magnitudes slice more finely than just noticeable difference; so perception of magnitudes, and the demonstrative modes of presentation it involves, can outrun the perceiver's recognitional capacity. This can be true even if the type of the magnitudes is not one whose instances are densely ordered—infinity is not required for making the point.

Under this treatment, there is a natural correspondence between the kinds of entity we need to talk about when we are applying an analogue/digital distinction to representations or vehicles, and the kinds of entity we need to talk about when we are applying an analogue/digital distinction to the intentional content of perception. In setting out his own characterization of an analogue/digital distinction, Goodman considered various possible relations that can hold between three things: the domain of marks, or inscriptions, or events; the characters those marks or inscriptions instantiate; and the domain of their references of the marks or inscriptions. I too have been considering various possible relations that can hold between three things: the domain of particular token perceptual experiences; the types those perceptual experiences can fall under; and the objects or event perceived in the experiences. The following correspondence exists between Goodman's categories and the kinds we need to consider in applying an analogue/digital distinction at the level of the intentional content of perception:

Goodman's category	corresponding category for classifying contents
marks/inscriptions/events	particular token experiences
characters	experiences typed by intentional content
references	objects or events perceived

Pairs of intentional contents involving modes of presentation that involve recognition of what is presented will be finitely differentiated, and differentiated more specifically in perception itself. A pair of intentional kinds in one of which something is presented as square, and in the other is presented as some other recognized shape, will be finitely differentiated from one another; similarly for any such pair in which something is presented as an instance of the symbol '4', and in the other of which something is presented as the symbol '2'; or as an utterance of the word 'France', and as an utterance of the word 'trance'.

The requirement of recognizability of perceptual kinds by an individual mind is the version for an individual mind of the requirement of recognizability of external, physical, and public characters if there are to be the usual reliable read/write mechanisms in the social transmission, transcription, and reproduction of external characters. The two requirements are obviously related, with the requirement of recognizability in an individual mind possessing the more fundamental status. External characters can be used in our everyday means of reproducing texts, scores, and the like reliably and knowably only if those characters are perceptually recognizable in the sense I have been discussing.

Demonstrative modes of presentation, including demonstrative modes of presentation of magnitudes, are *occasion-generated*. What makes them refer to the particular object or magnitude they do is a matter of which object or magnitude is the one perceived in a particular way in a particular experience on a particular occasion. To say that the mode of presentation is occasion-generated is not to say that the same mode of presentation of a magnitude cannot enter the content of two experiences on different occasions. It can. Being occasion-generated is to be distinguished from being occasion-specific. What is true, however, is that in the case of demonstrative modes of presentation of magnitudes, it need not be obvious to the subject that it is the same mode of presentation on different occasions. In the account of what gives a demonstrative mode of presentation of a magnitude its reference, there is nothing that requires recognition.[3]

Recognitional abilities, by contrast, do involve a capacity to identify from occasion to occasion and thus involve further representational capacities, and place correspondingly further demands on cognitive resources. The reference rule that individuates a recognitional notion or concept is correspondingly occasion-independent. What makes something the reference of a perceptual recognitional notion or concept—for example, a perceptual notion of the letter 'A'—is that it is a shape given in a way that can be present in the content of perceptions on many different occasions. There is no tie to any specific perceptual event in the condition that individuates the recognitional notion or concept.

Occasion-generated contents are all that are needed for many interactions with objects and events in one's immediate environment. For a normally functioning creature, it suffices to be able to act in relation to a direction itself, or distance itself, or shade itself, that it be so demonstratively presented. Many purposes of an agent will also be specific to an occasion in ways that do not require the ability to recognize the direction, the distance, or the shade as the same from occasion to occasion. What is explained by perception of magnitudes, in the presence of a suitable psychological background, is action in relation to the very magnitudes perceived. A subject may move her hands the same distance apart as she perceives to be the length of some object also given in perception. An animal repeating a call may make its sound the same duration as the call it just heard; and so forth.

---

[3] The notion of a mode of presentation of a magnitude must not be developed in such a way that modes of presentation are the same if and only if they seem the same. Since seeming the same is not a transitive relation, that kind of development leads to incoherence. Any coherent notion of modes of presentation in perceptual content must avoid the problems of the notion of 'precise apparent size/shape/shade' discussed in Peacocke (1981a).

These are actions explained under descriptions that relate them to the subject's environment. They are paradigms of externalist explanation (Peacocke 1993). It is this explanatory power that helps to explain the significance of the fact that the content of the subject's perceptual experience is externally individuated. But the occasion-generated character of the demonstrative modes of presentation of magnitudes also shows why no recognition of specific magnitudes is required in these explanations. Action in relation to a perceived length, duration, or other magnitude, including an intensive magnitude, does not at all require the ability to recognize or reidentify that length, duration, or magnitude from occasion to occasion. It suffices for the explanation of environmentally characterized action to perceive the magnitude on the particular occasion in question. That is part of the explanatory power of specifically analogue content.

Precisely because this formulation of the analogue/digital distinction is relative to a set of capacities, it can also be applied at subpersonal levels. At a subpersonal level, a notation may be recognized or recorded as the same again, and we can correspondingly draw a distinction between the analogue and the digital at that subpersonal level. This subpersonal application of the distinction could be used to elaborate the condition mentioned earlier on analogue computers, that none of its subcomputations be digital operations on digital representations.

To summarize: characters in usable read/write systems must be recognizable; this condition has application both at the level of public characters and at the level of perceptions of those marks; analogue contents, the purely demonstrative, occasion-generated perceptual modes of presentation of magnitudes, such as 'that height' and 'that duration', will not meet this recognizability condition, and they do not need to; and they will not meet it because of the nature of the underlying domain of magnitudes whose members are presented in perception.

5. A Response to Kuhn on Perception

Acknowledging the existence of the analogue content of perceptual experience, and in particular such perception of magnitudes, undermines the argument that Thomas Kuhn famously developed in section X of *The Structure of Scientific Revolutions*, titled 'Revolutions as Changes of World View' (1996). Amongst many other claims, Kuhn says that before and after a scientific revolution, scientists do not see the world the same way. Aristotle and Galileo, says Kuhn, would have seen the motions of a pendulum differently. Aristotle would have seen it as a heavy body falling with difficulty, constrained by its chain, moved by its own nature from a higher position to a state of natural rest at a lower position.

Galileo would have seen it as a body repeating the same motion over and over again (1996: 119). Kuhn says that his points "suggest that the scientist who looks at a swinging stone can have no experience that is in principle more elementary than seeing a pendulum. The alternative is not some hypothetical 'fixed' vision, but vision through another paradigm, one which makes the swinging stone something else" (128).

I disagree. The level of analogue content concerning such spatial matters as distance, direction, speed, and duration precisely occupies the level that Kuhn says does not exist. Aristotle and Galileo would have had, in respect of their perceptions of a given pendulum in motion, the same perceptual experiences at the level of analogue magnitude content in respect of all of the following: the length of the pendulum; the duration of each swing; and the angle through which it moves. For every other example that Kuhn cites, similar points can be made. He cites the duck-rabbit picture as an initial example (111). For both the person who sees the picture as one of a duck, and for the person who sees it as a picture of a rabbit, the lines can seem to be in the same place on the paper, the lengths of the lines ('that length') and the angles between them ('that angle') can seem to be the same, and so forth. The perceived distances between drops in the bubble chamber, and their distances in relation to parts of the apparatus, can be the same for the naïve subject and for one who knows them to be traces of particles.

Why does Kuhn not consider this very simple alternative to his position? He raises against himself the possible objection that "Many readers will surely want to say that what changes with a paradigm is only the scientist's interpretation of observations that themselves are fixed once and for all by the nature of the environment and of the perceptual apparatus" (120). I agree with Kuhn that observations are not so fixed once and for all by the environment and the perceptual apparatus. The duck-rabbit case, amongst many others, shows that perceptual experience can vary even while environment and perceptual apparatus are held constant. The problem is that the only candidates Kuhn considers for what might be constant in visual perception across scientific revolutions are retinal images and rich conceptual contents of experience. He is right that retinal image is far from determining perceptual experience (even the constancy phenomena show that). The rich conceptual content, if it exists, does vary the way Kuhn says it does. Kuhn's conception is that retinal states, together with rich conceptualization involved in the scientist's theories, produce experience. In his 1969 'Postscript' to the original text, he writes, "Mere parochialism, I suspect, makes us suppose that the route from stimuli to sensation is the same for the members of all groups" (193).

It is not mere parochialism. A relatively stable level of spatial analogue magnitude content of experience across different scientists contributes essentially to the explanation of the actions of those scientists that are constant across their competing theories. They will, from a given position, reach out the same distance to grasp the pendulum. They will have a common perception of the duration of one swing of the pendulum, something that contributes to their explanation in action of how long the swing took ('from now...to now'). A level of analogue magnitude spatial representational content common to the perceptual states of the different scientists earns its keep by such explanatory power. Kuhn is right that there is much computation intervening in the process from a retinal state to a perceptual experience, but wrong that every representational feature of the experience is influenced by the scientists' own scientific theories.

A different but related thesis, a thesis not denying the existence of the level of analogue perceptual content, is an anti-encapsulation thesis concerning the level. The thesis would be that different scientific views can cause differences in the analogue content of the experiences of two scientists in the same environment, and with the same proximal stimuli. On this position, competing scientific theories influence the analogue magnitude content of perceptual experiences in ways that may lead to confirmation bias, thus producing a serious epistemic problem. This is not the argument that Kuhn actually gives. His position is rather one that denies the existence of the level of analogue content altogether, but we can consider whether this variant supports his claims. Now the extent to which top-down concepts and theories in fact influence perceptual content is complex. While it is plausible that perceptual recognition and perceptual categorization are subject to top-down influence, much of the evidence that has been offered that there is top-down evidence on spatial content has rightly been questioned (on these issues, see Lupyan (2016) and Firestone and Scholl (2016)). But suppose that a scientist's perceptions were influenced by her physical theories in ways producing confirmation bias. Would this lead to the irresolubility, even using the evidence of their times, of the disagreement between Aristotle and Galileo? It would not. Even if someone's perception of the size or shape of an object is distorted by their scientific beliefs, that distortion can be shown to be the case by experimental results concerning how they act spatially in relation to the object. The experiments would concern matching perceived distance or duration with other distances and durations, and so forth. It would be important that the experiments concern perception, rather than judgement. The distortion can be shown without begging the question as to whether Aristotle or Galileo is right about the dynamics of falling objects. Experiments revealing features of a subject's perceptual experiences do not need to presuppose any particular physics of the motion of material bodies. They can be neutral as between Aristotle and Galileo. So I am inclined to conclude that there are neither perceptual nor epistemic challenges arising from these Kuhnian considerations. At a more general level, the role of the objective mind-independent magnitudes themselves in individuating the level of analogue content should give pause to anyone inclined to draw anti-objectivist conclusions from Kuhn's reflections.

3

Time and Temporal Content

1. Temporal Perception: Some Challenges

My aim in this chapter is to develop some elements of a positive constitutive, philosophical account of temporal perception. In particular, I aim to speak to some of the challenges, and some of the rewards, that arise from developing an account of temporal perception that respects two overarching constraints.

The first of these two overarching constraints is that the account be a metaphysics-first theory of the relation between the temporal events, properties, relations, and magnitudes, in the sense of the discussion in Chapter 1. It is certainly initially intuitive, to a contemporary philosopher, that the nature of temporal reality—the metaphysics of the temporal—is not to be explained philosophically in part in terms of the temporal intentional contents of mental states, or in terms of the meaning of temporal vocabulary. This contemporary view conflicts with some famous treatments in philosophy's history, from Kant to Husserl. Some of the arguments for a metaphysics-first treatment of temporal content and meaning are inferences to the best philosophical explanation. The actual explanations available to a metaphysics-first treatment will be crucial in defending the metaphysics-first status of this temporal case.

The second overarching constraint within which I will be operating is the realist account of magnitudes given in the Seven Principles formulated in Chapter 2. Those principles include the intelligibility, and widespread occurrence, of causal explanations by magnitudes. Correspondingly, those principles also include the existence of explanatory laws, possibly including the prima facie laws of the special sciences, that relate magnitudes of one or another kind to various types of *explananda*. That general realistic account of magnitudes applies directly to temporal magnitudes. That account provides the metaphysics on which I will be drawing in giving a metaphysics-first account of temporal intentional contents. One of the things that can be explained by two events' being separated by a certain duration (in a given frame of reference) is the perception, by a person at rest in that frame, that they are separated by that duration (also relative to that frame). The duration between two events can sometimes be perceived, as the distance between two objects can sometimes be perceived. In both the temporal and the spatial cases, the perception of the magnitude is unit-free, just as the magnitude itself is unit-free. We do not perceive the length of time since the person left the room in seconds or minutes, any more than we perceive the width of the desk in inches or centimetres.

In the spatial case, we specify how the world seems to be to a perceiving subject in part by specifying how the space around the subject has to be filled in for her spatial experience to be veridical. That is what I called scenario content (Peacocke 1992). In the temporal case, we similarly specify how the world seems to be to a perceiving subject in part by specifying how the recent past has to be filled out with events, at certain durations from the present, for her temporal experience to be veridical. Just as spatial magnitudes feature in the scenario content of perception, so temporal magnitudes should be included correspondingly in the representational content of perception. The notion of scenario content should be expanded accordingly, and given a temporal dimension. I will discuss the temporal component of scenario content and its philosophical significance in more detail later in this chapter.

There are three salient challenges that arise in elaborating an account of temporal perception that respect these two overarching constraints, and I will take them successively in structuring this chapter.

(1) The first challenge, really a set of challenges, concerns the nature of temporal intentional contents on any view that respects the two overarching constraints. The metaphysics-first account of the perception of magnitudes gives an objectivist account of the temporal content of experience, in the sense that the correctness of conditions of temporal experiences concerns in general mind-independent matters (unless their non-temporal contents are mind-dependent). In good cases, the temporal experiences represent the temporal conditions as they objectively are. Although this may at first blush seem like an uncontentious position, it is in conflict with two other much-discussed positions in the literature.

One is a subjectivism about time, something that can be traced back at least to Kant (1998). The subjectivism under consideration here is subjectivism about time and temporal properties and relations themselves. It is not just subjectivism about ways in which time and temporal properties are given in perception. That is a different, partially overlapping, and also interesting question, addressed by Lee (2017). Why has subjectivism about the metaphysics of time itself, as opposed to ways in which it is given, ever seemed tempting? Can we properly characterize and explain the sources of temptation to subjectivism about temporal reality, in ways that do not involve succumbing to the temptation?

The other—and entirely contemporary—position with which the particular metaphysics-first view of temporal perception I endorse is in conflict is given in the arguments developed by Brad Thompson (2010) and David Chalmers (2012). Their view is that perceptual experience can have only an internalist, narrow content. We will look at these arguments later, but it suffices for an initial formulation of the issue to note that narrow content is supposed to be constant across possible environments in which the relevant magnitudes vary. Here there are only three possibilities. Either the arguments to be offered in support of the thesis that magnitudes themselves are perceived are unsound; or else the arguments that perceptual content is narrow must be unsound; or else there is some deep reason that there really cannot be possible cases with the same narrow content and different wide content, so that there is a sense in which these superficially competing positions are reconcilable. Which possibility is correct?

(2) The second question concerns the status of temporal perception as something genuinely perceptual, representing something as temporal, rather than something weaker than perception, such as mere causal sensitivity to a magnitude that is in fact temporal. What is it, as a constitutive matter, for perception to represent temporal magnitudes, properties, and relations as such? We know that mere causal sensitivity to states of affairs of a given kind does not amount to representation of those states of affairs as being of that kind. So what more is required to represent temporal magnitudes, properties, and relations as such? This is an issue that needs to be addressed, whether one's view of temporal intentional content is wide or narrow.

(3) The metaphysics of time has been found to be almost uniquely mysterious amongst the various types of magnitude. The subjective character of temporal experience has historically played a role in generating puzzlement about the nature of time. The general project of this book is to show how the metaphysics of a domain is involved in the nature of intentional contents and meanings concerning that domain, and indeed is explanatory prior in the order of philosophical explanation in the case of temporal perceptual contents. I will be arguing that one of the rewards of a systematic development of a metaphysics-first view of temporal perception is that it allows us to give an analysis of certain temporal intentional contents that can help to explain away certain subjectivist illusions about the metaphysics of time.

Before I turn to those three tasks, I start with some preliminary remarks on the character of temporal experience itself. The experience of there being a particular duration between two events involves a distinctive temporal intentional content that is irreducible to other conscious intentional contents. The experience of a particular duration does not consist in the experience of various other non-temporal properties or magnitudes. It is representation of a temporal magnitude, as such, and in its own right. One can, prima facie, experience something as having a certain duration without experiencing any intervening events or changes. You may experience it as being a certain length of time since the sound occurred of the door shutting; a little later, you may experience the sound as being a longer duration ago; and so forth. This can all be so without your experiencing anything else. You could be otherwise anaesthetized, or be in a machine that cuts out other sensory channels, and not engaged in any active or passive thinking.

In *The Principles of Psychology*, a section of William James's famous chapter 'The Perception of Time' is titled 'We have no sense for empty time' (1910: 619). He says that "It takes but a small exertion of introspection" to show that we cannot "*intuit a duration . . . devoid of all sensible content*" (619–20, James's own italics). A little later, he continues,

be we never so abstracted from distinct outward impressions, we are always inwardly immersed in what Wundt has somewhere called the twilight of our general consciousness. Our heart-beats, our breathing, the pulses or our attention, fragments of words or sentences that pass through our imagination, are what people this dim habitat. Now, all these processes are rhythmical, and are apprehended by us, as they occur, in their totality; the breathing and pulses of attention, as coherent successions, each with its rise and fall; the heart-beats similarly, only relatively far more brief . . . And along with the sense of the process and its rhythm goes the sense of the length of time it lasts.   (620)

James's two words "along with" can cover at least two different theses here. A weaker reading of the words would have James claiming that only when combined with a sense of process and rhythm do we have a sense of duration, which is to be conceived as a further feature of subjective experience beyond what it goes "along with". That weaker reading is not at all faithful to the spirit of James's text, which reads as if there is nothing else to account for in a sense of duration once we have accounted for a sense of rhythm and process. We have to remember the thesis that forms his section title, 'We have no sense for empty time' (583).

The stronger reading of the words in question is that by "along with", James means that the sense of duration supervenes on experience of these other, allegedly non-durational, features of experience. With the claim involved in the stronger reading, I disagree. For any sequence of conscious events of the sort James describes here, one can conceive of its being spread out, in experience, over a shorter or longer period of time. The temporal magnitudes in the intentional content of the experience are something additional to the description of these processes, unless of course James's talk of, for instance, 'rhythm' is meant already to include specifications of duration—in which case his account would be circular.

There must be some subpersonal causal explanation, at the time the experience occurs, of the experience of a particular duration (Lee 2014). It is certainly fair comment that some current subpersonal magnitude or representation must be causally correlated with experience of a specific duration. It is also plausible that when there is other conscious mental activity additional to the experience of duration, that activity or its precursors may causally affect the size of the experienced temporal magnitude (Phillips 2013a). But neither of these points imply that there must always be in consciousness some further non-temporal feature whose presence is correlated with experienced duration. There need not be, and sometimes there is not.

The parallel with spatial perception is irresistible. With stereo vision, we can perceive the distance between two flashing lights in an otherwise dark region, and this subjective experience of distance does not supervene on any other qualitative, non-spatial features of experience. James more than once speaks of similarities between the perception of space and the perception of time (583–5). It is not clear that the comparison supports his position, rather than the opposite. He writes, again in italics, "*we can no more intuit a duration than we can intuit an extension, devoid of all sensible content*" (583). Even if the temporal endpoints of a duration must be in consciousness in some way, and the endpoints of a spatial extension must be experienced in some way, the qualitative characterization of how the endpoints are experienced will not, without temporal or spatial specification, fix the experienced duration or experienced spatial extension. There seems to be experience of temporal magnitude in its own right, just as there is experience of spatial magnitude in its own right.

2. The Illusions of Subjectivism

Kant held that there is a respect in which time is fundamentally subjective, its nature founded in the relations between mental events. His text makes clear that he conceived of these relations as themselves fundamentally subjective too. If Kant were right in these claims about time, it would be thoroughly erroneous, and confused about the nature of time itself, to hold, as I have been arguing, that our experience of temporal magnitudes is explained, *ceteris paribus*, by events being separated by certain temporal magnitudes themselves. It would be an attempt to explain the subjective by the subjective, and to explain it by something to which subjective properties could not, on Kant's view, even apply.

Here are some essential passages from Kant stating his position in the first critique, and his reasons for it:

time cannot be perceived in itself [für sich], nor can what precedes and what follows in objects be as it were empirically determined in relation to it. I am therefore only conscious that my imagination places one state before and the other after, not that the one state precedes the other in the object; or, in other words, through the mere perception the *objective relation* of the appearances that are succeeding one another remains undetermined.   (B233–4)

Time is not something that would subsist for itself or attach to things as an objective determination, and thus remain if one abstracted from all subjective conditions of the intuition of them...Time is nothing other than the form of inner sense, i.e., of the intuition of ourself and our inner state. For time cannot be a determination of outer appearances; it belongs neither to a shape nor a position, etc., but on the contrary determines the relation of representations in our inner state.   (B49)

Time is the *a priori* formal condition of all appearances in general.   (B50)

If we abstract away from our way of internally intuiting ourselves and by means of this intuition also dealing with all our intuitions in the power of representation, and thus take objects as they may be in themselves, then time is nothing. It is only of objective validity in regard to appearances, because these are already things that we take as *objects of our senses*; but it is no longer objective if one abstracts from the sensibility of our intuition, thus from that kind of representation that is peculiar to us, and speaks of *things in general*. Time is therefore merely a subjective condition of our (human) intuition (which is always sensible, i.e., insofar as we are affected by objects), and in itself, outside the subject, is nothing.   (A34–5/B51–2)

Such properties, which pertain to things in themselves, can never be given to us through the senses. In this therefore consists the *transcendental ideality* of time, according to which it is nothing at all if one abstracts from the subjective conditions of sensible intuition, and cannot be counted as either subsisting or inhering in the objects in themselves (without their relation to our intuition).   (A35–6/B52)

It should be clear from these passages that Kant's claim that 'time is the form of inner sense' goes beyond the anodyne proposition that states of inner sense are temporally ordered. That proposition is entirely compatible with a rejection of subjectivism about time. Kant's claim that time is "nothing other than the form of inner sense" is the claim that temporal properties and relations are in their very nature subjective. As he says at A35/B52 above, time "in itself, outside of the subject, is nothing". This formulation of his subjectivism, which is not at all anodyne, is incompatible with the position that emerges from the treatment of temporal properties and magnitudes given above, that there is a single uniform category of mind-independent temporal properties and relations that apply both to purely physical and to mental events and processes.

It seems to me to be an illusion that there is such a thing as purely subjective time, the nature of which is entirely independent of objective time. There is only objective time, relative to a frame of reference, and accurate or inaccurate representations of objective time relative to that frame. I call this position which says there is only objective time, and representation of objective time, objectivism about time (with apology, were any to be merited, to Ayn Rand). Here are three of the straightforward considerations that support objectivism about time:

(a) There does not seem to be any phenomenology that cannot be elucidated as representation or misrepresentation of objective time. A person who is enjoying some activity immensely, or who is on drugs, or who is in great danger may experience the interval of time between two individual events as much longer or as much shorter than it actually is. That is misperception of objective duration. It is not something that requires us to postulate some notion of subjective time not explicable in terms of the representation of objective time. Similarly, two people may experience one interval of objective time very differently. All that implies is that one or both of them then has an illusion of how long the interval was.

(b) If time were fundamentally subjective, we should be able to make sense of two subjects with very different subjective temporal experiences over time, even though the representational contents of their experiences concerning time are the same. It is not at all clear we can make any sense of this possibility (on which issue there is further discussion in Section 3).

(c) If time is genuinely subjective, it makes no more sense to say it applies to mind-independent events than it does to say that a relation of subjective similarity applies to unexperienced things. Such propositions can make sense only if some mind-independent property or relation is correlated with the subjective property or relation. Maybe the mind-independent property or relation is supposed to be or to involve objective time. But then there is a danger on a subjectivist view that objective time has consequently to be conceived as an unknown, theoretically postulated ground, not something itself perceived, and certainly not perceived as time. The position makes real time perceptually inaccessible. Kant, to his credit, acknowledged that that follows from his view. But the resulting position is problematic both in epistemology, and from the standpoint of a theory of understanding.

Kant writes that "time cannot be perceived in itself", and seems to take this as so obvious that he does not need to offer a reason for the claim. It must have been obvious to Kant that perceptual experience has, for instance, a present-tense content. It is implausible to think that Kant was denying that. When a great philosopher says something apparently contradicted by everyday experience, it is worth trying to see if we can identify a proposition nearby in the spirit of what the philosopher says, a proposition consistent with everyday experience. We can then go on to consider if that nearby proposition supports the conclusions the philosopher wants to draw from it. There is a very close parallel here, not only in abstract structure, but also in detailed diagnosis and parallelism, with Hume's claim that, try as he may, he can never find and attend to himself. As I noted in *The Mirror of the World* (2014a), Hume was certainly aware that he could see himself in a mirror, and could also look down and see himself. He would not have taken these everyday facts as contradicting the point he aimed to make. As I also argued in *The Mirror of the World*, one way of formulating Hume's point that yields a truth, one not contradicted by everyday experience, is that there is no such thing as attending to yourself when you are given in a purely first-personal way. Perceptual ways of being given are not purely first personal. Can we make a similar move on behalf of Kant's claim that time cannot be perceived?

There are notable parallels between the two cases. The way in which the present time is given in perception as *now* is distinctive. The present time is not thereby given in any particular sense modality. Kant would very likely say there is no intuition in which the present time is given in perception, no intuition of that time. Kant does say that the representation of time is an intuition, but there he is using 'representation' strictly. His point is just that we represent time in outer sense as a straight line "progressing to infinity" (B50). That point does not at all involve there being an intuition of the present time.

It also does not make sense to speak of attending to the entity which is the present time. This was noted too by William James (1910: 608), though his concern was to contrast duration with moments. Something can be an object of attention only if it is given in some specific sense modality, or in sensation, and since a time is not so given, it is not possible to have the present moment as an object of attention. That is to be distinguished from attending to some event that is happening now, which is of course possible and often actually occurs. It is also to be distinguished from attending to whether something is happening or changing now, where the object of attention is some object or event.

There is also a parallel with an indexical *here* which, when used in connection with a visual experience, refers *de jure* to the spatial origin from which objects are perceived in vision. Things are visually perceived in relation to this *here*. The perceiving subject does not, however, perceive the location that is the reference of *here*. The parallel can be reinforced by considering that just as the meaning of attending to the present time is problematic, the same applies to attending to the location that is the visual origin. There seems to be no such thing as engaging in either of these attentional exercises.

These points about the parallels between *now* in perception and both the first person and *here* stand. But they do not give any support at all to subjectivism about time, which is a claim about the level of reference rather than the level of modes of presentation. They do not give any support to subjectivism any more than they give support to the idea that *I* does not refer, or to the idea that *here* does not refer to an objective location. Even if the location that is the reference of this *here* is not perceived, the correctness conditions for an experience that represents a lamp as in a certain spatial relation to *here* still concern mind-independent space, and concern the mind-independent location to which *here* refers on this particular occasion. The correct observations about a certain parallelism between *now* and this distinctive *here* lend no support to subjectivism about time itself. Similarly, these points in no way support the idea that *I* does not refer to a subject. Any arguments for subjectivism about space or time, or no-subject theories of the self, would need to draw on entirely other resources. In short, the proposition that is nearby to Kant's claim that time cannot be perceived "in itself" is not one that supports his metaphysics.[1]

A different tack towards the goal of arguing that time itself is not perceived might start from the Leibnizian idea that only temporal relations between events, and not times themselves, are fundamentally real. Now obviously this line of thought is not going to rule out perception of the temporal relations themselves. Nor would it establish subjectivism about the temporal relations themselves. But could it do something to undergird the idea that times themselves are not perceived? It would be too strong to claim that a subject can perceive a time only by perceiving some event or object at that time. You can perceive that it's completely dark and silent now, just as you can perceive that there's nothing over there. The perception of absence is not the same as the absence of perception (Phillips 2013b).

So, is there some weaker starting point for a Leibnizian approach to these issues that would vindicate a claim that time does not enter the intentional

---

[1] Incidentally, the phenomenon under discussion in the preceding three paragraphs is not restricted to pure indexicals, in a natural nonlinguistic generalization of David Kaplan's sense of 'pure' (1989). While *I* and *now* are pure demonstratives in Kaplan's sense, the *here* of visual perceptual origin is not. It requires supplementation by at least a visual experience-type before any reference is determined in any given context.

content of perceptual experience? Suppose some form of Leibnizian position about the ontology of times is correct. Then the holding of a state of affairs concerning a certain time will consist in the holding of a complex of relations of that state of affairs to events, rather than to times. But from the fact that A consists in B, it does not follow that perception that A holds must consist in the perception of B. A subject may perceive that the number of apples on the table is four. The holding of that numerical condition about the apples very likely has some metaphysical analysis in terms of first-order quantificational conditions involving identity (see Chapter 5). It does not follow that perceiving that the number of apples on the table is four is perceiving that a complex first-order quantificational condition involving identity holds. The fact that a is F at time t and the perception of a's being F occurs just after t may consist in their having corresponding temporal relations to certain other events, in accordance with Leibnizian doctrine. But the perceiver need not mentally represent those systems of relations involved in the metaphysical analysis of times for such perception to occur. It is also true, if Leibnizian relationism about times is correct, that the explanation of perception by states of affairs holding at particular times must unfold into explanations that do not make essential use of an ontology of times. But again, this requirement does not put temporal representations that eliminate the representation of particular times into the mind of the perceiver. In short, this second attempt does not even take one as far as a plausible claim about perceptual experience, let alone all the way to subjectivism about time itself.

3. Phenomenal Externalism

I have been presuming that the perception of magnitudes contributes to the phenomenal character of perception. If this presumption is correct, then the account so far is a version of what has come to be called phenomenal externalism. It has some immediate attractions. In treating magnitudes themselves as perceptible, phenomenal externalism meshes straightforwardly with such ordinary attributions as 'she heard the rumbling last for a certain length of time'. We can form beliefs, and sometimes gain knowledge, about the magnitudes themselves by taking particular perceptual experiences of magnitudes at face value. Magnitudes themselves are cognitively accessible in perception itself.

The account also dovetails with the externalist character of what is explained in action-explanation (Peacocke 1993). Perception of a magnitude explains actions under relational characterizations, in relation to the very magnitude perceived. When asked how long the rumbling lasted, our subject may answer

'From now...to now', where the perception explains the magnitude of the duration between the two utterances of 'now'.

But for all these attractions, this form of phenomenal externalism is controversial. In particular, it contrasts strongly with the internalist functionalism about spatiotemporal notions, and more generally the internalism about perceptual content, endorsed in important and interesting discussions by Brad Thompson (2010) and by David Chalmers (2012).

Here I outline briefly the components of an externalist view of perceptual content involving magnitudes by addressing the considerations that have been offered in support of the Chalmers-Thompson version of an internalist, narrow-content functionalism. On the Chalmers-Thompson view, spatial and temporal expressions are 'Twin-Earthable':

> let us say that two possible speakers are *twins* if they are functional and phenomenal duplicates of each other: that is their cognitive systems have the same functional organization and are in the same functional states, and they have the same conscious experiences...We can then say that an expression E is Twin-Earthable if there can be a non-deferential utterance of E for which there is a possible corresponding utterance by twin speaker with a different extension. (Chalmers 2012: 317)

There is a similar notion, applied to concepts: that of *relational similarity* in Peacocke (1996: 150). The Chalmers-Thompson view is that spatial and temporal magnitude-expressions are Twin-Earthable because, they hold, two twins may be functional and phenomenal duplicates, but their spatial and temporal expressions refer to different magnitudes because, they also hold, different magnitudes may produce the same functional and phenomenal states in the twins.

I dispute the thesis of the Twin-Earthability of the spatial and temporal magnitude terms. An initial argument offered for Twin-Earthability of these terms is that it is not coherent to suppose that our experiences and judgements of magnitudes are massively illusory, throughout time in the actual world. For the spatial case of this argument, see Chalmers (2012: 326). I agree. But this verdict of incoherence would equally be delivered by the view that perceptual experience has contents concerning the magnitudes themselves, together with the thesis that which magnitudes those experiences have as their content is determined by which magnitudes normally cause them, when the conditions for genuine representation, and not mere sensitivity, are fulfilled. Chalmers (2012: 331, note 10) does note the availability of this response, and relies on the 'El Greco' cases in rejoinder, which I consider below.

Narrow-content theorists of perception also ask us to consider Doubled Earth, on which everything is doubled in length from actual Earth, or Slowed Earth, on which everything happens at half the speed on actual Earth. Their narrow functionalist view is that experiences of subjects on Earth and Doubled Earth, or Slowed Earth, can all be veridical. The phenomenal externalism I endorse also agrees with these intuitions and verdicts about veridicality. The inhabitants of Earth and of each of these variants of Earth all have largely veridical experiences.

Phenomenal externalism does not, however, agree that the experiences of the inhabitants of Earth, Doubled Earth, and Slowed Earth are phenomenally identical. They have different magnitudes in their content. When a perceiver on Earth sees something as having a certain length, his twin on Doubled Earth sees it as having twice that length; and so forth.

The subjects on Earth, Doubled Earth, and Slowed Earth are also not functional duplicates if our functionalism is of the 'long-arm' variety that takes into account functional relations beyond the boundary of the body (Harman 1982: 247). The experiences in the three kinds of world produce and explain actions in relation to correspondingly different magnitudes in the environment. The actions of a subject on Earth are explained in relation to a certain objective magnitude. The actions of his twin on Doubled Earth are explained in relation to a magnitude twice as large; and so forth.

The fact that one could trick a subject, at least temporarily, in carefully designed circumstances by moving her from one kind of environment to another does not establish that the phenomenal subjective contents are the same across the cases. Perceptual content is grounded in the relations to a baseline normal environment in which the subject is functioning properly. On the position which I am opposing to the Chalmers-Thompson view, the subjects on Earth, Doubled Earth, and Slowed Earth are not twins under the definition, and spatiotemporal magnitude-expressions are not Twin-Earthable.

The phenomenal externalist will sharply distinguish between Twin-Earthability and relativity to a frame of reference. Spatiotemporal magnitudes themselves are always nontrivially relative to a frame of reference. A subject can perceive a temporal or a spatial magnitude as it really is, relative to the frame of reference in which the subject is at rest. The fact that the magnitude between the two events will be different in a frame in which the subject is not at rest does not imply the Twin-Earthability of magnitude-expressions and concepts. In the temporal case, if a subject with a clock travelling in rapid motion relative to the Earth perceives his clock correctly, his phenomenal experience of that same clock will not be the same as those on Earth not in such rapid motion, because of the phenomenon of time dilation (see for instance Young and Freedman 2004: 1410). I doubt that there is any notion of phenomenal duplication on which the fast traveller's temporal experience of the clock must be a duplicate of those on Earth. Experience of a duration is always as of an objective duration, relative to the frame of reference centred on the subject.

One objection to phenomenal externalism is that it is committed to implausible verdicts on 'El Greco' examples. These are examples, originally suggested by Hurley (1998), in which everything in some part of the universe is stretched in the ratio 2:1 in the vertical direction. "Bodies that seem rigid within the environment will be nonrigid by standards outside the environment, in that they change their shape when they rotate. And beings in that world will typically say 'That is a square' when confronted by what outsiders would call a rectangle that is twice as high as it is tall" (Chalmers 2012: 330). Chalmers wonders what an externalist would say of the experiences of twin subjects in an 'El Greco' case: "will one have an experience as of a rectangle, despite insisting that she is confronted by a square?" (2012: 331, note 10).

Externalism about phenomenal content is consistent with pervasive illusions. The objects around subjects in the special part of the universe really are stretched in one direction, say by special forces, but they still look square. If perceivers discover this fact, they will come to realize that when they reach to touch the top and bottom of a seemingly square object, their hands are actually twice as far apart as when they pick it up from the sides. Even in the actual world, there is what is called the vertical-horizontal illusion. Vertical lines seem to humans to be 6–8 per cent longer than lines that are actually of the same length, but have a horizontal orientation (Rock 1973: 96–8). So even in the actual world, some things that look square in normal circumstances are not so. The externalist can consistently admit extensive and pervasive illusions, as long as these illusions gain their status as such from their relations to a base of cases in which subjects are perceiving correctly. The Muller-Lyer illusion is pervasive in the actual world, but it is not a counterexample to externalism about phenomenal content.

I do think that we can make sense of the classical inverted colour spectrum and of Ned Block's inverted Earth (1990). A narrow-content functional account of colour terms and concepts is highly plausible in these cases. So what then is so different, on my view, about the spatiotemporal cases? Why not treat the cases the same? A crucial difference is that there is no difficulty in imagining inverted-spectrum cases from the inside, and in making the case that this represents a genuine possibility. We have a notion of phenomenal similarity, of looking the same way, on which we can clearly make sense of the possibility that everything that is actually green looks the way things that are actually red look. Imaginability is indeed not always a guide to genuine possibility, but it matters here that what is imagined is something in the imagined experience of the inverted state of affairs, not just something merely suppositionally imagined (Peacocke 1985). Similarly, we have no difficulty in imagining that our colour experience is the same, but the reflectance properties of objects that cause those experiences are different from those which cause them in the actual world.

For the temporal case to be like the colour case, there would have to be a constant phenomenal temporal property common to an alleged pair of twins, one on Earth and the other a subject travelling very fast, subject to time dilation. There would also have to be a constant phenomenal temporal property common to an alleged pair of twins, one on Earth and the other on Slow Earth. I surmise that there is no such phenomenal property.

Similarly, for the spatial case to be like the colour case, we would have to be able to make sense of a world in which experiences are phenomenally the same as on actual Earth, but in which external objects are universally different in size. That is precisely what I have been arguing against earlier in this section.

There are further consequences of the Chalmers-Thompson position. If spatial and temporal magnitudes are not genuinely accessible in perception, it is not clear that they are accessible to thought and knowledge at all, given the fundamental role of perception in making possible thought and knowledge of spatial and temporal magnitudes. For the phenomenal externalist, spatial and temporal magnitudes are accessible to thought and knowledge via their perceptual accessibility.

Perhaps space and time are physically superficial, to be really explained in physics by deeper non-spatial and non-temporal aspects of physical reality. If so, our perception and thought are latching on to what is physically superficial. It should not be any part of phenomenal externalism to exclude that epistemic possibility.

4. Unavailability of Constancy Accounts in the Temporal Case

I now turn to address the second of the two challenges noted at the outset of this chapter: that of distinguishing genuine representation of temporal properties and relations as such from mere sensitivity to them. For an organism to be sensitive to a magnitude of a given type, to be in states causally explained by some object or event having that magnitude, is not yet for the organism to represent that magnitude as such. Sensitivity is not representation. The point is developed forcefully by Tyler Burge (2010: Part III).

In the case of genuine representation of spatial properties and relations in perception, Burge himself says that what makes the difference between representation of such a property or relation, as opposed to mere sensitivity to it, is the phenomenon of perceptual constancy. Varying proximal states, themselves caused by the same constant property, cause the same objective representational state representing that property, within a wide range of normal background circumstances. Different projected retinal sizes or shapes cause perceptual representation of the same objective size of a given object as the perceiver's distance from the object varies, or as her angle with respect to the object varies. Conversely, the same retinal size on two different occasions will cause states with representational contents concerning different objective sizes, when appropriate, and in a range of normal conditions. There are analogues of this for colour constancy too.

This constancy criterion for genuine representation does not carry over to provide a constitutive account of the representation of temporal properties and relations. The general problem is that in the spatial case, the very characterization of constancy involves either variation in three-dimensional conditions producing the same two-dimensional pattern of proximal stimulation, or else, as in colour constancy, it involves multiple environmental conditions, instantiated in normal circumstances, producing the same proximal stimulation property, retinal colour in the visual case. Conversely, one and the same objective length, for example, produces many different sizes of retinal image at various distances of that length from the perceiver. The retinal image of the length also varies with the orientation of the perceiver. But neither of these kinds of variation in three-dimensional relations, nor of varying normal environmental conditions producing the proximal stimulus state, applies to the case of duration and to other temporal properties and relations.

Consider as an example the perception of the whole duration of a temporally extended event, such as the sounding of a fire alarm bell. The proximal stimulus event is the series of events of sound waves hitting the eardrum, from the initial striking, up to their later cessation, just after the bell stops ringing. In normal circumstances, extended proximal events of this kind *will* be reliably correlated (and explained by) the objective complete duration of the ringing of the alarm bell. In ordinary circumstances, there is no highly variable range of environmental features of such a kind that a wide range of different such features will produce the same extended event of pressure on the eardrum. The correlation, in normal circumstances, between the objective duration of the bell ringing and the duration of the stimulation of the eardrum is uniform. Our perceptual systems are not in fact adapted, and do not need to be adapted, to circumstances in which there is no uniform correlation between the length of the objective event and the length of the auditory stimulation. This is a sharp contrast with the variability of projected retinal shape produced, according to the angle of the perceiver, of a given objective shape.

It is true that there is a limited subclass of cases in which the objective duration of some external event is not reliably correlated with the length of the proximal stimulus. There is in fact no reliable correlation in the special case in which the duration is an event of lateral motion across the visual field. The so-called Kappa effect is that the perceived duration between two events increases with the objective distance between those events, even when the corresponding retinal separation of those events is the same (Cohen et al. 1953). But there remains a reliable correlation when we are concerned with the perception of the duration of an event at a single location over time, and in many other cases than lateral motion. We have an obligation to explain philosophically why there is genuine temporal representation in the case of duration perception when there is reliable distal/proximal correlation. The Kappa effect is also not something that at all fits a model of constancy in which varying proximal stimulation is consistent with generally correct objective representation. On the contrary, the dilation effect of perceiving durations between distant events as longer means that some perceptions of durations between spatially separated events must be non-veridical, rather than correct.

So, does the inapplicability of the constancy criterion to a wide range of temporal examples mean that the distinction between representation of a property and mere sensitivity to it collapses in the temporal case? That does not seem plausible, for the notion of representation has real work to do everywhere. But what then is that work, if constancy is no longer the test of it in the temporal case?

Here we have to address two questions.

Question One: What is the nature, philosophically, of the distinction between mere sensitivity to temporal distinctions and representation of temporal distinctions, as temporal distinctions? This we can call 'the constitutive question of the representation of time'.

Question Two: Whatever is the correct answer to Question One, the constitutive question, what then unifies that answer with the constancy answer that is so plausible in such cases as spatial perception and colour perception? What makes all these kinds of cases genuinely representational? This is an equally pressing question, which we can call 'the question of representational unification'.

Burge's own proposal about temporal representation in *Origins of Objectivity* is as follows:

I believe that, at least in actual animal life, the functioning of temporal sensitivity in perception (and hence representational agency) is necessary and sufficient for temporal representation. A functioning psychological coordination of perception of *other matters* with temporal sensitivity is both necessary and sufficient for temporal representation in perception ... First, sufficiency. Suppose that an animal tracks a moving particular. The tracking relies on sensitivity to temporal order. The particular is represented as the same through the motion. The coordination of later perceptions with earlier perceptions in representing the particular depends on sensitivity to temporal order. Then temporal sensitivity is incorporated into perceptual representation of movement. One represents the particular's being in one position as temporally after its being in an earlier position ... Or a single diachronic perception contains a representation of temporally ordered change. Such perceptions are further coordinated with actional representations guided by perceptual memory ... Incorporation of sensitivity to temporal order in perception of change or movement is probably the simplest sort of temporal representation in perception. Similar points apply to sensitivity to temporal intervals.   (2010: 521)

Burge's proposal is then that in the temporal case, it makes a difference if mere sensitivity to temporal distinctions is coordinated with genuine perceptual representation of other matters. Earlier in the book he also wrote, "A perceptual system achieves objectification by—and I am inclined to believe *only by*—exercising *perceptual constancies*" (2010: 408, Burge's italics).

Here is a series of three examples that suggest that temporal sensitivity, even when coordinated with the genuine representation of other matters, does not suffice for temporal representation.

Example (i) Consider the nectar-feeding amakihi bird in Hawaii (Gallistel 1990: 292). The amakihi avoids flowers it has recently visited, because the nectar will not be replenished for a certain period of time. But it must also not leave a revisit too late, or else some other bird will consume the nectar. It has to be sensitive to a certain magnitude of duration to return to the flower at the optimal interval. This seems to involve only a sensitivity to duration, not a representation of it as a duration. But this sensitivity can certainly be coordinated with a functioning perceptual representation of other matters. The creature that is sensitive to duration may have perceptual constancies for objective shape and shade, and representations of shape and shade may influence its actions. But adding a sensitivity to duration that is integrated with these spatial representational capacities in coordinated action is not enough to ground the claim that the organism represents temporal duration as temporal duration. Saying that there is representation of duration simply on these grounds would make the notion of representation add nothing in the temporal case that is not already explained by temporal sensitivity to a duration. It would be a violation of a content-theoretic reading of Lloyd Morgan's famous canon:

In no case is an animal activity to be interpreted in terms of higher psychological processes, if it can be fairly interpreted in terms of processes which stand lower in the scale of psychological evolution and development. To this, however, it should be added, lest the range of the principle be misunderstood, that the canon by no means excludes the interpretation of a particular activity in terms of the higher processes, if we already have independent evidence of the occurrence of these higher processes in the animal under observation.   (Lloyd Morgan 1904: 59)

There is a way of making this vivid that can be helpful in thinking about the distinction between mere sensitivity and representation. All that is necessary to explain the actions of the amakihi bird is that after the relevant duration has elapsed, some system in the bird generates the means-end command 'To obtain food, go to such-and-such location'. The time at which this means-end command appears in the bird's systems is sensitive to the duration that has elapsed since the bird's last visit to the flower. Duration, however, does not enter the content of the command. Nor does the past tense enter the content of the command. The bird's actions are entirely explained by the presence of that command whose content does not mention duration and is entirely in the present tense. The philosophical question becomes: what is it that can be explained only by the presence of a notion of duration and of the past in the content itself?

This point illustrated by the amakihi bird should, incidentally, make us suitably demanding when presented with a claim that a creature has episodic memory of a past event. It is not sufficient to establish the claim of episodic memory that the creature's actions are sensitive to how long ago a particular event occurred in the creature's history. If such sensitivity can be explained purely by present-tense representations that arise after the corresponding dur-ation, further evidence is necessary to establish the existence of episodic mem-ories with a past-tense content.

Example (ii) We can make a similar case about organisms which are sensitive in their actions to which stage they have reached in some endogenously generated cycle. This is what Gallistel (1990: 240) calls a "phase sense". Bees will reappear at a feeding site twenty-four hours after the last of several daily feedings, even in circumstances of constant light. They will also reappear at a local feeding site in a contained space twenty-four hours after the last feeding, even when the container is flown from its home site in Paris to New York (Gallistel 1990: 255, citing work of Renner 1960). This kind of temporal sensitivity to the stage of an endogenously generated cycle could clearly be present in an organism with rich spatial repre-sentational capacities and constancies. But again, being sensitive to phase in this way is to be distinguished from representing temporal phase. Mere sensitivity seems to explain everything that needs to be explained here.

Again, we can put the issue in terms of what needs to be in the content of the creature's representational states and what does not. The actions of the bees are fully explained by the generation, at a certain stage of the endogenously generated cycle, of the instruction 'Get food now', and by the sensitivity of the time at which that command appears to the passage of a certain duration. Duration and the past do not need to be in the content of the representation.

Example (iii) Consider the case of fireflies that emit temporally distinctive flashes of light, and whose conspecifics are sensitive to such flashes:

Normally the flying male crisscrosses an area and rhythmically emits his species-specific flash pattern. In the simplest case this pattern is characterized by flashes of fixed duration emitted at fixed intervals. Stationary females, located in the underbrush, on bushes, or in trees, respond with simple flash answers whose latency is stereotyped, determined by their conspecific male's flash. Upon receiving an answer the male hovers in flight and orients his lantern toward the female, often dimming his lantern to locate the female more precisely. Eventually the male lands near the female and proceeds to her on foot.

(Copeland 1978: 341)

At dusk males can be seen flashing about 1 meter above the ground. Each flash lasts approximately 0.5 seconds at 20 degrees centigrade (flash timing is temperature sensitive) and is emitted during a short swoop that makes an upward arc of light. Flashes are repeated about every 7 seconds. Stationary females answer each flash with a 0.5-second flash of about 3 seconds latency.   (Copeland 1978: 341)

Now, I do not know whether fireflies exhibit spatial constancies in their perceptual systems. But again, we can conceive of a creature that makes and is sensitive to flash patterns, and also uses a perceptual system with spatial constancies to recognize and steer towards a female of the same species. This creature would exhibit temporal sensitivities in a way that is coordinated with genuine perception of other matters, viz. spatial properties and relations. I do not think this would suffice for this creature to represent temporal matters, as opposed to merely being sensitive to them. It is compatible with this description of the creature that it has no capacity for temporal representation beyond the sensitivity described, and no capacity to represent the past. Its actions are entirely explained by the temporal pattern of its reception of light stimulation. At no point in the explanation of this creature's actions do we need to appeal to anything beyond that. To put the point one last time in terms of content: the fireflies need to have something that represents the command 'Fly towards that light' that is sensitive to the number of flashes, and to the duration between the flashes. But duration, and the past tense, do not need to enter the content of these instructions or commands.

In these three examples, the mere sensitivity to temporal durations, or phase stages, or flash patterns stands in sharp contrast to what we need to invoke in explaining the actions of a creature with objective spatial representations. Those actions do not involve merely a sensitivity to retinal or proximal stimulation patterns. Explanation of such spatial actions involves sensitivity to the spatial representational content of the creature's perceptual states. This suggests a clue to formulating a different account.

5. Representational Preservation

By analogy with the case of spatial representation, the attribution of temporal representational content is well founded only if there are actions not fully explained by temporal features of proximal states, including properties of the time at which a command appears, but are explained rather by states of the creature whose content involves duration and the past. Our next task is to say what capacities could be explained only by such temporal contents. Equivalently, our task is to say what it is to grasp such temporal contents.

When you are functioning properly, in normal circumstances, you have some conception of the layout of the world around you at any given time, and have various experiences at that time. As time passes, some of this conception is retained, and is given a suitably adjusted temporal and spatial labelling. The conception needs to be given the right past-tense labelling, as time passes. If you have moved, the indexical spatial content in the conception needs to be adjusted too. If you have turned rightwards, then the earlier perception of the tree in blossom straight ahead of you needs to be adjusted to a representation of the tree in blossom to your left. Similar remarks apply to distance. The earlier perceptual demonstrative 'that tree' generates a corresponding memory demonstrative of the same tree; and so forth.

Such a process of preservation of a conception has three crucial and inter-related components.

First, there is some kind of preservation, as just illustrated, of a conception. It may be tempting to call this 'objectivity preservation', but that may be too strong. The conception can certainly contain elements concerning the subject's own experiences and other subjective states, so it is probably better to call what is in question 'representational preservation'.

Second, the later representation is sensitive to time itself. When all is working properly, the representation is given a past-tense label that is sensitive to how much time has passed. We are capable of thinking of a duration of a certain unit-free length, and, again when all is working properly, the adjusted representation represents the world as being a certain way that same unit-free length of time ago.

For the third component, which is arguably implicit in the first two, consider the subject's total representational conception at the later time, a total conception that concerns the state of the world both past and present. This total representational conception is one that registers certain identities between objects, events, or places that are represented as being a certain way at the earlier time and objects, events, or places that are given to the subject at the later time. If you have moved a certain distance from the tree in blossom, that tree that you represent as having been in blossom earlier is also represented by you as having a certain distance from your present position. If your left ankle hurt earlier, that ankle is, in your total representational system, represented as being one of the same ankles you have now; and so forth.

So we are concerned here with temporally sensitive representational preservation that registers identities over time. I will label this, with capitals, 'Representational Preservation' for brevity, the capitalized label being understood to cover all three components we just identified. There are obvious connections here with the notion of perspectival sensitivity I developed in *Sense and Content* (Peacocke 1983).

I propose the hypothesis that Representational Preservation is what distinguishes the representation of time and temporal distinctions, as opposed to a mere sensitivity to time and to temporal distinctions. When there is Representational Preservation, we have representation of objective temporal relations, durations, and properties. In a case of genuine perception of the duration of an event, that duration is fitted into the perceiving subject's local history of the world built up by the operation of Representational Preservation.

There is of course no one type of action we should expect when there is perception of duration, any more than there is just one type of action to be expected in the case of genuine perception of spatial extent. Any actions produced will depend on the appetites and projects of the agent. But when the duration of the ringing of the bell is perceived, a subject may be in a position to know what else was happening when the ringing began, whether someone would have had time to exit the building while the ringing continued, whether some other event occurred before or during the ringing, and so on. These are all species of objective temporal information of potential practical relevance, dependent upon the capacity to fit the duration of the bell's ringing into an objective temporal history of part of the world.

To say there is representation of objective temporal conditions is not to say that the subject who is representing temporal matters has a conception of objectivity, and is capable of representing the notion of objectivity. That would be a more sophisticated capacity, not required for minimal temporal representation. As in the spatial case, so also in the temporal case: we should always distinguish representing objective states of affairs from representing them as objective, which requires a notion of mind-independence. Both are distinct from the more primitive capacity of being merely sensitive to temporal states of affairs.

There is no Representational Preservation in the capacities we considered in the amakihi bird, nor in the bees whose actions are sensitive to the stage of an endogenously generated cycle, nor in the fireflies with their sequences of flashes. In all of these cases, there is indeed an explanatory and counterfactual sensitivity to temporal distinctions. If a certain duration has not yet elapsed since the amakihi bird last visited the flower, it will not return. This conditional is projectible to counterfactual situations that could easily have obtained. A similar point applies to the bees and the phase of their cycle that needs to be reached before they return to a food source. It is equally true that in the actual world and worlds that could easily have been actual, the fireflies will not respond to a non-standard number of flashes, or to flashing that is not at the regular interval. These cases illustrate the point that reliable counterfactual sensitivity can be present without any Representational Preservation.

What then are the kinds of actions that can be explained by the possession of temporal representation and which cannot be explained by mere temporal sensitivity? Obviously the requirement cannot be that present actions can explain what happened in the past. But it can be the case that present actions are rationally explained by what a subject represents as being the case in the past, together with the identities over time registered by the subject. Past states of affairs have significance for present action because of registered identities over time, or chains of identities over time.

Consider an everyday but still somewhat sophisticated case. You discover that your wallet is not in your pocket. You remember where you were the last time you used it, and you retrace your steps back to that location in searching for it. These actions are explained not only by what you represent as being the case in the past, but also by various identities over time that you register as holding. These identities include the identity of various places and objects that you now encounter with those you remember as encountering since you last saw your wallet. Your actions in searching for the wallet, the particular route you take, cannot at all be explained by a mere sensitivity to temporal properties and distinctions. How you represent the world as having been around you when you last saw your wallet is an essential part of the explanation, and so too is your route since that last sighting of your wallet. If those past-tense representational states were to have different contents, you would take or could have taken a different route now, and different actions of yours would be explained. Your searching actions cannot be explained entirely by simple conformity to an imperative 'Go to such-and-such location to obtain your wallet'. If such a practical maxim is eventually derived by the subject, it is derived in part from representational states with past-tense content.

The reference in this example to a continuing substance such as a wallet is inessential to illustrating the point. There could be a subject in a world of events, a subject who needs to relocate a continuing but moving event that provides a source of nutrition. The subject may make its way back to the event, wherever it now is, by a combination of memories of locations it occupied, and directions it took in the past, together with a conception of the layout of moving events, and their rate and direction of motion. This capacity relies on the subject's ability to identify currently encountered locations with those it occupied in the past. The capacity need not involve any exercise of an ability to reidentify continuing objects that are not events.

We can ask what would need to be added to the capacities and states of the amakihi bird to make it genuinely represent the past, and not, like that bird, to be merely sensitive to durations. Suppose we imagine a creature that needs to feed by consuming some organism, again at fixed intervals, but that the organism that it needs to consume moves around, and has to be located. The feeding creature needs to have information over what sort of distance it needs to look for its food source, and to preserve a representation of where the source was last time it visited and in what direction it was then moving, a representation whose content may vary from occasion to occasion. It needs to register identities between directions it perceives now and the direction in which its prey was moving earlier. Even if there remains a fixed interval at which the food becomes available from the source, with this modification it becomes much more plausible that the feeding creature is operating with past-tense representations that explain its actions. The creature's fitting the duration into an objective temporal conception of the history of part of the world plays a part in the explanation of the creature's actions. The creature's mental states with durational contents and identities over time form an essential component of the explanation of the creature's representation of the likely current location of its prey, and hence of the creature's actions.

Under this treatment, the answer to Question Two, the question of representational unification, is that both temporal and spatial perception contribute non-redundantly to the explanation of a creature's actions under environmental characterizations of those actions. Perceptual constancies are a sufficient, but not necessary, condition for such a non-redundant contribution to the explanation of action.

In emphasizing the importance of the registration of identities over time in a creature's past-tense representations, there is a point of contact, but only of extremely limited agreement, with Kant. Kant in various ways emphasized the importance of the identity of substances over time in our thought. From the above discussion, it should be clear that the conditions for the registration of identities over time can be met by the registration of identity of places over time, something much weaker than the identity of substance. But the enterprise in which I have been engaging is certainly Kantian in goal and spirit, if not in its conclusions. There is a common concern with the minimal constitutive conditions for the representation of temporal properties, relations, and magnitudes.

It is also a consequence of the fulfilment of the Representational Preservation condition that a creature that meets it will be able to use the same kinds of reasoning about how things are in the world at past times as it uses in the present tense about the world as it is around it now.

The capacities mentioned in Representational Preservation are those present when all is functioning properly. Subjects may not be functioning properly when ill, when taking drugs that affect the perception of time, when in some sudden life-threatening situation, or when suffering from damage that affects their ability to order remembered events, or even to remember at all. Subjects in one or another of these suboptimal conditions are still capable of representing, and misrepresenting, temporal properties, relations, and magnitudes, but only because there is some applicable notion of what is proper perceptual functioning for them.

Under the hypothesis that Representational Preservation is what matters for temporal representation, it is one thing for a subject to be able to represent particular past states of affairs, events, and objects, but it is another for the subject to represent causal relations between earlier and later events. Under the hypothesis that Representational Preservation is what matters, a subject can represent particular earlier events and objects, and leave it open which, if any, of them cause, or have properties which causally explain, later events and states of affairs. The temporal sensitivity involved in Representational Preservation, and the role of Representational Preservation in the explanation of action, already supply a foundation for the representation of temporal relations, and for thought about particular past events and times. Once Representational Preservation is in place, a subject can speculate about, and work out, which if any of the earlier events and objects have properties that cause the properties, or existence, of later events and states of affairs. But the subject does not need to exercise or rely on the notion of causation to grasp genuine temporal priority of particular events, or to represent particular past times, and perhaps does not even need to possess a notion of causation to do so. This is, evidently, a non-Kantian feature of the account.

6. Present-Tense Content: Varieties, Nature, and Deflationary Significance

Let us step back from the details for a moment to consider some general issues that arise in elaborating particular metaphysics-involving accounts of content and meaning. Sometimes, in elaborating such an account for a particular domain, we need to revise, expand, or produce a new metaphysics. That is what I argued in Chapter 2 for magnitudes. It is also a task in the metaphysics of modality for anyone who rejects David Lewis's modal realism. But for some domains, a necessary part of defending a metaphysics-involving account is the provision of a revised, expanded, or new account of the intentional contents or meanings that are the concern of the metaphysics-involving account. I believe this is so for the case of time and temporal intentional contents. I will argue and illustrate the case for the present-tense intentional content of perception, and mention some apparent consequences for positions in metaphysics. In doing so, I will be aiming to fulfil the third of the challenges noted at the outset of this chapter: that of explaining how highly distinctive features of the perception of time can be understood, and be shown to be metaphysically unproblematic, from a generally objectivist account of temporal perception.

Perceptual experience represents things as they are *now*. That is, the correctness condition for the content of perceptual experience concerns the time of occurrence of the experience itself. Perceptual experience presents objects as having a particular egocentric location now; a certain orientation, colour, and texture now. Perceptual experience presents events as having certain properties and relations now. These statements ought to be uncontroversial. They do not involve commitment to any particular metaphysics of time, or to any distinctive metaphysics of the present. The statement that the content of perceptual experience is present-tensed concerns not the nature of the time that the experience concerns, but rather how it is given in experience. It is given under the present-tense type of mode of presentation *now*. The most fundamental form of this kind of mode presentation is nonconceptual, as discussed in Peacocke (2014a: 13, 49, 83). The nonconceptual form of the present tense of course has conceptualized versions, which are expressed by the present tense in natural language.

There are, however, three important subtypes of present-tense content that need to be distinguished. Each subtype has a distinctive correctness condition and psychological significance. The elaboration of the nature of these subtypes is significant for an explanation of how the metaphysics-involving view can be correct for the case of time. The elaboration also bears on arguments about the metaphysics of time.

First kind: δP/δt content

Every property we perceive of an object or event we perceive either as constant or perceive as changing. We perceive the car as stationary, or perceive it as moving. We perceive the clarinet note at the start of *Rhapsody in Blue* as rising, and other notes we perceive as continuing the same. Human perception rarely if ever seems to be neutral on the issue of whether what the subject is perceiving is changing, or is continuing as the same.

This is not plausibly a general a priori truth. We can conceive of a creature that perceives in stroboscopic flashes, and receives snapshots of states of affairs that are given neither as constant nor as changing. (These would be different from our actual experiences in stroboscopic light, which are as of briefly glimpsed objects that are not changing.) But the fact that we almost always experience objects and events as either changing or experience them as constant does seem to be a deep-rooted psychological truth about humans.

An experience as of change may or may not be veridical. You may perceive the adjacent train you see out of your train window as moving, when in fact it is your train that is moving.

There is a two-way independence of whether you are perceiving something as changing in respect of a given property P from whether you have the experience of the thing as being different in respect of being P a moment ago.

(i) When you experience a change in an object as instantaneous, you do not have an experience of the object as chang*ing*. The object seemed to have a constant property a moment ago, and a different property a moment later.

(ii) You can experience something as moving, even though its position in relation to other objects has not apparently changed. There are versions of the waterfall illusion in which, after seeing motion for enough time, you are then presented with a stationary picture of e.g. a large Buddha, which seems to be moving towards you. Yet it does not seem, during this illusion, that the apparently moving Buddha is occluding more of the background as it apparently moves.[2]

---

[2] See www.michaelbach.de/ot/mot-adapt/index.html (accessed 8 March 2016). In the colour-ring illusion of J. Suchow and G. Alvarez (2011), the circular motion of a ring of coloured disks prevents correct experience of whether the disks are changing in colour or not. When the ring is not rotating, there is perception of the change of the disks. When the ring is rotating, there is very little perception of change of colour of the disks, even though they are changing in colour in the same way as when the ring is not rotating. For a demonstration, see visionlab.harvard.edu/silencing (accessed 8 March 2016). If the correct interpretation of this experiment is that there is changing experience of some of the disks without experience of change of those same disks, that is another example of the point of

There is a natural account of an underlying subpersonal mechanism that explains empirically this first kind of $\delta P/\delta t$ present-tense content. The explanation uses the notion of an object-file, or an event-file. For each property P (under a mode of presentation) the object or event is represented as having in its object-file or event-file, there is a $\delta P/\delta t$ slot in the file structure. This slot is required to be filled, specifying whether the property is constant or changing. What is sometimes called the WALK light illusion suggests that, at least for event-files, the default filling is that the property is constant. When you see a regularly flashing light, such as the WALK light on US pedestrian crossing lights, the first moment you see it, it seems as if it is on longer than in subsequent flashes. Your perceptual system assumes, as a default, that it has been on and has not been changing, before the next flash forces revision of that default assignment in the $\delta P/\delta t$ slot.

These points about experience of constancy and experience of change apply to some other states of consciousness. Your pain may be experienced as unchanging, or as changing, in some particular way. Your mood may be experienced as changing. The same applies to your attentional state.

When your perceptual systems are working properly, what explains your experience of change or constancy is change or constancy itself. There will be interesting and complex sensory and computational procedures involved in such explanation. But there is nothing metaphysically puzzling or problematic about the general status of such explanations in general. In general, when all is working properly, your experience of $\delta P/\delta t$ for a particular property P can be explained by the actual value of $\delta P/\delta t$.

The identification of present-tense content of this second kind has a bearing on theses some have suggested about the metaphysics of time. I suggest that it is the presence of $\delta P/\delta t$ content in phenomenology that has caused some theorists to think, wrongly in my view, that there is such a thing as objective temporal 'passage' of which we have experience. Such 'passage' is supposed to be something distinct from, and additional to, time's having a direction. Characteristic descriptions of this supposed experience of passage—not all of them formulated by believers in the objective existence of passage—include the following: "we *find* passage . . . we are immediately and poignantly involved in the jerk and whoosh of process, the felt flow of one moment into the next" (Williams 1951: 466); "there is hardly any experience that seems more persistently and immediately given to us than the relentless flow of time" (Schlesinger 1994: 257).

the text above. The interpretation is controversial. For philosophical discussion, see Watzl (2013) and Phillips (2014).

We in fact need only change over time in the world, without any further element of passage in the world, to explain these experiences. Theorists of objective temporal passage have been right to think that subjective experience is not captured solely by present-tense content which is described merely as representing how things are now. They would also be right to think it is equally not captured by a specification of how things seem now when combined with a specification of how they seemed a moment ago. Those theorists have, however, been wrong to think that only a metaphysics of objective passage can explain the distinctive phenomenology that is not so captured. $\delta P/\delta t$ content captures that distinctive phenomenology without in any way endorsing a metaphysics of objective temporal passage. $\delta P/\delta t$ content can be correct in a universe that has just an earlier/later distinction, and no additional objective passage.[3] Our distinctive experience of change, when analysed using $\delta P/\delta t$ content, allows it to be veridical without postulating some further form of temporal passage in the world.

Even the experience that nothing around one, and none of one's internal sensations, is changing—an experience that for any experienceable P, $\delta P/\delta t$ is currently zero, if you will—is a distinctive experience-type. This allows us to explain why theorists of temporal passage are inclined to say that we have an experience of time flowing even in the absence of any experience of change. We do have such an experience, but it is fully accounted for by saying that such an experience is one in which, for any experienced property P, the experience is one whose representational content includes the condition that there is no positive (or negative) rate of change of P. In this sense, there can indeed be a pure experience of time flowing without the veridicality of the experience requiring anything about the flow of time in reality, beyond facts about past and future, and rates of change.

The believer in some kind of objective passage may be tempted to reply that the earlier/later distinction itself cannot be explained without appealing to some kind of temporal passage not captured in the descriptions physics gives of the universe. But that would then have to be a purely metaphysical argument, rather than one drawing upon the nature of conscious temporal experience. The phenomenology of $\delta P/\delta t$ content in experience is entirely neutral on the metaphysical issue, and cannot be used to support a metaphysics of objective passage.

---

[3] This point is also made with great clarity (I discovered some years after writing the first draft of this chapter) by Adrian Bardon (2013: 95). The "certain sensible quality that does not seem to be captured by the notion of our having successive beliefs about part of the motion or process being future, present, or past" of which he writes is the $\delta P/\delta t$ content of experience.

It will be adaptive for an organism's perceptual systems to have states with $\delta P/\delta t$ content insofar as conditions important to survival and reproduction are captured by $\delta P/\delta t$ content. The representation of changes in motion, direction, auditory volume, and much else will be important in avoiding danger and protecting offspring. The environmental character of these conditions only further emphasizes the objective character of $\delta P/\delta t$ content.

Second kind: happening-now

This subkind of present-tense content can be illustrated by your experience of hearing two knocks on your door in rapid succession, or by your experience of hearing an utterance of the syllable 'she', rather than of 'sho'. It seems, in these happening-now contents, that a certain temporally structured event is happening now. The events involved in happening-now content all seem to be occurring now, not a moment ago. Happening-now content is quite distinct from what seemed to be happening a moment ago. Happening-now content is neutral on what happened a moment ago, and cannot be analysed in terms of a sense of what happened a moment ago. What distinguishes happening-now content is that there is no time at which it seems to the perceiving subject that an earlier event in the happening-now content has occurred, without the later events having yet occurred. When you hear the double knock on the door, there is no moment at which it seems that the first knock has occurred, but the second has not yet occurred. When you hear a normal utterance of 'she', in the case of normal speech, there is no moment at which it seems to you that the 'sh' sound has occurred, but the ending has not. A natural hypothesis is that happening-now content is computed subpersonally in units that are grouped together, and that there is no perception of the elements of the group until the grouping has been computed. This would help to explain psychologically the defining characteristic of happening-now content.

As with the first kind of present-tense content, there is no problem in principle in the happening-now content of experience being explained by what it represents. The sequence of knocks on the door can explain your experience of their so occurring. An utterance of a syllable can explain your experience of its being uttered now, and as having a certain structure.

Some thinkers have used the notion of the specious present to capture the fact that at any given moment, we may be aware in perception of more than is happening at that moment. (This is not the only use of the specious present in the literature. It does not capture everything involved in William James's notion of the specious present, which we will consider a few paragraphs hence.) For this second kind of present-tense content, there will be a temporal interval, for each perceiver, in given circumstances, which determines the boundary within which perceived events must fall for that perceiver, in those circumstances, if they are both to feature in happening-now content, as opposed to content concerning what happened a moment ago. Theorists are right to insist on that distinction within phenomenology, and in that limited sense, the specious present is psychologically real in that happening-now content is psychologically real.

Could the proposition that present-tense awareness is of an interval, in the case of happening-now content, help to explain the nature of δP/δt content? The idea would be that the perception of motion, for instance, could be determined by the perceived distance travelled by an object in the duration of the specious present, or some part thereof (see for instance Ismael's elegant paper (2011)). If this is meant to be a proposal not about the temporal backward reach of subpersonal mechanisms but about conscious representational content, I think it cannot meet the need. The problem is that in the phenomenology of experience, as soon as one sees an object, one may see it as moving, or may see it as stationary. In such cases, there is no relevant prior perceived temporal interval on which a computation of distance in relation to duration might be computed. The same applies to the rising pitch of a clarinet, or of a fading lamp—such perceptions with δP/δt content can occur as soon as one hears the clarinet, or as soon as one sees the lamp. This objection would not of course tell against subpersonal computations that take into account distance travelled just prior to the onset of the conscious experience, if that were in fact how the experience came about. But the specious present was not intended by its advocates to be something unconscious. I myself am in agreement with Sean Kelly's arguments and conclusion that no account of the specious present is capable of explaining the experience of change, the δP/δt content discussed above (Kelly 2005).[4]

These first two kinds of present-tense content in perceptual experience each have corresponding versions for the content of action-awareness. For subjects capable of using the first person, the content of action-awareness has the present-tense and first-person form 'I am φ-ing now'. We can equally distinguish the case in which I have an action-awareness of keeping the pressure of my fingers on a keypad as constant from the case in which I have an awareness of increasing or decreasing the pressure, at a given time. We can also distinguish the case in which I have an action-awareness of knocking twice in rapid succession on the door now, or uttering 'she' now, where the content of my action-awareness is of the production of a temporally structured event with more than one element. The

---

[4] For contrasting views on the issues of this paragraph, see Ismael (2011: 464–5).

distinctive happening-now content that enters perception can also enter the content of action-awareness—and, of course, of intention too.

Third kind: trailing envelope

Suppose you hear the first four notes of Beethoven's Fifth Symphony. There certainly is a time at which you are hearing the fourth note, and no longer hearing the first note. So this is not a case of the second kind, of happening-now content. Yet your relation, when hearing the fourth note, to the first note is quite different from your relation to the conversation you had before the performance started. Also, when you hear those four notes in the middle of the first movement, your relation to the notes that immediately preceded them is very different from your relation to those, say, twenty bars or measures back. What is this relation?

In the case of music, one can hear the current note (or notes) as part of a phrase structure that includes the earlier notes. Similarly, in the perception of language, you may hear an utterance of the word 'horse' as part of the noun phrase 'the horse'. But syntactic structure cannot be essential to the phenomenon in question here. When you perceive an event, such as someone walking across a road, you may perceive the swinging of the pedestrian's right arm as following the skipping of a child on the sidewalk. There is no syntactic structure here. Even when there is syntactic structure, we want to know what the distinctive psychological relation is of the current event to that which it is related to syntactically, and it seems to be the same relation as is present when there is no relevant kind of syntax. When syntax is present and recognized, the earlier note or utterance is not currently perceived; yet it does not seem to be merely remembered. What is the criterion for and nature of this distinctive phenomenon?

Intuitively, it seems to be part of your current experience that certain things have just happened (in a certain order, each with a certain duration and certain durations between the events). Your experience now is that current events are related in such-and-such temporal fashion to certain other events, present in auditory, visual, or other memory, of a kind which makes available memory demonstratives like 'that earlier note', 'that skipping by the child'. The conscious mental states that make available such demonstratives are there because you have just seen, heard, or otherwise perceived the events. This gives out over longer durations, after which you have only memory-that, or memory images produced in a different way. It is an entirely contingent psychological matter how far back this distinctive conscious availability of earlier events stretches.

This aspect of the temporal intentional content functions as an envelope of trailing temporally related perceptual awareness. We could call this intentional content 'the perceptual past-envelope' that exists in current perceptual

present-tense awareness. This perceptual past-envelope content is a third distinctive kind of perceptual content, not determined by or reducible to the other
two kinds. The perceptual past-envelope, like the previous two kinds, has a
straightforward objective correctness condition. The correctness condition concerns the location and durational relations of events in objective time, in relation
to the time of the experience itself (and, as always, relative to a frame of reference;
in this case, the frame centred on the perceiver).

Of the three kinds of present-tense intentional content I have been discussing, this trailing envelope content is much the best candidate for a statement of
what William James meant by the 'specious present' (1910: 609ff.). James said
of the specious present, as he conceived it, that "we seem to feel the interval of
time as a whole, with its two ends embedded in it" (610). By contrast, the $\delta P/\delta t$
present-tense content of an experience is not an experience as of an interval at
all. James also wrote of the specious present as an "intuited duration" (630),
and said that "our maximum distinct *intuition* of duration hardly covers more
than a dozen seconds" (630). A dozen seconds is clearly vastly greater than the
interval whose contents contribute to happening-now content. Even if James's
estimate of twelve seconds for his specious present is too large, he clearly intends
something distinct from happening-now content, for which no one could claim
twelve seconds is the interval whose objective events explain happening-now
content.

I should add that in saying that the trailing envelope content is the best
candidate of these three for being a version of James's conception of the specious
present, I do not mean to endorse everything he said about the specious present
involving "the foretaste of those ['objects'—CP] just to arrive" (606). "Foretaste"
is a metaphor, but if it is intended to mean experience either of future events, or
as of future events (whatever that would mean), nothing I have said implies
commitment to that feature of James's conception. The most that can be said is
that an event experienced as occurring now may be experienced in a way that is
specified by a structure that continues one way into the future rather than
another. That is a matter of a subject's enjoying a perceptual expectation, as
when you hear the first seven notes of a rising tonic scale being played. Your
perceptual system represents the last of these notes as the seventh of a scale, and
perceptually expects the tonic an octave above the starting point to occur next.
But that is not the same as experiencing the future. Nor is it experiencing
anything as the future. Similarly, one should not say that when one perceives
the front of a house that extends to one's right beyond the region one sees, one's
sight extends to the right beyond what is normally classified as one's visual field.
As in the temporal case, the more plausible description is that you see the object

as a house, and that unifying description of what you see involves perceptual expectations in what is located in the unseen region just off to your right.

It is with the trailing envelope that Brentano was concerned when he discussed what he called 'protoaesthesis'. Brentano is reported as having discussed the developing perception over time of a melody. In Chisholm's translation, Brentano wrote, "When something that had been given as present appears as more and more past, it is not the case that *different objects* are apprehended as existing; rather the same object is apprehended throughout, but in *different ways*, with a different mode of apprehension" (Chisholm 1979: 11). There is in the trailing envelope a distinctive mode of presentation, a mode Brentano would have called protoaesthetic, of a note, the particular token sound-event, heard recently. It is important that this protoaesthetic mode of presentation cannot be identified with a memory image. Having a memory image of the first note of Beethoven's Fifth Symphony, even as occurring the right length of time ago, is not the same as experiencing it as being in the trailing envelope. Having the memory image in that way is consistent with not experiencing the current note as related to the initial note. The following principle, however, does seem to be true. Just as a memory image is a memory of a certain experience-type, so a proto-aesthetic experience of a note, or anything else, is a protoaesthesis of it as given in a certain experience-type. A place must be found for protoaesthesis in the psychology of perception and temporal experience, along with more familiar kinds of memory.

That concludes this short discussion of these three kinds of present-tense temporal intentional content. The significance for metaphysics of these three kinds of present-tense content illustrates the distinction, noted in Chapter 1, between order of discovery and order of explanation in metaphysics and the theory of intentional content. Initially, we can identify the different kinds of $\delta P/\delta t$ and of happening-now content, and of the trailing envelope, before thinking about metaphysics at all. We can, after identifying them, then argue that nothing in the nature of relations of these experiences can be used to support a metaphysics of temporal passage. Nor does anything in these experiences tell against objectivism about temporal perception. The final theory we reach will still be a metaphysics-first account in the order of explanation of the nature of these contents, even if the philosophical arguments about the metaphysics come later in the order of discovery. What it is for a state to have contents of each of these three kinds will involve at least sensitivities (of certain kinds) to the holding of their correctness conditions, which are causally and constitutively prior to an account of what it is to be in states with these contents.

It was a thesis popular with earlier writers on time that our thought about times other than the present is to be elucidated as thought about times that stand in certain relations given in present experience. James writes, "To think a thing as past is to think it amongst the objects or in the direction of the objects which at the present moment appear affected by this quality. This is the original of our notion of past time" (1910: 605). Later, he writes, in italics, "*the original paragon and prototype of all conceived times is the specious present, the short duration of which we are immediately and incessantly sensible*" (631). Brentano makes the different but similar claim that the very source of our concept of time is the experience of protoaesthesis described above (Chisholm 1979: 3). Given the discussion in Section 5 of Representational Preservation, we need to distinguish here sharply between two theses. One is the thesis that events occurring at times other than the present are thought of as standing in some complex relation of duration to durations that we experience. That may be true, and it is a thesis about certain kinds of thought. A different thesis is that we can explain what it is to think of duration relations in which events at times other than the present stand to the present time simply by considering the phenomenology of temporal experience, and without requiring that temporal experience be embedded in a certain structure of relations in the subject's psychological economy, relations that involve explanation by past-tense contents of the subject's actions, and a distinctive relation to the temporal world. If the thesis of Representational Preservation is true, and temporal representation is answerable to its indispensable role in the explanation of the subject's actions, then that second thesis is false. Temporal representational content is not autonomous and independent of the explanatory powers of states with temporal representational content, any more than spatial representational content is.

*   *   *

This chapter represents only the first steps towards the development of a metaphysics-first treatment of temporal intentional content. But I hope to have made it plausible that the apparent obstacles in the path of such an account can be overcome; that we can give an account of genuine temporal representation, and not just temporal sensitivity, within the framework of such an account; and that the detailed work involved in developing such an account of temporal intentional content can provide us with tools for analysing the distinctive features of temporal consciousness, and for assessing claims about their metaphysical significance.

4

The Self

1. The Metaphysics of Subjects and the Nature of the First Person

Can we develop a plausible metaphysics-first account of the first-person concept? It is the goal of this chapter to develop such an account.

I have come to think that we need to improve on previous accounts, my own included, of the relation between mental states and events and the subjects who have or enjoy or suffer them. We also need to improve on our accounts of the nature of the first-person concept or notion by which we represent such subjects. In short, we need deeper accounts of both the metaphysics and the theory of content in the case of subjects and the first person. I will be arguing that improved accounts of these matters undergird a metaphysics-first account for the first person.

My discussion of these issues will fall into four parts.

First, in Section 2, I will try to say something explanatory about principles relating the nature of mental states and events to the subjects who enjoy or suffer them. This account bears on the nature of the subjects of these states and events.

Second, in Section 3, I will discuss the relation between the account of subjects emerging from this discussion and treatments of subjects in terms of subject-stages or person-stages. The latter treatments include the sceptical views of subjects implied in Mark Johnston's (2017) discussion of what he calls 'personites'.

Third, in Section 4, I will try to say something about how in first-person thought we succeed in latching on to the very same entity that is the subject of mental events as described in the metaphysics of subjects. No account of subjects is going to carry much conviction unless the subjects it is talking about are the entities to which each of us refers in using the first person in thought and language. This part of the enterprise demands the improved account of the first person.

Finally, in Section 5, I will try to draw out some of the wider ramifications, both positive and negative, of this account of the first person for general issues in the philosophy of mind.

2. Some Metaphysical Principles and Their Explanation

Consider this Principle (C) about mental events and subjects: that it is in the nature of the property of being conscious that conscious mental events have a subject. We can make clear the content of this principle using Kit Fine's notation for "it is in the nature of entity o that P", viz. $\square_o$P (Fine 1995; the notation here is simplified for the case in which we are speaking of the nature of only one entity). With Fine's notation, Principle (C) would be regimented:

$\square_{\lambda x(x \text{ is conscious})}(\forall e(\text{if } e \text{ is a conscious event, then } \exists x \ (x \text{ is the subject of } e)))$,
or better, using binary quantification that omits the conditional that is also absent from the English (Davies 1981: ch. VI, sec. 2),

$\square_{\lambda x(x \text{ is conscious})}(\forall e \ (e \text{ is a conscious event, } \exists x \ (x \text{ is the subject of } e)))$

(Perhaps a better intuitive formulation would be: it is in the nature of being conscious that being conscious involves having a subject—I skip the issue of regimenting that formulation.)

This subject-involving Principle (C) is plausible. Principle (C) has been an important resource in the case against neo-Humean constructivist views of the subject of experience. If Principle (C) is correct, then conscious mental events are not ontologically prior to the subjects of those experiences. So conscious mental events are not available for some intended construction of subjects from what is ontologically prior to the existence of subjects.

Principle (C) has intuitive support, deriving from the more detailed principle that is constitutive of an event's being conscious that there is something it is like for the subject of that event; and that requires the event to have a subject. The requirement for consciousness is not just that it be as if the event has a subject, but that the event really does have a subject.

This sound reasoning in support of Principle (C), however, takes us only so far. It leaves three questions unanswered:

(1) The first question is one that arises for all true propositions of the form 'It's in the nature of . . .'. Of any such proposition, we should always ask: what is the explanation, the source of its truth? Why is it in the nature of so-and-so's that such-and-such holds? We need an explanation, starting from a specification of the nature of the so-and-so's, from which it follows that such-and-such holds.[1]

---

[1] One might equally ask: *how* is it in the nature of so-and-so's that such-and-such holds? But when one is concerned with natures themselves, there does not seem to be much of a distinction between the how-question and the why-question. Contrast questions of grounding of kinds, where the question of how there is grounding of one kind of fact in another plausibly does not yet settle the why-question.

(2) Does a version of the subject-involving Principle (C) 'It's in the nature of...' also hold for nonconscious mental events? That is, do unconscious mental events have subjects, as a matter of their very nature? If they do, then the explanation of the holding of a version of Principle (C) in the nonconscious case cannot involve consciousness. The explanation must appeal to something else.

The nonconscious mental events for which a version of Principle (C) holds include much more than just unconscious events in the life of a subject who is conscious. Subjects that have perceptual states only from the older, dorsal route may never be conscious at all. The unconscious mental events of these subjects cannot attain their status as requiring subjects simply by their relation to conscious events in the same conscious subject. For this subclass of unconscious mental events, there is no possibility of cantilevering relations built out from conscious events. There are no such conscious events in the lives of such subjects. So for these unconscious mental events, the explanation cannot appeal to consciousness at all, not even in an indirect way.

(3) If the explanation in the nonconscious case does appeal to something else, is that explanation in fact also available in the conscious cases? And if it is, must that not mean that this more general explanation is more fundamental?

I propose the following explanation of why such constitutive principles as (C) hold for the case of mental events of perception and action. In the case of perception, what it is to be a perceptual state involves potential significance for the subject of the state, in respect of its future actions and nearby possibilities of action. An event of perception, by a subject x, of the world as having a certain layout around the subject has potential significance for the same subject x's actions in the future. The significance is potential significance for that very same subject.

This significance is present even at what I called Degree 0 in *The Mirror of the World* (2014a). At Degree 0, we have a genuine subject, but one who does not self-represent. A subject at Degree 0 may, for instance, have perceptions that represent an object of a certain sort as being in a particular direction from a perceptually determined *here*. The explanation I just offered of the explanation of the constitutive principle (C) applies to the perceptions of this subject at Degree 0 too. The significance of perception for present and future action involves just being the same subject. It does not need to involve any representation in the first person of being the same subject. The significance will also of course have consequences for the first-person representations of subjects at higher Degrees.

What is the corresponding explanation of the significance of Principle (C) for the case of those mental events that are actions, which also seem to need, in their very nature, an agent? In the case of actions intentional under some description, they make sense given they are produced by a subject with a continuing identity over time, and certain projects, needs, appetites, emotions (this last to cover expressive actions). A subject's actions make sense in relation to the subject's perceived and previously experienced environments. It also needs to be the same subject that is both the subject of perceptual events and the agent of actions.

Some events are actions that occur in organisms too primitive to be properly characterized as performing actions intentional under a description, for instance the swimming of a jellyfish, in one of Burge's examples of a primitive action (2010). These are events produced by an organism which are produced because they are of a certain kind, where the 'because' adverts to a natural selection explanation, rather than anything that has to presuppose content-involving states. But the explanation in terms of natural selection involves an organism with a continuing identity over time. The explanation of the action occurring is that it is of a type whose instances have promoted the continuing existence and reproduction of agents (producers) of its type.

These are identity-involving explanations of instances of the metaphysical Principle (C) that mental events must have subjects. These explanations apply uniformly and equally whether the mental events and actions are conscious, and whether the mental events and actions are unconscious. These explanations seem to answer all of the initial questions (1) through (3), at least for mental events with intentional contents.[2]

The preceding points imply that there can be wholly unconscious subjects with unconscious perceptions. Whether there can be unconscious perceptions has been the subject of a vigorous debate between Ned Block (2016) and Ian Phillips (2016) in philosophy, and between many prominent psychologists too.

---

[2] Is there an argument that mental events must have continuant subjects even in the case of nonrepresentational states, such as the sensational properties I talked about in *Sense and Content* (1983), or even their unconscious analogues, if they are allowed? The argument so far in the text would still be of interest even if its conclusion applied only to states with objective intentional content. But there are some relevant considerations even in the nonrepresentational cases. Sensational states, whether conscious or unconscious, must be capable of influencing action, and action must be action of a subject (albeit possibly highly primitive) that is acting. Without that connection with action, we would have no reason to speak here of sensational states or events, rather than just events or states nomically correlated with environmental or internal conditions. That is not yet an argument that the subject must be a continuant, persisting through time. But for any organism that acts, even when the action is influenced only by sensational, and not by representational, states, there must be some unit or assembly in the organism that connects sensational states with action. This will involve either a primitive integration apparatus, or perhaps a precursor thereof, and that apparatus will have an identity over time, determined by its function in connecting sensation and action. So the availability of arguments requiring mental events to have continuant subjects may not be restricted to the cases of events with objective representational content. The issue merits further investigation.

We would have to veer way off-course from the intended destination of this chapter to address these issues fully here. But it is still important to identify a position in the space of options on the issue of unconscious perception that vindicates and dovetails with the preceding points on subjects, perception, action, and consciousness. To that end, I briefly outline a position on these issues that is distinct both from Block's and Phillips' positions.

What makes an event or state one of perception is, in part, that its meets this condition:

(Percepn):   An event or state with representational content is a perception only if its content is available to the subject in forming a conception of the layout, spatial and temporal, of the world around it and the properties and relations of objects given in that layout.

The conception of the layout of the world in (Percepn) is one that endorses the content of the putative perceptual state or event. A perception will thus be capable of contributing to the explanation of actions performed by the subject in part because the world is given as being a certain way around it, and similarly capable of contributing to the explanation of the emotions of the subject. In the case of action, a perception will contribute to the explanation of events that are intentional under certain descriptions because they are made rational under that description by the subject's conception of his, her, or its environment, given the intentions of the subject.

This condition (Percepn) can be met by the events and states of a wholly nonconscious subject, one whose representational perceptual states are produced wholly by the older dorsal route. The contents of such events and states in a nonconscious creature can contribute to the conception of the layout of the world around it that the creature builds up. These contents can correspondingly explain the subject's actions in relation to its environment, under the descriptions under which those actions are intentional. If it is asked how an unconscious state can have the fine-grained kind of perceptual content that our own conscious perceptions possess, one answer is that the analogue contents identified back in Chapter 2, with their distinctive correctness conditions and explanatory role, can be present in wholly unconscious events and states.

On the other hand, in creatures that are conscious, such as humans, there can be states with content, and which even explain certain features of behaviour and of the occurrence of mental states, but do not explain in the way required by the condition (Percepn), and hence do not have the status of perceptions. I mention two such cases briefly.

Spering, Pomplun, and Carrasco (2011) designed an experiment in which subjects were presented with two orthogonally drifting gratings, each presented separately to a different eye. The results showed that the reflexive eye movements made in this situation were diagonal, tracking the vector average of both gratings, tracking in effect the resultant combined motion of the total pattern. Each subject, however, reported experience of only one component of the motion, either vertical or horizontal. Here it is clear that the unconscious direction of motion of the stimulus affects the diagonal eye movement. But it does not seem to the subject that anything in the environment is moving diagonally. Nor is it plausible that the diagonal movement of the eyes is intentional under some description involving the property of diagonal movement. In such subjects, there is plausibly some state with a content-involving motion in the direction that is not consciously perceived and reported, but that state does not meet the condition (Percepn).

For a second example of states with rich content that can exist without meeting (Percepn), consider the resourceful experiments of Mudrik, Breska, Lamy, and Deouell (2011). The experiment involves a form of continuous flash suppression (CFS). One eye was shown a random 'Mondrian' pattern; the other eye was shown a photo that slowly increased in contrast. Some of these experiments involve anomalous photos, such as a photo of a chessboard being placed in an oven. The anomalous photos surface in consciousness faster than an ordinary photo, such as that of a tray of biscuits being placed in the oven. Such experiments do make it highly plausible that, prior to conscious awareness of the photo of the chessboard being placed in the oven, there is some state in the subject with a rich content concerning a photo of a chessboard being placed in an oven. The experiments do show too that something in the subject's psychological economy is sensitive to the anomalousness of a chessboard being placed in an oven. But prior to its presence in consciousness, the state with the content of a chessboard being placed in the oven is not available to the subject for updating the subject's conception of the layout of the environment. If it were, it would after all meet the condition for being perception. Nor is something's coming to awareness at a certain time an intentional action at all. So the state with a rich content concerning the photo of a chessboard does not meet the condition (Percepn). This is not because it is unconscious, because, as noted, unconscious states and events can in other cases meet (Percepn). It is rather because of the limited explanatory role of the state.

The principle (Percepn) is intended as a partial characterization of a psychological natural kind that is uniform across conscious and unconscious perception. It gives a more specific, and thus more restrictive, characterization of the natural kind than is implied in Block's writings.

Endorsement of (Percepn) thus amounts to an intermediate position between those of Block and Phillips. It is with Block in permitting unconscious perception, but only if the conditions in (Percepn) are met. It is with Phillips in agreeing that some of the unconscious states cited by Block do not meet the conditions for being perceptual states, not even if they involve content of a personal-level kind, and even if (as in the Mudrik et al. cases) there are phenomena explained by the presence of that unconscious state.

There is much more to be said on these issues about perception, but these remarks may be enough to indicate a position on the issue that comports with the preceding discussion about subjects and consciousness. Let us return to that topic, and to the earlier claim that the intertwining of the identity of subjects in the very nature of perception and action contributes to an explanation of why the subject-involving Principle (C), and its version for unconscious events, are both true.

The identity-involving explanation offered above of why the subject-involving Principle (C) holds means that there is a certain superficiality in trying, as I did in earlier writings, to explain the need for subjects in conscious events by appealing to the characterization of phenomenal consciousness inspired by Nagel (1974). That proposed explanation was simply that for an event to be conscious is for there to be something it is like for the subject of that event. The contrasting explanation I have just offered of Principle (C) and its version for unconscious mental events suggests the following rather different way of looking at the matter. The subject-involving Principle (C) states a constitutive connection between the status of an event as conscious, and properties of the subject when the event is conscious. But the explanation of *why* the event, even a conscious one, has to have a subject at all is something more general, having to do with the very nature of perception and action, and the more general explanation applies both in conscious and unconscious cases. The Principle (C) about conscious events merely characterizes a relation that holds between a mental event and its already required subject when the event is a conscious one. It is a restriction to the conscious case of something that holds more widely, and the explanation of the general case has nothing particularly to do with consciousness.

Neo-Humean moderate reductionists about subjects sometimes claim that 'every experience has an owner' is merely a way of speaking, and nothing more. Thus Derek Parfit writes, "We do in fact ascribe thoughts to thinkers. Because we talk in this way, Descartes could truly claim, 'I think, therefore I am'" (1986: 226). The identity-involving explanation of Principle (C) and its analogue for unconscious events contradicts the claim that we have here nothing more than a way of talking. The explanation of Principle (C) that I have been endorsing is drawn from the metaphysics of particular kinds of states and events. On this approach, the principle that mental events of action and perception have to have subjects has its source in the very nature of mental events and actions, rather than anything to do with language and mere ways of talking.

The preceding arguments also imply that perceptual events and actions are not ontologically prior to subjects.

The position on subjects reached at this point in the discussion then presents us with further issues. It may be helpful to formulate the issues at this juncture in Humean terms. In the preceding discussion, we have rejected Hume's idea that "all our particular perceptions" "may exist separately, and have no need of any thing to support their existence" (2000: 164). On the contrary, particular perceptions constitutively require the existence of a subject whose perceptions they are. Now the claim that particular perceptions "have no need of any thing to support their existence" was one of the two principles that Hume, in his extraordinarily insightful, honest, and devastating Appendix to the *Treatise*, said he could not reconcile with one another. The second of those two principles was that "*the mind never perceives any connexion amongst distinct existences*" (2000: 400, Hume's own italics). What of that second Humean principle?

Under the treatment I have been advocating, we do not need to be involved in the intrinsically impossible enterprise of trying to find what connects allegedly distinct existences together into bundles that form the perceptions of a single subject. We are not facing the problem which faced Hume and faces neo-Humeans, the problem of trying to find a reductive account of ownership, by a single subject, of perceptions that allegedly "may exist separately", in Hume's phrase.

Nonetheless, there are at least two pressing questions remaining at this point, and that are very much in the spirit of a Humean enquiry. One is of course:

(4) Can we say more about the nature of identity over time of these subjects that mental events and actions must, in their nature, possess?

The preceding argument that there must be such subjects may constrain the answer to this question, but a proper answer to it has to say much more.

The other pressing question is one in the spirit of Hume's question of where the idea of himself comes from, given, he says, that he has no impression of himself. We can reject the claim that every idea must be individuated in terms of its relation to corresponding impressions. We still need, however, a substantive account of the first-person way of thinking and representing, an account not based on impressions, one which says what it is to be employing the first-person way of thinking, and which explains how the way of thinking refers to the subject that the metaphysics says mental events must have. (Or we need some demonstration that it is an illusion that any such account is needed—some of John Perry's views (2002b) instantiate this latter position.) So our other pressing question is:

(5) How should we conceive of the relation between being a subject of mental events and the agent of actions, on the one hand, and on the other, the ability to employ the first-person way of representing oneself, either in states and events with nonconceptual content, or in states and events with conceptual content?

An entity can be a subject without using the first person in any form at all. That was the case I made in *The Mirror of the World* for the existence of examples of subjects at what I called Degree 0. But it does seem that when a subject does enjoy states and events that have a first-person content, of however primitive a kind, then that first-person component of the content, both in perceptual content and action-awareness, must refer to the subject whose existence is required by the metaphysical considerations above. Can we say more about what this involves?

This is really a threefold question:

(a) What is the nature of the first person?
(b) What the nature of the subject?
(c) What is the relation between the two, in virtue of which first-person thought and reference to subjects, with all their distinctive features, are possible?

On Question (4) above about the nature of the identity of subjects over time, I suggested this principle in *The Mirror of the World* (2014a: 66):

(Int) subject *x* is identical with subject *y* if and only if *x* and *y* have the same material integration apparatus.

An integration apparatus takes information from the subject's various sensory, perceptual, and action systems, and integrates that information by placing predicative materials drawn from those various sources into an integrated representation concerning what is represented as a single *here* and as a single *now*. In the case in which the subject represents itself first personally, the integration apparatus places the relevant information into a file containing the information the subject represents as holding of himself (Peacocke 2014a: 15, 20–2). An integration apparatus is broadly characterized in informational terms, but it will have some material realization. (Int) is intended to be a nonreductive contribution to an account of the nature of subjects themselves.

According to David Wiggins's general account of identity, for any object x and any object y,

x = y iff there is some sortal F such that x is the same F as y.   (Wiggins 2001: 17)

I am inclined to regard the biconditional (Int) about the condition for the identity of subjects as a further metaphysical analysis of 'same F' for the F that verifies "x = y iff x is the same F as y" in Wiggins's account of identity, for the special case of subjects. The biconditional (Int) is intended to provide further elaboration of the principle for tracing the same subject through time.

The biconditional (Int) is not meant to be a reductive biconditional. The elucidation of what it is to be an integrating apparatus will need to mention perceptual states. Perceptual states are in turn intelligible only as states of a subject. The biconditional (Int) is meant rather to state a principle linking elements of an ontology that involves a nexus of items—subjects, action, perception, and so forth, and their material realization. I doubt that any one item in this nexus is ontologically prior in Fine's sense to the notion of a subject. Maybe the whole of this ontology can be reduced collectively to nonpsychological entities and properties and relations. The biconditional (Int) about the identity of subjects can, however, be important without any commitment to such reduction. For similar reasons, being an integration apparatus is not, on this account, an intrinsic property, in the sense David Lewis aimed to articulate, of the material object that is the integrating apparatus.

3. Contrasting Subjects and Personites

I now turn to the relation between the account just outlined, and to the work of Johnston (2017) and Leslie and Johnston (forthcoming) on what Johnston calls 'personites'. Personites are, Johnston writes, "shorter-lived very person-like things extending across part, but not the whole, of a person's life" (2017: 617). Johnston's view is that these personites and ordinary persons are ontologically on a par. For him, personites differ only in their temporal extent from persons. Persons do not, for Johnston, have any deeper ontological or more fundamental significance than personites. He conjectures that personites have as much claim on our practical reason and moral concern as ordinary persons.

Clearly the relation between this conception of personites and the treatment of subjects that I have offered is one of incompatibility, in respect both of the underlying metaphysics of the two positions and their verdicts on examples.

Here I just state the ways in which I think the advocate of the conception of subjects I have been outlining should respond to the personite conception and the arguments supporting it.

(i) The personite conception takes for granted an ontology of person-stages, from which personites are composed (or it takes for granted mental events standing in certain relations). I do not object to the notion of a person-stage; but on the conception I have been defending, person-stages are a kosher element of an ontology only if they are seen as temporal slices of entities, subjects, that have a genuine relation of identity over time, something to be elucidated on my view in terms of the identity of integration apparatus. If the ontology of person-stages, some of which are composed to constitute persons, is meant to be legitimate without any such presupposition, then substantial philosophical work needs to be done. In particular, the identity-involving significance of perceptual states and intentions would need to be accommodated somehow.

There is a contrast here with an example cited as a supporting case in Leslie and Johnston's 'Essence and Accident' (forthcoming): that of the boat and its planks. Leslie and Johnston discuss such entities as a boat-17, which is such that it definitely does not exist when only seventeen planks are left after removal of all the others from a boat; and a boat-25, which is such that it definitely does not exist when only twenty-five planks are left after removal of all the others from a boat; and so forth. Leslie and Johnston write, "Now imagine an advocate of real definition or of real characterization trying to settle the essentialist question of under what conditions certain very boat-like entities case to be. He should throw up his hands" (forthcoming: 12). I agree. Planks are certainly ontologically prior to boats, and they have a nature and existence conditions that do not in any way need to mention boats. This, on my view, is in contrast with person-stages. If what I have said is correct, an account of what makes something a person-stage has to mention persons. So any conclusions drawn from the case of boats and planks do not necessarily carry over to the case of persons.

(ii) On Johnston's conception, for any given time in what we ordinarily take to be the life of a person, there is a personite—in fact there are many—whose existence comes to an end at that time. He writes, "that there is an individual corresponding to each period is... very odd, but it is a direct consequence of four-dimensionalism's reliance on unrestricted mereological summation: for any plurality of person-stages there is a sum, i.e. an individual made up of just them" (2017: 619). On the conception for which I am advocating, it matters that such a personite's integration-and-action apparatus persists after the demise of the personite. In such cases, that apparatus persists properly embedded in a fully functioning body and brain of a person. So the subject whose integration-and-action apparatus it is also persists.

A corresponding point applies to the 'latter-day personites' discussed later in Johnston's paper (2017: 628–30). These latter-day personites include all the personites who cease to exist when you do, but who come into existence at some time after you do. The integration-and-action apparatus of such a latter-day personite existed before that personite came into existence. So the subject whose integration-and-action apparatus it is also existed before the latter-day personite came into existence.

Because they have different persistence conditions, personites are not subjects. I do not dispute the intelligibility of the ontology of personites. But since they are not subjects, a multiplicity of personites associated with a given body at a given time does not imply a multiplicity of subjects associated with that body at that time. The state of affairs of one subject with multiple personites does not seem to me to be any more problematic than the state of affairs of the existence of one table at a location at a given time, consistently with there being multiple table-ites there then.

(iii) In another highly engaging passage, Johnston discusses the step of extending the circle of moral respect to personites. "The step itself represents—relative to the four-dimensional ontology—a natural expansion of the circle of our respect for persons, an expansion to things that differ from persons in merely extrinsic ways" (620). On the rival view I have been presenting, the difference between a person and a personite is not merely extrinsic. The temporal boundaries of personites do not respect the persistence of their corresponding integration apparatuses, whereas the temporal boundaries of genuine subjects do respect such persistence. My general view, relevant to several of Johnston's positions on moral status, is that a being's moral status can turn on whether it is a subject or not.

(iv) It would be an entirely legitimate response to these points so far that they simply do not take into account the very wide-ranging significance and applicability of Leslie and Johnston's points about multiple objects and multiple essences. For of course those points, if correct, apply equally to an ontology that includes integration apparatuses. On their view, there will, for each integration apparatus, be a huge range of what we can call 'integrationite' apparatuses, almost all of which have temporal boundaries distinct from those of the integration apparatus, but which share some of its temporal parts. What, then, it can fairly be asked, is so special about an integration apparatus, rather than an integrationite apparatus? And if this question cannot be answered satisfactorily, the reliance on the notion of an integration apparatus in what I have already said actually provides no defence of the position at all. For in addition to subjects, whose identity involves sameness of integration apparatus, there will be subjectites, whose identity rather involves sameness of integrationite apparatus. The position would become identical with that of Leslie and Johnston, unless this question is properly answered.

What then is so special about an integration apparatus; what property does it have that is not correspondingly possessed by an integrationite apparatus? One property that distinguishes an integration apparatus from its multiple integrationite rivals is unified and maximal explanatory power without redundancy. Consider first integrationite apparatuses that either omit or add capacities to what I would call a canonical integration apparatus. One kind of integrationite apparatus might, for instance, omit integration with the precursors of sound experience. Any conception of a subjectite founded on such an integrationite apparatus is not going to do very well in explaining why it is something that turns intentionally towards the source of a sound, and is capable of forming rational beliefs about sounds on the basis of experience of sounds. On the 'without redundancy' part of 'explanatory power without redundancy': if we consider an integrationite apparatus that requires, for instance, also the identity of the apparatus that produces bodily homeostasis, this seems to add nothing to the explanation of the corresponding subjectite's actions that would not equally be explained by the canonical integration apparatus combined with whatever apparatus the organism has for maintaining homeostasis, whether that homeostatic apparatus is the same over time, or is replaced by some new mechanism in the organism.

A different kind of integrationite entity would not remove or add capacities from a regular integration apparatus. It would rather retain the same capacities, but, like personites, have different temporal boundaries from a regular integration apparatus. One integrationite entity overlaps in its initial stages with a regular integration apparatus, but stops existing at a time after which the regular integration apparatus continues to exist. The very notion of an integration apparatus, however, presupposes the notion of sameness of subject, in that it produces perceptual experiences with representational content. I have argued that the nature of these experiences cannot be elucidated without appealing to the notion of sameness of subject. If that is correct, and an integrationite apparatus is just a proper temporal part of an integration apparatus, then its nature presupposes the notion of sameness of subject.

(v) A further point of contrast between the present treatment of subjects and the multiple-essence view concerns the relation between the metaphysics of subjects on the one hand, and their representation and epistemology on the other. Leslie and Johnston very pertinently remark that on their multiple-essence, personite-permitting view, "Here, metaphysical and epistemological considerations against the limited variety of essence work smoothly together. The metaphysical demand for exquisite sensitivity when it comes to available essences makes it correspondingly unlikely that we as a species have naturally developed a conceptual scheme that maps the entities that exhibit the supposed limited variety of true essences" (forthcoming: 18). This raises important questions that certainly need an answer.

On the view I oppose to Leslie and Johnston's description, we can begin with a metaphysics of subjects, subjects that can exist at what in *The Mirror of the World* I called Degree 0. These are entities that are genuine subjects, who represent objects and events, and a *here* and a *now*, but do not self-represent. On the account I defend, their identity over time constitutively requires the identity of integration apparatus. Grasp of first-person notions or concepts, however primitive, requires a suitable sensitivity of mental states containing the first-person notion or concept to states and events involving the subject, states, and events that are possible even for a creature at Degree 0. I say this not by way of non-question-begging defence of the position, but by way of elaboration of the further tasks that face someone defending the conception I have outlined. If there is a secure and defensible metaphysics of subjects that can exist even at Degree 0, then—while we certainly are under an obligation to say much more about the relation of self-representation to that more primitive level—nothing here requires an exquisite and empirically implausible sensitivity to philosophically arbitrary distinctions, or to an artificially carved-out ontology. Our ordinary first person requires a sensitivity of representational states involving it, and in the conceptual case a sensitivity of first-person judgements, to the states of and events involving an independently articulated ontology of subjects.

The nature of that sensitivity is precisely my Question (5) above: that of how we should conceive of the relation between subjects and the first person. In Section 4, I turn to address that question. It is harder than it may seem, and much in the philosophy of mind turns on the correct answer to the question.

4. What Makes the First Person Refer to a Subject?

(i) *A Problem*: We can introduce one of the problems in explaining what is involved in explaining first-person reference to subjects by considering a subject who uses an expression 'I', but for whom a complete account of what is involved in this use is as follows. This subject accepts

I am in front of a window

when and only when he accepts

Here [the location of his perceptual point of view] is in front of a window.

Similarly, he accepts

There is a tree in that direction from me

when and only when he accepts

There is a tree in that direction from here.

That is, in general he accepts something of the form

I stand in relation R to things and events that are F

when and only when he accepts

Here stands in relation R to things and events that are F.

In this case, the seeming first-person acceptance is just a stylistic variant on the content of the second sentence of each of these pairs. If this is the full account of this person's use of an expression, that expression is not the genuine first person. This use of the expression 'I' also does not give any new spatial content, a fortiori, not even by complex inference. It conservatively extends the subject's knowledge of propositions not involving 'I'. If we want to invoke the spirit of a Kantian point, we could say that this is a purely formal use of 'I'; it is a 'merely logical subject'.

The force of these considerations for present purposes is that exactly the same point applies at the level of nonconceptual content. Suppose there is a component c of nonconceptual content for which it is a full account of the subject's grasp of it that

c stands in relation R to things and events that are F

is equivalent to

Here stands in relation R to things and events that are F.

For the same reasons of redundancy, such a nonconceptual component c would not be the genuine nonconceptual first person (would not be i in the notation of *The Mirror of the World*).

Exactly parallel points apply to a subject for whom a full account of its use of 'I' in

I am lying down

is that it is equivalent to

This body is lying down,

and similarly for whom

My left arm is extended

is equivalent to

This body's left arm is extended;

and more generally for whom it is a full account of their grasp that

I am F

is equivalent to

This body is F.

Again, the same points apply to a component c of nonconceptual content for which the above would be an exhaustive account of its role in a subject's psychological economy. Such a c would not be i.

Such notions as *this body* and *this hand* may be made available to a subject by proprioception of the subject's own body. There are also notions of the body and of limbs that are made available by the fact that the body or the hand in question is under the subject's control in action. A creature can represent something as *this hand*, even when not perceiving it proprioceptively, if the creature can reliably act with the hand in question. It can plan actions with that hand, thus represented. But thinking of a body, or limb, even in an action-based way, still does not by itself involve first-person content. Neither proprioception nor action-based modes of representation of the body and its parts bring a subject into the referential truth-conditions of *this leg is bent*—into its content. The content *this leg is bent*, even based on proprioception, or capacities for action with the leg, or both, is not yet the content *my leg is bent*.

The combined effect of both of these points, about *here* and *this body*, means that it does not suffice for having states with first-person content that one has both an atlas of a world around a body that's *here*, and a history of that same body over time. The atlas and the history do not require more than a *here*, appropriate temporal updating, and perception of a body that's normally at that point of view, with memory of its movements over time.

The question then becomes pressing: what more is required to make a nonconceptual content c the first-person nonconceptual content i? In the terminology of *The Mirror of the World*, this is equivalent to the question: what is it for an organism to be at Degree 1 of self-representation rather than Degree 0? It is also equivalent to the question: what is minimally required to bring a subject into the referential content of a mental state?

A thinker brought up in the Western philosophical tradition may be inclined to smile at this question, and to answer it almost as a matter of reflex by saying, "Well, someone who is employing the genuine first person, and not merely something equivalent to *here* or to *this body*, will be able to make sense of the possibility that by some kind of brain transplant he might have had a different body; and similarly he might be representing himself in thought or imagination even when there is no perceptual *here* to get a grip, because the subject is not perceiving the world, but is still conscious."

It is true that we can correctly entertain these possibilities and these kinds of thoughts and imaginings, and it is correct too that using the first person is essential to doing so. But it is wholly implausible that the capacity to entertain these possibilities, thoughts, and imaginings has to be mentioned in a foundational, constitutive account of the nature of the grasp of the first person. Many creatures have mental states with a specifically first-person content without the capacity for such sophisticated modal thought. Even when the capacity for sophisticated modal thought is present, it seems that its presence, and the genuine possibility of the propositions entertained, rest on the nature and grasp of the first-person component itself. There must be features of the first-person component at a more basic level that make possible the sophisticated capacity to entertain these possibilities. Our task is to say what those features are.

(ii) *A Proposal*: It is uncontroversial that there are two different kinds of case in which a content

This body is moving

can be true. The body in question may be passively moved, as when one is in an elevator, on an escalator, or on a moving walkway at an airport. In the other case, the subject whose body it is is moving the body, in a case of agency. I suggest that for possession of a first-person notion or concept, the subject must be capable of representing the state of affairs that he or she or it is performing some action-type, such as that of moving, running, or extending an arm. The subject must also be capable of using in bodily attributions the same way of representing itself as is employed in those action-attributions. These are, in central cases, severally necessary conditions, and they seem to be jointly sufficient for a way of representing something to be the first-person way.

More formally and explicitly, I suggest that in central cases the following conditions are each necessary, and taken together are jointly sufficient, for a nonconceptual component c of intentional content employed by a creature to be the genuine first-person i:

(1)   there is a range of action notions A for which the creature must be capable of being in mental states or of enjoying mental events with the content

c is A-ing

where the state or event is produced by the initiation of an A-ing by the reference of c; and

(2)   there is a range of notions F of bodily properties, spatial properties, and past-tense properties F such that the creature is capable of being in mental states or enjoying mental events with the content c is F; where in these attributions,

c is F

is accepted (in central basic cases) if and only if

this body is F

is also accepted.

The range of notions F of bodily and spatial properties in condition (2) is to be understood as including the merely bodily and spatial properties involved in the creature's falling under one of the action notions A in condition (1), such as the merely bodily property one has when one raises one's arm. The 'this body' in (2) is either a proprioceptive or an action-based notion or concept of the creature's own body.

The range of action notions A in condition (1) can include demonstrative notions of actions (*I am doing this*), as well as nondemonstrative notions such as *walking*, as in *I am walking*.

Condition (1) links transitory events (initiations, actions) with a continuant, persisting entity, a subject. Certain kinds of binding must be in place for this to be possible.

Condition (1) alone would not be sufficient for a content c to be i. In the absence of condition (2):

c is A-ing

would have as its correctness condition merely that there is an event of A-ing, or that some particular event is an event of A-ing, an event that is in the circumstances an *A*-ing by the creature itself. That would not be a predication of a continuing entity. States with contents governed only by condition (1), and not by condition (2), could be produced simply by an action-awareness, from the inside, of the relevant event of *A*-ing. A continuing entity would not be involved in the content itself. The earlier nonredundancy arguments would apply again. The earlier arguments about nonredundancy also already show that condition (2) by itself would not be sufficient by itself for *c* to be *i*.

As I just implied, condition (1) can be fulfilled by the creature enjoying a distinctive action-awareness, in phenomenal consciousness, of its own actions. But that is not the only way. Primitive first-person nonconceptual content is possible for a creature that is not conscious at all. Such a creature may still be an agent: there are probably many such in the universe. There can be unconscious states with a content, *i am A-ing* that are produced in the creature by the events which cause the action, or by the initiating event that is the action on Hornsby's account (1980). That content would still be distinct from a content, *i am being moved*, when for instance the creature is passively moved by a strong tide or current in its surrounding water.

If conditions (1) and (2) are, in central cases, severally necessary and jointly sufficient for content *c* to be the first person, it should not be surprising that the capacity to represent spatial relations, certain bodily properties, and even a bodily and spatial history too, are not sufficient for first-person representation. For none of these capacities involve the ability to represent something that has to have the capacity for agency.

All these considerations support the view that there is a much deeper role of agency in the first person than I indicated in previous writings. Henceforth I call the thesis that conditions (1) and (2) are, in central cases, jointly sufficient and severally necessary for a notion (and corresponding concept) to be that of the first person, *i*, 'the agency-involving account'. I return to non-central cases further below.

The agency-involving account has implications for the correct characterization of the functional psychological organization of a creature that self-represents. I argued in *The Mirror of the World* that the identity of a subject over time depends on the identity of an integrating apparatus. At the subpersonal level, the integrating apparatus operates to produce a file that contains representations that underlie how the world seems to be to the subject whose integrating apparatus it is. The implication of the agency-involving thesis is that this file is properly labelled as a self-file only if it includes representations of actions of the subject, where the inclusion of the representation is, in central cases, produced by the subject initiating an action of the type represented. A self-representing subject, a creature at Degree 1 rather than Degree 0, must not only be capable of action, but also at least some range of its actions must be connected to representations of action, and to the file that is the output of the integrating apparatus, in the way just described. This requirement was not included or discussed in *The Mirror of the World*.

It is natural to wonder how this agency-involving account is related to the claim—also endorsed in *The Mirror of the World*—that the first-person notion, like any other notion or indeed concept, is individuated by its fundamental reference rule. Does the argument above suggest that something more than the fundamental reference rule is involved in the individuation of the first-person notion? And if not, what is the need for all this argument, for can we not answer the question of what it is to be using the first-person notion by saying that it is the notion individuated by the fundamental reference rule that on any occasion of its occurrence in a mental state or mental event, it refers to the subject of that state or mental event?

We can indeed say that. But we still have to address the question of what it is for a subject to be employing one intentional content rather than another. What is it for a subject to be in mental states with the first-person *i* in their intentional content rather than, for instance, a content of a type individuated by the rule that in any mental state or event, an instance of the type refers to the body of the subject enjoying that state or event? That was precisely the issue we were discussing at the start of this section. Note that a similar point applies to the pure indexical *here*. We have a clear fundamental reference rule for *here*. The pure (non-perceptual) indexical *here* refers, in any mental event or state, to the location of the subject enjoying the event or state. Still, reference to locations can be properly attributed to a thinker only if the thinker has some grasp of identity of locations over time. Without that grasp, the attribution of reference to locations would be an over-attribution, and some more austere attribution (if any) should be made in properly characterizing the intentional contents of the thinker's states and events.

These are not *ad hoc* points. Rather, on any plausible conception of sense and intentional content, they apply for reasons of principle to all senses and intentional contents. We may individuate the sense of the classical logical constant *or* by giving as its fundamental reference rule that *A or B* is true just in case either *A* is true or *B* is true. We still have the philosophical and substantial task of explaining what would make it the case that a thinker is employing a sense individuated by that classical rule, rather than some other sense. More generally, if an arbitrary sense or intentional content is individuated at the most fundamental level by the relation in which a thinker must stand to some entity in order to be thinking of thinking of it under that sense or intentional content, then for each sense or intentional content, we have the task of saying what that relation is. A fortiori, that task exists for the first-person intentional content *i*. Conditions (1) and (2) are intended as a contribution to executing that task.

The first person is distinctive in that agency has to be mentioned in an account of its very nature. It was argued several decades ago that psychological explanation of action on or in relation to a particular object requires the agent to employ some indexical or demonstrative mode of presentation of that object (Perry 1979; Peacocke 1981). The agency-involving account is far more specific than merely being an instance of that more general point about indexical and demonstrative modes of presentation. We should distinguish between what is consequential on the character of modes of presentation of a given kind, and what is actually written into the very nature, the individuation, of a particular kind of mode of presentation. The claim of the agency-involving account is that it is written into the very nature of the first person that its presence has certain connections with action and its representation. In the case of indexical and demonstrative modes of presentation in general, or more accurately a proper subset of them, the connections with action-explanation are more plausibly consequential on their nature than written into their very individuation. Their nature involves certain kinds of relations holding between their use, the subjects who use them, and their references, and it is the general character of these relations that underwrites the connections with the psychological explanation of action on particular objects. It would take us too far off track into the theory of modes of presentation to argue in detail for this point here. I make the claim just to indicate more sharply the position in the space of philosophical options that is occupied by the agency-involving account of the first person.

In advocating the agency-involving account, I am rejecting a rival kind of experience-involving account. This rival view holds that what makes something the first-person notion *i* is that it is the *c* such that the subject represents it as being the case that

c has this experience

where 'this experience' refers to the subject's current experience. There are at least two problems with this proposal. First, this cannot be a necessary condition for a notion to be the first person, because a subject can have representational states with a first-person content without being able to represent its experiences as such at all. The representational states can, for instance, concern the relations in which the subject, represented in the first-person way, stands to things and events around him, without the subject representing the experiences in which those things and events are presented. To be able to represent one's own experiences as such is a much more sophisticated matter than enjoying mental states and events with first-person content. Second, organisms that do not have phenomenally conscious mental states and events at all—perhaps organisms that only have the older, faster, dorsal route that leads to perceptual states—can still have states with first-person content.

These two objections do not apply to the agency-involving account. A subject can be an agent without being able to represent experiences as such. An organism can be an agent even if it only has the older dorsal route that ends in the production of nonconscious perceptual states.

The agency-involving account of the first person is formulated in terms of the capacity for attributing bodily actions. A creature may find itself in circumstances in which it cannot engage in bodily actions, perhaps because its efferent nerves have been blocked. A human being in these circumstances could continue to use 'I' in thought, and with the sense of the first person. That is so because the person in these unfortunate circumstances would still know what it is like to act, indeed for he himself—first person—to act. This is one of the non-central cases alluded to above. The case is non-central because its status as use of the genuine first person is a matter of its relation to the central cases meeting conditions (1) and (2). In the case in which a paralysed subject no longer knows what it would be like to act, and whose use in thought of 'I' involves no more than the uses of *this body* and *here* that we noted earlier in this section, we would have a case in which the subject is no longer employing the first-person notion or concept.

But could there be a creature capable only of mental action, action of a kind not fundamentally parasitic on the possibility of bodily action? Though I doubt that is possible, the question of its possibility would require at least a further chapter. Part of the issue would turn on what kinds of contents would be available to such a subject. If there could be such a creature, I think an account of the first person in terms of agency would still be correct. The account would just need not to require that the agency be bodily agency. The possibility of such a case would mean that the reference to bodily agency in the above formulation of the agency-involving account would have to be removed. Many of the consequences noted below of the agency-involving account would still apply. Those consequences noted below that concern bodily action would need to be restricted to those subjects using the first person who also enjoy embodiment.[3]

---

[3] Two writers who have emphasized the importance of agency in first-person representation are Bill Brewer (1992) and Lucy O'Brien (2007: chapter 5). There are important insights in both these contributions. I may differ from Brewer in holding that there can be objective representation at Degree 0; and from O'Brien in holding that awareness is not required for first-person representation.

(iii) *Instantiation-Dependence*: Under the agency-involving account, a subject's ability to think about itself using the first person is made available by its being a subject, capable of action. A creature is able to represent itself in the first-person way only because it is suitably sensitive to the very events and states involving agency that make it a subject. This is not just a modal claim, but a constitutive claim. There is a way of representing, the first-person way, that in its nature requires what is so represented to be of a certain type (a subject), and requires sensitivity on the part of its possessor to what makes it of that type.

Just as there are phenomenal concepts of phenomenal states made available to a subject by the subject's being in those states, so the first-person notion is made available by its user being a subject, capable of agency. Phenomenal concepts— concepts of an experience of red, of pain, or of joy—have the characteristic that grasp of them requires the ability to apply them in response to a very instance of the property they pick out, an instance that is in the concept user's own consciousness.

We can, in a similar spirit, introduce the idea of an *instantiation-dependent notion*. An instantiation-dependent notion is one whose fundamental reference rule requires its reference to be of a certain kind, and grasp of the notion, for constitutive reasons in the nature of the notion, is possible for a creature only if it is suitably sensitive to it itself being of that kind. In the present case, the kind is that of being a subject. If what I have said is correct, the first-person notion is instantiation-dependent. It is only because the subject is an agent, and its action-ascriptions are suitably sensitive to the events that are its actions, that it can meet the conditions for using the first-person notion.

The ways of thinking expressed by a person's use of a personal proper name, such as 'Napoleon', or a perceptual demonstrative *that person*, equally require their references to be subjects. But they do not require, purely in virtue of the nature of these ways of thinking, that the subject who is employing them be suitably sensitive, in his representations *Napoleon is thus and so*, or *that person is thus and so*, to the conditions that make the thinker himself a subject. Suppose Napoleon himself is thinking of himself in the third-personal way, as Napoleon (as such a person might well do). In that case, although Napoleon's representations of what Napoleon is doing are sensitive to what makes Napoleon, namely himself, a subject, that is not so purely in virtue of his use of the third-person notion *Napoleon*. The sensitivity depends also on his being Napoleon. By contrast, concerning the sensitivity required of any user of the first person to the states and events that make the user a subject: there is no such dependence on the subject being identical with something given in a third-personal way. The sensitivity to what makes the thinker himself a subject is required simply in virtue of the nature of the first-person notion itself.

These points also illustrate a metaphysics-first view of the domain of subjects and their properties in relation to the first-person way of representing them. The metaphysics of subjects, as agents, is explanatorily prior in philosophy to the nature of the first-person notion, and to the nature of the corresponding concept. An account of the nature of the first-person notion needs to refer to subjects as agents, and to the representational states that such agency makes available to subjects. If the agency-involving account of the first person is correct, the relations in which a thinker must stand to something to be representing it in the first-person way involve a sensitivity of its action-ascriptions to the precursors of actions by that very entity. There is a level of action by a subject, the actions that are possible even at Degree 0, to which a subject's action-ascriptions can be so sensitive. It is because there is a genuine possibility of a subject that perceives and acts, but does not yet self-represent, that the metaphysics-first view can be shown to be applicable in the domain of subjects and the first person.

Perhaps the fact that the first-person notion and concept are instantiation-dependent can make understandable, and even partially justify, the idea of some writers that a special mode of acquaintance with its reference underlies the ability to employ the first person (see, for example, Kripke 2011). When acquaintance is construed as a causal notion, I have objected to that claim in *The Mirror of the World* (chapter 4, section 3). The hapless Cartesian subject who is deceived by the evil demon may have many beliefs about himself that are not caused by his being as those beliefs represent him to be. This hapless subject can still be using the first person to think about himself, even though he cannot use perceptual demonstratives to refer to things. If, however, we construe the kind of relation a subject can have to his own actions as a mode of acquaintance, such a mode of acquaintance with oneself is, on the present view, involved in the capacity for first-person representation. On the account I have been proposing, agency-based acquaintance does indeed have a special role to play in an account of first-person representation. The point may be a resource for elaborating the ideas of some of those wanting to give a special place to acquaintance and to being a subject in an account of the first person.

5. Consequences of the Agency-Involving Account

Consequence 1: predicative transfer and its ramifications

The agency-involving account implies a certain functional organization of a subject at Degree 1. Consider a subject at Degree 1 who represents it as being the case that

this body is next to a ravine

where 'this body' is a notion made available by proprioception, and refers to what is the subject's own body (not represented as such, of course, by the notion 'this body'). Unlike the subject at Degree 0, the subject at Degree 1 will in normal circumstances make a transition from representation of the displayed content as holding to representing it as being the case that

   i am next to a ravine.

This is a nontrivial transition, unlike the status it is accorded in the discussion of examples at the start of Section 4. It is nontrivial precisely because the first-person component of the second content has agency-involving and hence subject-involving connections that are not implicated in the first content itself. Here we have what we can call predicative transfer from predications involving *this body* to those involving the nonconceptual first person *i*.

   There will equally, for a subject at Degree 1, be predicative transfer for representations concerning *here*, where that refers to a subject's perceptual point of view. From

   here is in the shade

the subject at Degree 1 will make the transition to

   i am in the shade.

Such transitions, both at the nonconceptual and conceptual level, thus connect spatial representations about the body with the subject's desires, emotions, and intentions, when the subject also has the capacity to self-ascribe these mental states.

   Consequence 1 opens up an explanation of the possibility of perceptual experiences with first-person content in which the subject does not perceive herself. From Consequence 1, it follows that when a subject at Degree 1 has a perception with the content

   that object is coming towards here

such a subject will also represent, and may perceive, it as being the case that

   that object is coming towards me.

But of course a subject can perceive something as coming towards here without perceiving any part of her body at all, either in proprioception, or by ordinary external perception of her limbs and body parts. In such a case, the subject can perceive that something is coming towards her without perceiving her body in any way at all.

Consequence 2: the agency-involving account can explain why it is the same first-person concept that features both in judgements based on taking action-awareness at face value, and in judgements based on perception

When two judgements with a common element in their content come to be known in very different ways, it is always a reasonable question why it is the same element in both contents. This is widely accepted as a challenge that needs to be addressed in the case of first-person and third-person ascriptions of mental states. Theories that do not address the challenge, or respond with implausible answers, are rightly regarded as defective. Challenges of this sort arise for predicative concepts in cases beyond the psychological. It is, for instance, a challenge needing an answer to explain why it is the very same shape concept that can be known to be instantiated in perception of an object, and known also, by inference, to hold of an object not perceived by anyone. Challenges of this form also apply to singular concepts too, and one such challenge is the one that Consequence 2 states can be addressed by the agency-involving account. Why is it one and the same singular concept that features in *I'm speaking* and *I'm in front of a desk* when these contents are known in such different ways, one taking action-awareness at face value, the other taking perceptual experience at face value? Saying that this is unproblematic because both action-awareness and perception have first-person content simply pushes the question back. What makes it possible for such different kinds of states and events both to have first-person content?

The combined effect of clauses (1) and (2) of the agency-involving account of the first person provides the resources for addressing the question. Action-awareness can have a first-person content going beyond mere awareness of an action-event only if that first-person content features in nonpsychological contents accepted on the basis of perception or proprioception, as per the arguments for clause (2) of the agency-involving account. Moreover, the requirements of clause (2) imply that in normal circumstances, the subject of which, in acting, a subject has action-awareness will be identical with the subject referred to in *I'm in front of a desk* when that is judged on the basis of perception of being in front of a desk.

When a thinker accepts *I'm speaking* on the basis of action-awareness and accepts *I'm in front of a desk* on the basis of visual perception, she is entitled to infer *There is something that is both speaking and is in front of a desk*. This holds even if the thinker is profoundly deaf, and has no perceptual experience of speaking, but only an action-awareness. The first person is no more ambiguous in its various occurrences than is the concept of pain in first- and third-person occurrences, or the concept of a particular shape in perceptual and non-perceptual occurrences. This lack of ambiguity is a structural precondition for much epistemology of the first person and metaphysics of the subject.

Consequence 3: the metaphysics of first-person ownership

What makes a body mine is that it is, in normal circumstances and when all is functioning properly, the body whose movements I control. Some would elaborate this further by saying that it is the body controlled by my tryings (Shoemaker 1984a). Whether elaborated in terms of tryings or not, this statement about what makes a body mine is in itself entirely neutral on the metaphysics of ownership. The statement simply links ownership itself—not representation of ownership—with the first person, and with tryings if the statement is so elaborated. When, however, this statement is combined with the agency-involving account of the first person, we have a metaphysics-first account of ownership. For under the agency-involving account, what makes something the first-person notion can be explained in terms of a certain kind of sensitivity of the subject's first-person representations to the precursors of action, where action and the precursors of action are not explained in terms of the first-person notion. Actions and the precursors of action, and indeed in my view even the ownership of a body by a subject, can be present at Degree 0. They can all be elucidated without mention of the first-person notion, without the subject whose actions they are possessing the first-person notion at all.

Subjects who represent themselves, often reliably and knowledgeably, as agents of particular actions, and as owning body parts, succeed in doing so because of the systematic relation of their notions of themselves, of action, of ownership, to this metaphysically prior level of agency that does not need to involve the first person. Misrepresentations and illusions of ownership, as in the rubber hand illusions, are illusions that, for instance, the rubber hand is part of a body largely under one's own control.

Consequence 4: individuation without everyday knowledge of what individuates

We are faced with an interesting and potentially puzzling combination. What makes for the identity of a particular subject over time is the identity of integrating apparatus, together, as I would now add, with an action-initiation apparatus.

But the first person does not refer to this complex subpersonal apparatus. Nor does the ordinary user of the first person, whether their first person is nonconceptual or conceptual, need to have any conception or knowledge of this apparatus. Yet on the other hand, there must be something about the representing subject that makes it the case that in perception, registration, knowledge, memory, and the rest, the representing subject is latching onto a subject or person, rather than a mere body, or a mere point of view in space. "So we are grasped by what we cannot grasp" (Rilke)—or at least by what in everyday life we do not need to grasp.

I suggest that what makes it the case that we succeed in latching on to a subject with an action-involving integration apparatus is the constitutive link of the first person with representation of the subject's own actions, as outlined in the agency-involving account. Only a subject with an integrating apparatus and action-initiation component can be the producer of an action. A point of view in space cannot be the producer. Insofar as it makes sense to say that a body is the producer of the action, that can mean only that the subject whose body it is is the producer. The constitutive link of the first person with agency means that the first person must refer to something whose identity condition over time involves an integration apparatus and associated action-initiation apparatus.

I suggest also that it is the constitutive link of the first person with the representation of agency that is the ultimate source of our temptation, mentioned earlier, to cite the possibility of brain transplants and the like when we initially object to attempts to identify *i* and *this body*. Ordinary thinkers do not need to have contemplated or to have taken a stance on such possibilities for their first-person notion to be distinct from notions like *this body*. Ordinary thinkers' use of the first person respects the constraints formulated in the agency-involving account. The agency-involving account is inextricably involved with the existence of a subpersonal action-initiation component. A subject's integration apparatus and action-initiation component are preserved if her brain is connected to a new body. The first-person intelligibility of a subject's own persistence without persistence of what *this body* refers to is something founded in the agency-involving nature of subjects, and in the agency-involving nature of the first person, rather than having some kind of primitive modal intelligibility on its own.

Consequence 5: a constitutive account of the first person does not involve the intersubjective, the second person, or social matters

The agency-involving account of the first person bears on the position of such diverse thinkers as G. H. Mead (1967) and Jean-Paul Sartre (1992) that there is no conception of self as object until a subject is involved in social relations of one kind or another. Mead is in my view convincing in his insistence that thought and perception concerning the body are not yet representation that involves the first person. "The self has the characteristic that it is an object to itself, and that characteristic distinguishes it from other objects and from the body" (1967: 136).

Mead's own positive view is that "it is impossible to conceive of a self arising outside of social experience" (1967: 140), and that "the language process is essential for the development of the self" (135). The agency-involving conception of the first person suggests that the positive claims of Mead are much too strong. The agency-involving account employs materials that do not make any mention of either social relations or language.

Sartre says that uses of the first person that seem to be independent of a subject's involvement in relations with other persons can all be understood as really reference to the body—"Body as illusory fulfillment of the I-concept", as he titled one table in his book *The Transcendence of the Ego* (2004: 90). But as I argued above, uses of the first person in contents whose truth involves agency of the subject cannot be understood in purely bodily terms. There can be rich and extensive such attributions of agency without a subject participating in any social world at all.

The fact that there is no explicit mention of the social in the agency-involving account does not of course exclude the possibility that what it mentions does require, in less obvious ways, some relation to a social world. One claim for such less obvious involvement is that anyone capable of mental states with first-person content must be capable of being in corresponding states with third-person content, states that attribute actions, for example. Gareth Evans's Generality Constraint (1982), with its Strawsonian origins, and perhaps considerations of recombinability, might be cited in support of this claim. But those principles apply only to conceptualized content, not to nonconceptual content.[4] Though it is also a matter for some other occasion, the nature of nonconceptual content, and the attributional, quasi-predicative contents it involves, are answerable to explanatory roles that do not need to involve the generality and recombinability that are distinctive of conceptual content, meaning, and judgement.

I am thus inclined to conclude that a full account of the nature of what is involved in possessing the notion of the first person at Degree 1 undermines the thesis that interpersonal relations must be involved in first-person representation. The Mead/Sartre arguments are but a small sample of the arguments that have actually been canvassed, and might plausibly be canvassed, for that thesis.

---

[4] Some of the arguments for recombinability and generality are clearly restricted to judgement and to the level of nonconceptual content. See Peacocke (1992: chapter 2).

All such arguments merit a detailed consideration. Nonetheless, I think that the agency-involving characterization of the nature of the first person tells against all of them.

This conclusion may make it seem that a good theory of the first person has nothing to contribute to a philosophical understanding of intersubjective relations and our conception of many minds. The very next consequence of the action-involving theory, Consequence 6, however, implies that quite the opposite is so.

Consequence 6: despite Consequence 5, the agency-involving account of the first person connects it with resources that contribute to the explanation of our access to features of the minds of others; to the explanation of the character of our psychological ascriptions to others; and to the explanation of features of an agent's interaction with other subjects, once a subject does have a conception of other minds

There are at least two ways in which the agency-involving account bears on the possession of the conception of multiple subjects. One point of contact concerns the range of predications made of other subjects, and the resources that aid in rationally making such predications that are available even in advance of possession of a conception of many subjects. The other point of contact concerns the conception of the nature of those other subjects themselves.

We can consider the first point of contact, on the range of predications made rationally of other subjects. Events that are the subject's own actions can be represented in ways that involve both action and perception, as in the phenomena so extensively discussed by the mirror-neuron theorists (for an overview, see Iacoboni 2008). A subject can perceive what is in fact the action of another subject, and know exactly how to perform such an action himself, without inference at the personal level. Similarly, if the subject himself acts in a certain way, he can perceive whether some action on the part of another is of the same kind as he has just performed. When events are so represented in this unified action/perception way by a subject capable of first-person representation, that subject will be capable of seeing events which are actions, but actions performed by others rather than himself, as actions; or at the very least as events with a teleology. This subject may not yet possess a conception of many subjects, but has already made a crucial step towards it. If this subject wonders what unifies and explains these events over time, occurring in a given body, the answer will be the presence of a subject, of the same general kind as he is. In connecting grasp of the first person with agency, the agency-involving account contributes to an explanation of the significance of the resources available even in advance of possession of the conception of many minds for an explanation of possible modes of acquisition of the conception of many minds. In fact, in the case of humans, there is extensive evidence that even quite young children expect events that are actions not merely to have a teleology—a goal—but also to be produced by an agent (Carey 2009: chapter 5). What the present remarks imply is that when the subject does have the conception of many minds, events that are perceived in the unified action/perception way, available in advance of the conception of multiple subjects, can give reasons for making action-ascriptions to other minds.

The position I have just been outlining has a complex and interesting relation to Vittorio Gallese's important conception of a shared manifold of intersubjectivity, provided by the content of unified action/perception representations of events (2005). Gallese writes, "it is by means of this shared manifold that we recognize other human beings as similar to us" (2005: 115). I wholly agree; for Gallese's work can be seen as an elaboration of the underlying representational states and formats that can sustain the points of the previous paragraph. Gallese also says that the representational format underlying unified action/perception representation of events meets the condition that there be an "indifference of the representational format to the peculiar perspective spaces from which referents project their content; in other words, indifference to self-other distinctions" (2005: 107). It is true that representations underlying the unified action/perception way of representing an event can be applied both to one's own action and to those of others. We do, however, need to distinguish between the self/other distinction and the self/nonself distinction. To say that the shared intersubjective manifold contributes to our grasp and application of the self/other distinction is not to say that it contributes to our grasp and application of the self/nonself distinction. According to the agency-involving account of the first person, we do not need to invoke the shared manifold—the unified action/perception ways of representing events—in an account of first-person representation. On the agency-involving account as I have developed it, a subject can enjoy self-representation without other-representation. In fact, one can, to use Gallese's language, recognize other human beings as similar to oneself only if one already has some grasp of the first person. The agency-involving account specifies the nature of that prior grasp of the first person.

Consider a subject who employs the first person, even the conceptual first person, in thought. This subject may employ predicative concepts, true or false of particular events, such as *is a raising of a hand, is a reaching for a cup*, and these concepts may have the unified action/perception character we mentioned. These predicative concepts may, however, require for their satisfaction only that the events in question have a certain teleology, a goal-directed explanation, and not require that they be produced by a continuant agent, with a past and future and all the other structures normally involved in agency. For such concepts, we should not identify the contents *I'm A-ing* that the agency-involved account says are essential to the first person with the occurrence of such a merely teleologically specified event of A-ing in the body of the subject. That would not be sufficient. There can be such an event without its being an action of A-ing on the part of the subject. The phenomenon of anarchic hand, illustrated by Dr. Strangelove's Nazi salutes, exemplifies this possibility (for discussion and further references, see Marcel 2003). Real events of anarchic hand, such as undoing a series of buttons on the shirt the agent is wearing, contrary to the intentions—and to the immediately preceding actions of the subject in doing up the buttons—evidently have a teleology. The anarchic hand is a hand of the subject's body; but that does not make the undoing of the buttons one of the subject's actions. "*I'm* not undoing the buttons, it's not under my control, this wretched hand is doing it on its own!" would be a true utterance by the unhappy subject suffering from anarchic hand. The upshot of this point is that the sense in which a subject enters the truth-conditions of the action-predication *I'm A-ing* goes far beyond the occurrence of an event with the characteristic teleology of A-ings occurring with the participation of the agent's body.

In one of the later chapters of *The Mirror of the World*, I emphasized that capacities for certain kinds of self-consciousness can combine with other capacities to explain a certain kind of intellectual achievement on the part of the subject. An example I offered there is the way in which perspectival self-consciousness and reflective self-consciousness can combine to explain the operation of what Bernard Williams called "the absolute conception" (Peacocke 2014a: chapter IX; Williams 1978). Here I suggest that a subject who has perspectival self-consciousness, and grasps the first person, already has the resources rationally to make other-ascriptions, even if he has not yet reached the point of marshalling those resources in that service. To oversimplify in ways that do not matter here, to be perspectivally self-conscious is to be capable of thinking of oneself, as such, as someone who is given in a way that is also third personal. Such a person may see a subject who is in fact himself acting, and not realize it is himself. When he does gain the further information that the person given in a third-personal way is himself, he is in a position to see that he had a basis for ascribing a genuine action, of a subject, to someone presented in a third-personal way. Since someone presented in that third-personal way need not be him, this subject is operating with a basis for genuine other-attributions of actions (going beyond acknowledgement of merely an event with a teleology). For a subject who is perspectivally self-conscious, and who also enjoys the unified action/perception ways of representing events, the move from self-attribution to other-attribution is no huge leap.

The other point of contact of the agency-involving account with the conception of many subjects concerns our thought about the nature of those subjects. This contact exists both at the constitutive level and as an epistemological matter. According to the constitutive account that I offered in *Truly Understood* (2008), to think of something as a subject is to think of that subject as something of fundamentally the same kind as oneself. To think of multiple subjects is to think of multiple entities of fundamentally the same kind as oneself. This gives the first person a constitutive place in the account of thought about other minds. Now if other subjects are conceived of the same general kind as me, and thinking of oneself involves conceiving of oneself as an agent, it follows that our thought about other subjects is thought about them as agents. This, I would argue, is indeed the basic form of perception of another as a subject, viz. as an agent. Our interaction with other subjects, in conversation, in contact attention, in joint activities and the formation of joint attitudes, is interaction with them as agents.

The constitutive role of the first person in thought about subjects in general can help to explain why the first person has a special role to play in the epistemology of attribution of mental states and events to other subjects. The first person has a distinctive epistemological role under the 'Like Me' thesis of Andrew Meltzoff (2007), according to which a basic way of coming to know propositions about other subjects involves appreciating that they are like oneself. If to be a subject is to be of the same fundamental kind as me, then attributing mental states and events to others in accordance with an overarching principle that they are Like Me has a default reasonableness.

*   *   *

In this chapter, I have tried to give a metaphysics-first treatment of the first person. I hope this is the beginning of an investigation, rather than a conclusion. The large and fascinating domain of mental action needs an extensive investigation, of a kind it is only just beginning to receive in the philosophical literature. For that investigation, a proper understanding of the first person, its relation to the nature of subjects, and its role in a subject's awareness and production of mental action is a necessary precondition. Beyond the intrinsic interest of their topic, the materials of this chapter are also meant to be of service in that further investigation.

5

Numbers

1. Tasks

In this chapter, I aim to show how the Primary Thesis can be true of ways of thinking of elements of a domain, even when there is no causal interaction between the elements of the domain and those who think or represent elements of that domain. More specifically, I will be arguing for a metaphysics-first view of the relation between our ways of thinking of the natural numbers and of the real numbers, and those numbers themselves.

My strategy in arguing for the metaphysics-first view for abstract objects can be summarized in a three-word principle: Individuation Precedes Representation. 'Precedes' here concerns the order of philosophical explanation, rather than temporal priority. It is in the style of the existentialists' claim that Existence Precedes Essence (why should the existentialists have all the good slogans?). The intended force of 'Individuation Precedes Representation' is twofold. First, a good account of what is involved in representing abstract objects of a given kind has to make specific use of a theory of what individuates objects of that kind—a theory of their metaphysics. Second, the account of representing abstract objects of a given kind, when properly formulated, does not have to draw on more than that metaphysics. This second condition means that we could also call this a case of 'Individuation Determines Representation'. But for vividness, I will keep the parallel with the existentialists' slogan, and stick with 'Individuation Precedes Representation'.

It is important to appreciate what a striking and unusual property is present in cases conforming to the principle that Individuation Precedes Representation. For the material objects and events that we perceive, for the particles, entities, and magnitudes of theoretical physics, for the mental states of belief, desire, and intention, it is one task to say what is constitutive of them, to give a metaphysics for them. It is a further task, one which has to draw on much more, to say what it is to employ certain modes of presentation, concepts, or notions of those entities in thought or perception. However, in cases in which the principle 'Individuation

Precedes Representation' holds good, that further task involves only drawing in the right way on the metaphysics of the entities in question. It is an open question, on which I return to make some remarks at the end of this book, how wide is the range of cases in which Individuation Precedes Representation.

In the case of the natural numbers and the real numbers, I call the metaphysics of abstract objects for which I will be arguing 'Individuationism'. More specifically, it could be called 'Applicationist Individuationism', but I will sometimes use only the second word for brevity.

In Section 2, I illustrate and develop Individuationism for the case of the natural numbers. Individuationism can be considered as a doctrine in its own right, independently of our general concern with issues about the relative priority of metaphysics and the theory of content and meaning. For the case of the natural numbers, Individuationism deploys familiar resources in a less familiar way. I will, within the metaphysics of abstract objects, try to sharpen the focus on what Individuationism involves by contrasting it with other prominent views about abstract objects.

From there, I will go on to say how we can build an account of concepts and language about natural numbers from an Individuationist account, and thereby defend the metaphysics-first view for the case of natural numbers. Then I will proceed to widen the focus beyond the natural numbers, to sketch an Individuationist treatment of the real numbers, and I conclude with some more general reflections.

The materials I deploy in this chapter have been around for decades, and in some cases centuries. What may be new here is their deployment in an argument for a metaphysics-first view of ways of thinking of numbers, and also the role of the metaphysics of magnitudes in that argument.

2. Applicational Individuationism for the Natural Numbers

Here are some plausible theses about the individuation of particular natural numbers.

What makes something the number 0 is that it is the number n such that for an arbitrary concept F, for there to be n Fs is for there to be no Fs.

What makes something the number 1 is that it is the number n such that for an arbitrary concept F, for there to be precisely n Fs is for there to be something that is F, and to be the only such thing (that is, for $\exists x(Fx \& (y)(\text{if } Fy, \text{ then } y = x))$ to be true).

What makes something the number 2 is that it is the number n such that for an arbitrary concept F, for there to be precisely n Fs is for $\exists x \exists y(Fx \ \& \ Fy \ \& \sim(x = y) \ \& \ (z)(\text{if } Fx, \text{ then } z = x \lor z = y))$; and so on.

These are constitutive statements. In fact they are doubly so. They contain 'what makes . . .'; and they also contain 'is for . . .'. They are also statements about the numbers themselves, those entities, rather than being statements about a way of thinking about, or representing, a number, or about the sense of an expression for a particular number. These individuating statements may determine certain ways of thinking about the objects they concern, but that is a matter of determination, not of what these principles actually state.

Since its individuating condition is meant to be a full account of what individuates a natural number, there is nothing more to being any given number than is given in the individuating condition.

This is Applicationist Individuationism about the natural numbers because it founds the individuation of natural numbers in their conditions of application to concepts that need not be concepts of abstract objects. One concern about some versions of Platonism about numbers is that they do not properly answer such questions as these, as formulated by Philip Kitcher: "Why should these abstract objects be so important to us? Why is it that by studying them we improve our ability to describe and explain the behavior of more familiar objects? Why do premises about abstract objects play such an important role in our reasonings about physical things?" (1978: 130). Applicationist Individuationism starts from a point at which the very nature of abstract objects is explained by their application conditions. I will continue with this approach when we turn to the real numbers further below.

For any particular natural number to exist is for it to have an individuating condition of the common form instantiated by the above individuating statements. Not only existence-conditions, but also identity-conditions, are determined by these individuating principles. The idea of individuation is that each of these principles determines which abstract object is in question, not merely that some or other abstract object is in question. A natural number n is identical with a natural number m if they have the same individuating condition. If it is possible that the constitutive condition for there being n Fs can hold without the constitutive condition for there being m Fs holding, then n and m are distinct natural numbers. As always, constitutive conditions have modal implications, even if the constitutive cannot be reduced to the modal.

The present chapter relies on the existence of an acceptable metaphysics, epistemology, and theory of understanding for metaphysical modality. It also relies on accounts of these matters that do not already presuppose a metaphysics of the natural and the real numbers. For some discussion of the wide-ranging issues relevant to the availability of such accounts, see amongst much else Chalmers (2002), Peacocke (1999: ch. 4), Peacocke (2018), Roca-Royes (2010), Rosen (2002), Vaidya (2015), and Yablo (2008).

There are other ways in which a theorist might attempt to respect the priority of applications in the individuation of the natural numbers besides the Applicational Individuationism developed here. A theorist might attempt to individuate natural numbers by the condition for being the object that is the number of Fs (NxFx) for an arbitrary concept F, rather than by their role in numerical quantifiers. That approach faces a problem of explanatory order in metaphysics. Issues of ontological priority and explanation arise for operations and properties as well as for objects, and this theorist's account would take it that in any statement of the individuation of a particular number, the operation *being the number of*, NxFx, is available as ontologically prior to the individuation of that number. That seems to be the reverse of the correct order of metaphysical explanation. What it is for something to be, in general, the entity that is the number of Fs seems to presuppose an ontology of numbers, which is what we are out to elucidate. There could be at most simultaneous, joint explanation of the nature of particular natural numbers, and the nature of the operation NxFx. We cannot take the latter as available in advance in the explanation of what it is to be a particular natural number. Applicational Individuationism does not take NxFx as available in advance in that way.

A different alternative account that can lay claim to taking applications as fundamental is one that treats numbers as concepts of concepts. With a sufficient background of higher-order properties of properties, or concepts of concepts, this different alternative could be concerned simply with definition, rather than individuation. It would aim to say, for instance, which of the already existent second-order concepts is referred to by 'four', rather than being concerned to individuate a new recognized entity. This alternative theorist does, however, need to give some account of the apparent treatment in the language of numbers as objects. If the proposed alternative account does that in the same way as Applicational Individuationism, it will not be a genuinely distinct option, but will coincide with it on numbers as objects.

The proposed alternative account might instead give a fictionalist account of numbers as objects, while treating discourse in which numbers can be taken as concepts of concepts literally. This is the approach to numbers as objects in the illuminating discussion in Hodes (1990). Hodes writes, "Natural numbers are, loosely speaking, fictions created to encode cardinality-quantifiers, thereby clothing a certain higher-order logic in the attractive garments of lower-order logic.

More precisely: arithmetic singular terms that appear to quantify over numbers really encode higher-order quantification over cardinality-quantifiers; predicate-phrases, whose logico-syntactic behavior makes them of level one, really do the semantic work of expressions of higher levels" (1990: 350). Under Applicational Individuationism, by contrast, there is no pressure to endorse fictionalism. The natural numbers are genuine objects; they are in the range of unrestricted objectual quantifiers; the operation *the number of* can be applied to concepts of natural numbers; there is no need for two notions of existence; and a referential semantics for discourse about natural numbers is legitimate. What distinguishes the natural numbers from other objects is rather their distinctive metaphysics.[1]

Frege famously worried that one of the accounts of numbers that he considered did not settle the question of whether a particular number is identical with Julius Caesar. There is no such problem for Applicational Individuationism. A natural number is individuated by its application conditions, in numerical quantifications. Any object that is not individuated by its application conditions in numerical quantifications is not a natural number. Julius Caesar is not so individuated. So no natural number is identical with Julius Caesar.

There is no indeterminacy in the truth-value of '1 = Julius Caesar'. It is determinately false. There is, by contrast, an indeterminacy of truth-value in that statement according to accounts that (a) use the notion of a 'representor' object, one corresponding to each second-order number concept, and (b) suppose that this representor must come from a domain that does not already contain natural numbers (cp. Hodes 1990: 361–2). Such accounts then go on to doubt that there is any such thing as a standard representor. From the standpoint of Applicational Individuationism, that is a self-generated problem that does not arise under the proper development of an Applicationist view. If the domain of objects the theorist is considering does not already include the natural numbers, then none of them is the number of Fs for some finite concept F. If the domain does include the natural numbers, then there is no need to be looking for a 'standard' representor. The domain already includes the unique number that is the number of any given finite concept F.

---

[1] In the English expression 'there are n Fs', the position occupied by 'n' does not unequivocally behave as a singular-term position. 'There are the number of planets children in the room' would receive either an asterisk or at least a query in any discussion in linguistics. Yet 'There are 5 + 3 children in the room' does not sound so bad; nor does quantification into the position, as in 'For any number n, if there are n^2 tiles of a certain shape, they can be arranged in a certain pattern'. Perhaps there are restrictions on well-formedness in English that correspond to no fundamental philosophical distinctions. Maybe a combination of pragmatics and linguistics will supply further help with these phenomena.

The next task for the Applicational Individuationist is to say what it is for n to be the successor of m (or more strictly, *a* successor, but uniqueness is easily proved). Intuitively, for n to be the successor of m is for a certain relation to hold between the individuating condition for n and the individuating condition for m. The relevant relation is this: the condition for there to be n Fs that is mentioned in the individuating condition for n requires there to be one more F thing than is required, in the individuating condition for m, for there to be m things that are F. The formal statement of this intuitive condition runs as follows. As a preliminary, let '$Con_{i,j}[not(x_i = x_j)]$' abbreviate the conjunction of all propositions of the form '$not(x_i = x_j)$', where i is distinct from j. '$Con_i[not(x_i = z)]$' is to be construed similarly. Then we can say that for n to be the successor of m is for these conditions to hold:

> m has the individuating condition that for there to be m Fs is for there to exist $x_1, \ldots, x_m$ such that $Fx_1 \& \ldots \& Fx_m \& Con_{i,j}[not(x_i = x_j)]$, & (y)(if Fy then $y = x_1$ v....v $y = x_m$);

> and

> n has the individuating condition that for there to be n Fs is for there to exist $x_1, \ldots, x_m$, z such that $Fx_1 \& \ldots \& Fx_m \& Fz \& Con_{i,j}[not(x_i = x_j)]$ & $Con_i[not(x_i = z)]$ & (y)(if Fy then $y = x_1$ v $y = x_2$ v....$y = x_m$ v $y = z$).

Again, this is meant to be a constitutive account of the successor relation. There is no more for two natural numbers to stand in the successor-of relation than the displayed condition's holding.

In saying 'and so on' and in giving this schema for individuating the successor relation, we are using natural numbers in collecting together individuating conditions of a certain form. But the conditions in each case for a numerical quantification holding do not mention natural numbers. Remember, we are not here giving an account of grasp of the sense of numerical vocabulary, but rather a statement of what individuates the numbers themselves, and what individuates the successor relation. There is no circularity in using natural numbers to specify these entirely non-numerical individuating conditions.

Addition and multiplication are inductively defined in terms of the successor operation in the standard ways, with a limiting clause. For addition:

> n + 0 = n; n + the successor of m = the successor of (m + n); and a number is the sum of two (natural) numbers only on the basis of the preceding two clauses.

So in giving an account of the successor operation, the Individuationist conception has the resources to give a characterization of addition and multiplication too.

We can, in the first instance, regard the talk of 'arbitrary concepts' in the individuation of a natural number as ranging over concepts not of natural numbers, and even as ranging only over concepts of concrete, entirely non-abstract objects. Now it is plausible that for each natural number n, there could exist at least n non-abstract objects. If that is so, then under the Individuationist conception, there is the required denumerable infinity of natural numbers. Here we are relying on a modal truth, not on any particular logic of modality. If it is true that for each natural number n, there could exist at least n non-abstract objects, then the Applicational Individuationist has all the required natural numbers in her ontology.

We can contrast this position with one considered by Hodes (1990: 378–91), which attempts to reconcile the 'representor' position described earlier with the existence of only finitely many non-numerical objects by using modal considerations. Hodes suggests such a theorist is going to have to use a non-actualist *number of* operator, and says that that theorist will in the end do "best to accept an actual infinitude" (1990: 391). If we do not accept the 'representor' position, and hold that actual abstract objects may be individuated by what could be the case, then using modality in our theory will not require us to accept an actual infinitude of non-abstract objects.

Applicational Individuationism is, however, in agreement with Hodes's insistence that we need some justification for thinking that terms apparently referring to natural numbers do genuinely refer. The basic difference between the positions is on the question of whether such a justification exists.

Having individuated the natural numbers, we can then consider a concept K applying to natural numbers, such as the concept *even* or the concept *less than 17*. For any natural number n, the condition for there to be n natural numbers that are K is the same as the condition for there to be n concrete things that are F (with K replacing F in the individuating conditions given above). So we can also make sense of the idea that there is a natural number that is the number of natural numbers meeting a certain condition. We could individuate the first infinite cardinal in a similar way if we are allowed the use of infinite conjunctions and disjunctions, which can be introduced using inductive means and a limiting clause.

Under this way of developing the Individuationist conception, there are infinitely many natural numbers even if the non-abstract universe is finite in all respects. Contrasting positions according to which, in committing ourselves to the infinity of the natural numbers, we thereby commit ourselves to infinity in the non-abstract world seem to me quite implausible. Those positions are hard to square with facts about how we come to know about the natural numbers. We are not in danger of running out of natural numbers because of facts about the actual concrete universe. We do not make any commitments at all about the concrete universe in saying that for each natural number, there is a successor of that number. Observations from radio telescopes about the size and contents of the actual concrete universe are not relevant to the explanation of why every natural number has a successor. Nor are they relevant to how we come to know that proposition.

So far, this Applicational Individuationist position deploys very familiar resources to its own particular ends. But the simple position just developed contrasts sharply with some other familiar positions in the philosophy of abstract objects. I take structuralism first.

Charles Parsons describes the structuralist view of mathematical objects thus: "By the structuralist view of mathematical objects, I mean the view that reference to mathematical objects is always in the context of some background structure, and that the objects involved have no more to them than can be expressed in terms of the basic relations of the structure" (1990: 303). On the Individuationist view, we are not required to identify abstract objects of a given kind with entities, such as sets or classes, in some further structure. Each of the natural numbers, real numbers, functions, ordered pairs, and ratios are entities in their own right. A correct theory of each of them may be interpretable in the theory of some other kinds of object, but that is not at all something that is a prerequisite for their legitimation. Individuationism is a kind of Platonism, and from the perspective of Individuationism, abstract objects of any given kind have existence and identity-conditions that do not mention or presuppose the mapping of objects of that kind into some other structure. By contrast with the doctrine of structuralism as Parsons characterizes it, there is no further background structure of abstract objects that is relied upon in the above Individuationist account of the natural numbers.

Some forms of objection to structuralism argue that there is a background structure as the structuralist describes for many kinds of abstract objects, but that there must be a single fundamental level of abstract objects that has some non-mathematical characterization. That is not the Individuationist's position. Some particular kinds of abstract objects may be individuated by reference to the elements of some further domain, as I will be arguing in the case of the real numbers further below. That is a matter specific to particular kinds of abstract objects, and when present, involves genuine relations of ontological dependence and priority. For the Individuationist, there will be several kinds of abstract objects, directions and sets included, whose individuation is not founded in one uniform non-mathematical domain.

Here again my position contrasts with that of Philip Kitcher, who writes in a paragraph worth quoting in full,

Problems begin to arise when the Platonist tries to produce *the* abstract objects which embody the structure in virtue of which arithmetic is true. His theory gives him too many abstract instantiations of that structure, the von Neumann numbers, the Zermelo numbers, and so forth. Sensitive to the original idea that talk of abstract objects is a way of talking about structure, he tries to isolate what is common to these various sequences of abstract objects... However, since he regards functions as abstract entities he has no way of resisting demands to reduce his ontology by identifying functions with sets. Canons of economy and explanatory unification direct the Platonist to see his realm of Platonic entities as a universe of sets. But the notion of set is insufficient to yield a mathematical theory which can be interpreted as describing the abstract structure of the world. As we have seen, purely set theoretic developments of mathematics must arbitrarily assign a special status to particular instantiations of mathematical structures. (1978: 131)

The Platonist who is of the Individuationist variety will say that each category of abstract object is of its own kind, individuated in a distinctive way, so that the Individuationist Platonist is not faced with a uniqueness problem in answering the question, 'Which are the objects in virtue of which arithmetic is true?'. In the case of arithmetic, they are the natural numbers as individuated in the account of Applicational Individuationism.

Is this reply violating canons of economy and explanatory unification? The Individuationist should say that the canons of economy and explanatory unification are met rather at a higher level, at the level of the more general theory of what is required to individuate abstract objects of any given kind. Those general requirements are met by the Applicational Individuationist accounts of each of the various kinds of abstract objects. In fact, it seems to me that the form of Platonism that requires a special unique role for set theory is itself open to the charge of lack of unification. For it is not only set theory in which other domains of abstract objects are interpretable; and there are many varieties of set theory too that allow such a general interpretability. Kitcher's arguments are effective against the Platonist who gives a very special role to set theory, and requires other abstract objects to stand in a certain relation to sets. His arguments do not seem to me to apply against the Individuationist variety of Platonism, which does not accord that special status to set theory.

The Individuationist also aims to respect and vindicate the genuine insight that talk of abstract objects is very broadly a way of talking about structure. The structure articulated by talk of abstract objects of a given kind is the structure articulated and exploited in the individuation conditions of particular objects of that kind. For the case of natural numbers, the Individuationist account maintains that it is structure that is applied to concepts, and is captured in first-order quantificational logic with identity. The structure of the successor relation, and everything defined in terms of it, is determined by that quantificational structure.

3. Relation to Neo-Fregean and Postulationist Views

What is the relation of the present Individuationism to the neo-Fregean abstractionism extensively developed and defended by Crispin Wright and Bob Hale for more than three decades (Wright 1983; Hale and Wright 2009; amongst many other writings)? The neo-Fregean abstractionist focuses on such biconditionals as these:

> The number of Fs = the number of Gs iff there is a one-one relation between the F's and the Gs ('Hume's Law')
>
> The direction of line l = the direction of line k iff l and k are parallel
>
> The set of Fs = the set of Gs iff ∀x(Fx iff Gx)

Some neo-Fregean abstractionists have claimed that the left-hand sides of such biconditionals merely 'recarve' the content of the right-hand side. Some have said that these biconditionals are analytic. In a review of what has been an extensive debate, Øystein Linnebo labels as the 'fundamental problem' with neo-Fregean abstractionism the point that if the right-hand sides of these biconditionals suffice for the truth of the left-hand sides, how can they be any less problematic? "If φ genuinely suffices for the truth of ψ, how can ψ have smaller ontological commitments than φ or be philosophically less problematic? One would have thought that any commitments or problems attaching to ψ would be inherited by φ" (2012: 146).

The Individuationist position of the sort I am expounding holds that natural numbers, directions, and sets are entities in their own right, individuated by their application conditions. So according to the Individuationist, the ontological commitments of the left- and right-hand sides of the displayed biconditionals do differ. The left-hand sides of these biconditionals do in each case mention abstract objects that are not mentioned on the right-hand sides. The two sides of the biconditionals cannot be seen as 'recarving' the same content. What single content would it be? At the level of reference, the entities referred to on each side of such a biconditional are different, under the Individuationist view. When we are considering the level of reference, Frege's strictures against creative definition apply if we suppose that entities can be defined into existence by conditions that do not mention those entities. At the level of sense, the right- and left-hand sides are also clearly different. Hale and Wright are of course aware of these concerns, and have addressed them (2009); and I return to their position further below.

Nonetheless, despite this divergence between the Individuationist and the neo-Fregean abstractionists, there is an important point about the biconditionals on which the abstractionists rely, one which the Individuationist should also emphasize—even if the correctness of the point does not take one as far as neo-Fregean abstractionism. The point concerns an *asymmetry of individuation*. Natural numbers are individuated by their relations to concepts, and as we have seen, these concepts do not need to be concepts of numbers. But concepts in general are not individuated by their relations to natural numbers. Directions are individuated by their relations to lines, but lines are not individuated by their relations to directions. Sets are individuated by their relations to their elements, but those elements do not need to be individuated by the sets of which they are members.

These asymmetries of individuation are truths about ontology, about the metaphysics of the relevant objects, if you will, rather than anything to do, in the first instance, with the notion of sense. The asymmetries and their importance can be recognized quite independently of an endorsement of neo-Fregean abstractionism. Though it would take us off-course to pursue the point here, these asymmetries suggest a division of cases, and a research programme relating to the division, according to the materials used in the individuating condition for entities of a given kind. Only concepts, logical operations, and identity feature in the individuating conditions for individual natural numbers (together with constitutive notions). In the individuating conditions for material objects, sortal kinds would feature. The correct account of what is to be mentioned in the individuating conditions for social objects is equally of great interest. Asymmetries of individuation in all of these cases, and their consequences, constitute a starting point for a general investigation of which the present treatment of natural numbers is just a special case.

There is another point of contrast between the Individuationist account of natural numbers and the neo-Fregean abstractionist account when we turn to the issue of the means of establishing simple arithmetical truths. It concerns Kit Fine's very reasonable objection (2002) to Wright's proposed demonstration of the distinctness of 0, 1, 2, etc., under the neo-Fregean abstractionist definition of numerals for these numbers. Fine observes (2002: 98) that under the predicative understanding of 'the number of Fs = 0', the abstractionist principles on which the neo-Fregean account relies are of no help in determining whether the sentence '0 = 1' is true or not, since they give conditions for identity only in the case in which the concepts involved are concepts of non-numerical individuals. Saying the abstractionist principles are impredicative and already apply to numbers would be to abandon the central feature of the neo-Fregean abstractionist position.

For the Individuationist position as I have been developing it, by contrast, natural numbers n and m are identical only if the condition for there being n Fs is necessarily equivalent to the condition for there being m Fs. Since there can be zero Fs without there being one F, 0 is distinct from 1. Similarly, 1 is distinct from 2; and so on. The same reasoning applies even if the number of concrete, non-abstract objects in the universe is finite—k, let us say. On the Individuationist treatment, k is distinct from k + 1 because there could be k objects that are F without there being k + 1 objects that are F.

It can be helpful at this point to compare this position with that of Fine's Procedural Postulationism, as developed in his book *The Limits of Abstraction* (2002). There are both affinities and differences. There are three clear affinities.

(i) Fine describes his Procedural Postulationism thus: "instead of stipulating that certain statements [such as Hume's Law—CP] are to be true, one specifies certain procedures for extending the domain to one in which the statements will in fact be true" (2002: 100). The procedures of which Fine speaks for extending the domain are analogous in his framework to principles individuating the natural numbers in the Applicational Individuationist treatment by reference to conditions on concepts that are not concepts of natural numbers.

(ii) Moreover, both Fine and the Individuationist require that these procedures and principles be subject to certain constraints. Fine offers a treatment of the generation of the natural numbers, in fact a treatment of which he writes that it "is very natural and, indeed, it is hard to think of reasonable alternatives" (28), a treatment under which "Any number, for example, must be the number of some concept. Moreover, it must be possible so to choose the concept that it can be specified without reference, either direct or indirect, to the number in question" (27). This is the version in Procedural Postulationism of the Applicational Individuationist's requirement that in the individuation of any particular natural number, the individuating condition not involve quantification over, or involve reference to, that very number whose individuation is in question. In both cases, this is a fine-grained articulation of the asymmetry of individuation we already noted.

(iii) Both Procedural Postulationism and Individuationism treat Hume's Law (for finite numbers) as consequences of the correct account of the nature of natural numbers, rather than as something primitively written into the fundamental nature of natural numbers. In this respect, both Procedural Postulationism and Applicational Individuationism contrast with the neo-Fregean treatment of Wright and Hale. For the Individuationist, applications in numerical quantifications, 'there are n Fs', are fundamental to the nature of natural numbers, rather than being available as a consequence of Hume's Law. Under Applicational Individuationism, Hume's Law is not justified by some general doctrine that term-forming abstraction operators, applied to concepts, always refer when certain conditions are met. Trying to say what those conditions might be, and restraining the otherwise great power of abstraction operators, has been a source of difficulty for abstractionist positions, starting of course with Frege's Axiom Va. Those difficulties are simply bypassed in Applicational Individuationism. Applicational Individuationism does not rely on any general doctrine about the conditions under which abstraction terms refer.

Now for some differences between Individuationism and Procedural Postulationism as formulated in Fine's *The Limits of Abstraction*. On the Individuationist's treatment, the individuation of the natural numbers has a twofold feature. First, for any particular natural number, it does not give any individuative significance to any particular concept or property or entity involving particular objects that have that number. Second, it is completely independent of the way the non-abstract actual world is. These seem to me to be metaphysically and epistemologically desirable properties.

It is a very delicate matter whether Procedural Postulationism on its own can be formulated in a way that achieves these properties. Consider the individuation of the natural number 0. This is discussed in two sections in *The Limits of Abstraction*: in the Philosophical Introduction (Part I.2) and in the discussion of minimal models in the Analysis of Acceptability (Part III.5). In the Philosophical Introduction, Fine writes, "What we are proposing is that each number (not numeral) has a definition of the form 'the number of Cs' (it is essentially of that form for suitable C)" (2002: 31). In the preceding paragraph of the text, the real definition of the natural number 0 itself (not a linguistic definition of the expression '0' or of a sense) is that it is the number of objects that are not self-identical (30–1). Despite the distinguished historical precedent for this real definition, it seems to me implausible that the negation of self-identity plays a special, distinguished role in the individuation of the number 0. Why fix on that concept rather than some other? The number of propositions such that p & ¬p would equally have served; so would the number of things x such that for some property or predicate F, x is F and x is not F; and so forth. The Individuationist account of what individuates the number 0 itself does not distinguish a privileged position for one particular concept under which nothing falls. Rather, what makes something the number 0 is that it is the number n such that for an arbitrary concept F, for there to be n Fs is for there to be no Fs. No particular concept F is given a more fundamental role than any other in this account. That seems to me to be a positive feature of the account. Similar points apply to accounts that treat the number 0 as the null set (as does Fine's example of a minimal model (2002: 119)). An ontology of sets does not seem to me to play a fundamental role in what individuates the number 0 itself.

We should consider the possibility that these comments are focusing on inessential, easily revisable properties of Fine's formulations, and do not go to the heart of his proposal. How might a revised version of Procedural Postulationism run? A very different way of developing Procedural Postulationism would be to take each natural number as individuated by the concepts that have that number. As in effect noted in the discussion of Hodes's suggestions, this proposal comes into conflict with the second of the two desirable properties noted above. However we construe 'concept' in the proposal, it would be too tightly tied to the contingencies of the actual world. If concepts are functions from objects to truth-values, it would make the individuation of a natural number depend on the identity of the objects that happen to exist. Similarly, if concepts are taken as properties, there would be dependence on the contingency of which things have which contingent properties; and so forth. We obviously need to speak of one and the same number being, say, six, however the actual world may be. The Individuationist treatment provides that element of noncontingency.

These differences from Fine's position in *The Limits of Abstraction* should not at all be regarded as fundamentally damaging to the conception he outlines there. On the contrary, it seems to me that the differences just noted point to the desirability of a marriage between the central points of Procedural Postulationism and a position that takes applications as fundamental to the individuation of the numbers. Constraints linking the procedures of Postulationism with conditions for the application of the abstract objects those procedures introduce could easily be introduced into Fine's framework. Conversely, the metaphysical stance of Applicational Individuationism as I have outlined it here is obviously indebted to the conception of ontological priority and its significance that is found in

Fine's work. The metaphysical stance that Applicational Individuationism shares with Procedural Postulationism has evidently been important in distinguishing the present Applicationist position both from the neo-Fregean position of Hale and Wright, and from the partially fictionalist position of Hodes.

Hale and Wright have replied extensively to critical discussions of neo-Fregean abstractionism, particularly in their paper 'The Metaontology of Abstraction' (2009). In reply to their critics, they discuss an "anxious metaphysical" stance (2009: 206) that fears that the right-hand sides of the relevant biconditionals may fail to determine a reference for numerical terms, and they repeatedly emphasize the absence of any risk of reference failure on the abstractionist conception: "Properly viewed, the very stipulative equivalence of the two sides of an instance of an abstraction principle is enough to ensure both that it is not to be seen as proposed as part of a project of reference-fixing and that there *is no significant risk of reference failure*" (2009: 207, their italics). That point may be well targeted against some critics of the abstractionist programme, but I suggest that it does not apply to Applicational Individuationism. Applicational Individuationism does not say that there is an epistemic risk in individuating or postulating abstract objects that meet the right requirement on application conditions. The abstract entities described by Applicational Individuationism exist necessarily, just as Hale and Wright are inclined to say about the abstract objects as described by abstractionism (2009: 206). Of course there is always epistemic risk in a philo-sophical account, but that is not what Hale and Wright were talking about—and that general epistemic risk applies to neo-Fregean abstractionism too. What Applicational Individuationism is insisting upon is not a matter of epistemic risk, but rather an asymmetry of individuation, and a hierarchy of individuation, related to conditions of application. On the side of epistemic issues, we should be as confident that there is a natural number 5 individuated by the condition for there being five Fs as we are of the possibility of there being five Fs for some or other concept F. This lack of epistemic risk is entirely compatible with the asymmetries of individuation, and the special role of application in the individu-ation of natural numbers and real numbers.

Partly because it is of great interest in itself, I also comment briefly on a parallel Hale and Wright suggest with the logical connectives. Their view is that reflection on the determination of the reference of the logical connectives can help the abstractionist case. Their view is "that there is a statement-forming operation associated with any connective of which it is possible to succeed in imparting a satisfactory understanding by natural deduction characterization of its inferential role, and that this operation may be conceived as the reference of the expression in question" (2009: 199). It seems to me, by contrast, that the case of the connectives reinforces a challenge to abstractionism. The relevant inferential role for a connective has to determine, at the level of reference, a function from truth-values to truth-values if it is to fix a genuine sense. This is always a substantive further condition that needs to be established, beyond constraints specified at the level of inferential role (Peacocke 1998). Hale and Wright state, "The conferral of sense upon a connective precisely ensures that there will be a statement formed whenever the connective is applied to an appropriate n-tuple of sentences each of which possess a prior sense" (2009: 199). In any classical truth-conditional theory of sense, no sense will have been determined for the complex sentence with a given connective as its main operator unless it has been determined how the truth or falsity of the complex sentence is a function of the truth or falsity of its constituents.

4. From Individuation to Representation

So how, if we are defending a metaphysics-first view, do we move from ontology to representation, from the metaphysics of natural numbers to senses, ways of thinking, or modes of presentation of the natural numbers? It seems to me plausible that to think of a natural number as 1, for instance, is to have tacit knowledge that for there to be 1 F is for it to be the case that there is something that is F, and nothing else is. This condition aims to elucidate grasp of the way of thinking of something as 1 with the very condition that individuates the number 1. More generally, for an arbitrary natural number n, we make the ascent from metaphysics to ways of thinking or representing by recognizing this condition:

> to think of a natural number n in a canonical primitive (unstructured) way τ is for the thinker to have this tacit knowledge: that for there to be τ Fs is for a certain condition logically equivalent to the constitutive first-order-with-identity condition for there to be n Fs to obtain.

The 'certain condition' in question may be different for different thinkers. There are multiple conditions equivalent to the constitutive condition for there to be five Fs. There is the condition that the Fs can be mapped one to one on to the numerals from '1' to '5'. For a thinker capable of immediately perceiving, without counting or conscious inference, that there are five things of a certain kind in the scene around her, there is the condition that the Fs are in one-to-one correspondence with things so perceived. These are different senses of the natural number 5 itself, and the different senses correspond to different patterns of epistemic possibility and informativeness, just as for any distinct senses or modes of presentation of the same thing. They are all senses of the natural number 5 itself because of their equivalence to the condition in first-order logic and identity for there being five Fs.

For someone capable of thinking of a range of natural numbers, the ability to use the first-order quantifications with identity will often be a parasitic on the possession of a system of numerals. Such a thinker will think of the condition of there being five Fs as the Fs being in one-to-one correspondence with the Arabic numerals from '1' to '5'. Children think of the cardinal numbers this way, and there is evidence that they acquire mastery of an ordinal sequence of numerals before using them so as to refer to cardinals that number concepts and sets (Wynn 1990, 1992). This is a distinctive way of thinking of the number 5. It is to be distinguished from the way of thinking of 5 available to someone who can just look at a collection of objects of a certain kind, and see that there are five. For such a person, it can be informative that the number he can identify visually is the same as a certain number reached by counting up in numerals from '1'.

Similar points apply to understanding of a symbol for the successor relation, and for addition and multiplication. The understanding-conditions for such expressions make reference to conditions that involve the individuation of these functions themselves. For a sense σ to refer, primitively, to the successor function is for the thinker to have tacit knowledge that for a natural number n to be σ(m) is for n to stand in some relation to m that is equivalent to the condition given above that individuates the successor relation in terms of numerical quantification conditions.

This is an account in which Individuation Precedes Representation, a metaphysics-first account, because the condition for thinking of a natural number n mentions the condition, constitutive of n, for there being n Fs. If there were more to being n than that relation to numerical quantification holding, no doubt we would require more for thinking of or representing n. But no more is required for being the natural number n; so there is no such additional requirement on thinking about or representing n. The condition displayed above is sufficient for thinking about a particular natural number n. That condition for thinking about n draws on an individuating condition for the natural number n that does not itself mention thinking about n, nor does the individuating condition for n mention any other mental representation of n. This is what makes the treatment a metaphysics-first account.

The displayed condition for thinking about a natural number holds without there being any requirement that natural numbers interact causally with subjects who represent natural numbers. So, as promised, this is a metaphysics-first case without causal interaction between the subject matter and those who represent it.

So far I have been considering natural numbers only in their role as cardinal numbers, as giving the number of things having a certain property. What of the ordinal numbers? Applicational Individuationism can be developed for the ordinals too. In Applicational Individuationism for the natural numbers as cardinals, a foundational role is given to a natural number being the number of things having a certain property. There is no more to the nature of a cardinal number than the condition for the property to meet the condition of having that cardinal number of instances. Similarly, in Applicational Individuationism for the ordinal numbers, a foundational role is given to an ordinal specifying the position of an object under a given well-ordering. There is no more to the nature of an ordinal number than the condition for an object to have the position specified by that ordinal in a given well-ordering.

Applicational Individuationism can then treat the ordinals as follows. I use underlining to indicate terms for, and variables over, the ordinals.

(1) What makes something the ordinal number $\underline{1}$ is that for an arbitrary object x to have position $\underline{1}$ (to be $\underline{1}$st) in well-ordering R is for there to be nothing that stands in R to it (i.e. for $\forall y\ (\sim Ryx)$).

(2) What makes something the successor ordinal $\underline{a}'$ is that for an arbitrary object x to have position $\underline{a}'$ (to be $\underline{a}'$th) in a well-ordering R is for there to be something y that has position $\underline{a}$ under R and x is the least under R of things greater under R than y (i.e. $Ryx\ \&\ \forall z\ (Ryz \supset (Rxz \lor z = x))$).

In a further formal development, we could introduce a less-than relation on the ordinals so individuated, and then use that relation to individuate limit ordinals.

In accordance with the claim that for the domain of ordinals too, Individuation Precedes Representation, we can then plausibly assert that thinking of the ordinals, as such, involves tacit knowledge of the individuating conditions (1) and (2), and of the version for limit ordinals. There is no more to the individuation of the ordinals than their role in specifying position in a given well-ordering. There is no more to thinking of ordinals as such than having an appreciation, shown in judgemental practice, of this relation of ordinals to specifying position in a well-ordering.

5. Applicational Individuationism for the Real Numbers: A Sketch

The materials for developing the idea that there is a close connection between the real numbers and ratios of magnitudes has been with us since ancient Greece.

The ratio between the length of the hypotenuse of a unit right-angled triangle to the length of one of the triangle's other sides, in Euclidean plane geometry, is a ratio between magnitudes, lengths in particular. The ratio between these two magnitudes was known by the Greeks, and to teenagers to this day, to be irrational. Frege stated clearly that real numbers are ratios of magnitudes: "If we now understand by 'number' the reference of a number-sign, then *real number* is the same as magnitude-ratio" (2013: Vol. II §73: 85). The idea that reals are ratios of magnitudes was also in the German air before Frege wrote. Richard Dedekind, an opponent of the idea, wrote in 1872 that "the way in which irrational numbers are usually introduced is based directly upon the conception of extensive magnitudes . . . and explains number as the result of measuring such a magnitude by another of the same kind" (1901: 4–5).

I will sketch a case that the treatment of real numbers as ratios of magnitudes, when developed in a certain way, can be an implementation of Applicational Individuationism for this particular domain of abstract objects. Accordingly, the treatment can support a metaphysics-first view of our ways of thinking of real numbers, under our general rubric that for abstract objects, 'Individuation Precedes Representation'. The treatment relies at a crucial point on the metaphysics of extensive magnitudes developed in Chapter 2.

This, so far, is just a statement of aim, the aim to provide a treatment of real numbers as ratios of magnitudes. As Frege said at a corresponding point, "So far, we only have words that point roughly in the direction where a solution is to be found" (2013: Vol. II §73: 85). Any realization of this aim has to address multiple issues. These issues include the question of what conception of the ontology of magnitudes is suitable, or even so much as available, for coherent use in an account that claims to be a form of Applicational Individuationism. They also include the question of the full force of the requirements of being faithful to Applicational Individuationism. The issues that arise are both metaphysical and epistemological.

More particularly, there are at least four constraints on a good account of the real numbers that respects Applicational Individuationism. I label them Noncircularity, Uniformity, Noncontingency, and Full-Faith Individuationism. I take them in turn.

(1) Noncircularity. What are magnitudes? On a widely held view, to say that some object or objects have a certain magnitude of a particular type (mass, distance) is to say that it or they are mapped onto a particular real number by a certain kind of mapping. The mapping respects certain qualitative and comparative, non-numerical properties and relations concerning the magnitude-type, and it selects a certain object or objects as the unit for that magnitude-type. This

is an approach that emerges from the important and successful project of Patrick Suppes and many colleagues in developing theorems in the theory of measurement, in the framework of Tarskian model theory (Suppes 1951; Suppes and Zinnes 1963). Since the theory of the qualitative and comparative non-numerical relations for the magnitude-type in question would now be classified as a 'synthetic' theory, in the style of Hilbert's axiomization of Euclidean geometry (1971), I call this the synthetic account of magnitudes.

I objected to this synthetic account of magnitudes back in Chapter 2, and in Peacocke (2015). The proposed equivalences offered by the synthetic account are not substitutable in counterfactuals, or in explanatory contexts. Something could have had a length of 5 metres even if whatever physical object is taken as the standard metre were never to have existed. It could also have had that length even if its spatial relations to other objects had been different, for they could have had different lengths. I will not labour the point any further. What matters for present purposes is that this widely held synthetic account of magnitudes is inconsistent with the theory of real numbers as ratios of magnitudes, at least if that theory is to have any philosophical significance as a theory of the nature of the real numbers. The two are inconsistent, because on the synthetic theory of magnitudes, attributing a magnitude already involves the ontology of real numbers. So under the synthetic theory, saying that real numbers are ratios of magnitudes may be true, but as an attempt at a philosophical explanation, it would be explaining the nature of the real numbers in terms of the real numbers again. If our aim is philosophical explanation, we must either abandon the conception of real numbers as ratios of magnitudes, or revise our conception of the ontology of magnitudes.

I suggest that we pursue the second option, in accordance with the realistic conception of the ontology of magnitudes outlined in Chapter 2. Under that conception, magnitudes of a particular type are entities in their own right. Given certain conditions, and a choice of unit, they can be mapped onto the real numbers; but the possibility of that mapping is not what makes the magnitudes what they are. The account of real numbers as ratios of magnitudes should be combined with a realistic treatment of magnitudes that is distinct from the widely held synthetic account. A realistic conception of magnitudes is an essential component in an elaboration of the real numbers as fundamentally ratios of magnitudes.

Here it can help to address Dedekind's critical remarks against the conception of the real numbers as ratios of magnitudes. Dedekind's mathematical work is justly famous. His statement that "the problem is to indicate a precise characteristic of continuity that can serve as the basis for valid deductions" (1963: 11), written in 1872, seven years before the publication even of Frege's *Begriffschrift*, would merit the strong approval of even the young Frege. But my concern here is with Dedekind's philosophical position and motivations, rather than his mathematical contributions. In his philosophical discussion, Dedekind first remarks that the conception of extensive magnitudes "is nowhere carefully defined" (1963: 9–10; this is in the material covered by the elision '...' in the earlier quotation about the way in which irrational numbers are normally introduced). The proper characterization of what it is for a magnitude-type to be extensive is indeed crucial to the Applicational Individuationist development of the position that reals are ratios of magnitudes, for this characterization must be restricted to extensive magnitudes. In fact clear definition, with sharpening well beyond the intuitive idea of an extensive magnitude-type as one whose instances can be added, was provided in the later literature well after 1872. Axioms for what makes a magnitude-type extensive were developed by Hölder (1901) and improved by Suppes (1951) and Suppes and Zinnes (1963). These axioms use what is intuitively a notion of an addition-like operation on the extensive magnitudes in question, and they employ the natural numbers. They do not mention, and do not need to mention, the real numbers. These axiomatizations seem to me to meet Dedekind's legitimate demand for a proper explanation of the term 'extensive magnitude'.

The contrast between the philosophical and the more strictly mathematical applies also when we consider Dedekind's own discussion of the distinctive axiom of the continuity of the reals. Dedekind writes, "I find the essence of continuity... in the following principle: 'If all points of the straight line fall into two classes such that every point of the first class lies to the left of every point of the second class, then there exists one and only one point which produced this division of all points into two classes, this severing of the straight line into two portions'" (1963: 11). A few lines later he writes, "I am utterly unable to adduce any proof of its correctness, nor has any one the power. The assumption of this property of the line is nothing else than an axiom by which we attribute to the line its continuity" (12); "if we knew for certain that space was discontinuous there would be nothing to prevent us, in case we so desired, from filling up its gaps, in thought, and thus making it continuous; this filling up would consist in a creation of new point-individuals and would have to be effected in accordance with the above principle" (12). We need to distinguish Dedekind's characterization of continuity, a major contribution, from the question of the philosophical justification for the existence axiom for cuts, or, equivalently, to the axiom that for every set (of point, or ratios, etc.) bounded from above, there exists a least upper bound. For the Applicational Individuationist, Dedekind's remark that even if real space is discontinuous, we can conceive of completions of it that accord with the continuity axiom, is crucial. For the Applicational Individuationist, the least upper bound of any set of lengths bounded from above also exists, because it is possible that instances of that length-magnitude exists, even if it is not actually instantiated. To each of the cuts Dedekind postulates on the real line, there is a possibly instantiated distance magnitude, a possible distance for a possible point from the 0 point on that line.

The difference between Dedekind's philosophical position and that of Applicational Individuationism comes out sharply in their respective justifications for the axiom that cuts, or least upper bounds, always exist. For the Applicational Individuationist, the axiom is justified by the existence of a possibly instantiated magnitude of some type that stands in the relevant comparative relations to a set of magnitudes bounded from above. The real number is individuated by its ability to measure ratios of magnitudes, whether actually or merely possibly instantiated. For Dedekind, the cut or upper bound is postulated. There is of course no general objection to suitably constrained postulation, as indeed I have been emphasizing in the discussion of the natural numbers. But Dedekind and the Applicational Individuationist will differ in respect of their conception of the relations of magnitudes to the postulated real number. For Dedekind, these reals can be used to classify ratios of magnitudes. But so can any other set-theoretical objects, or function-theoretic objects, or anything else that replicates the structure and continuity of the reals. For the Applicational Individuationist, by contrast, it is important that there is nothing more to the reals than is determined by their ability to measure ratios of magnitudes, just as there is nothing more to each natural number than its ability to number concepts. The reals and the natural numbers have in themselves no properties other than is required for their respective applications.

It would be open to Dedekind to recognize an ontology of abstract objects constrained to possess only the minimal properties required for the relevant applications. But for that ontology, Applicational Individuationism would be correct.

Dedekind does have several other objections to the conception of reals as ratios of magnitudes. Of that conception, he writes, "The apparent advantage of the generality of this definition of number disappears as soon as we consider complex numbers" (1963: 10, fn). Complex numbers are also explained in terms of their application to magnitudes, but in a different way. Consider a physical system that behaves as a cosine wave function, given by $z = x + iy$, where $x = r \cos A$ and $y = r \sin A$, and where the angle A is a constant function of time ct. The physical magnitudes mapped on the axes behave over time in accordance with the equation for z. Mathematical operations can be performed on the complex number z that provide information about the evolution of the physical system. This can all be developed within the spirit of applicational individuationism.

Immediately after formulating this objection to the conception of reals as ratios of magnitudes of the same type, Dedekind also writes, "According to my view, on the other hand, the notion of the ratio between two numbers of the same kind can be clearly developed only after the introduction of irrational numbers" (1963: 10, fn). I agree that we need to explain the nature of the real numbers first, and then use that explanation to legitimate talk of the ratio of two complex numbers. But the Applicational Individuationist can and should do so too. This point about the order of ontological elucidation and explanation of the real numbers is consistent with applicational individuationism applied to the complex numbers.

Dedekind also writes, "I demand that arithmetic shall be developed out of itself" (1963: 10). An Applicational Individuationist cannot accept precisely that demand. For the Applicational Individuationist, arithmetic is developed out of first-order quantificational logic with identity. In any case, Dedekind is not really developing arithmetic—he should really here say "analysis"—out of arithmetic alone. He himself is using set theory essentially in his characterization of continuity. The Applicational Individuationist can at most accept a weaker claim, perhaps overlapping in spirit with Dedekind's 'demand'. The Applicational Individuationist can say that the ratio corresponding to a cut, or least upper bound, is the same kind of thing as a rational ratio developed from the natural numbers, because it, like them, is the ratio of a pair of possible magnitudes.

In developing a positive account of the real numbers, the Applicational Individuationist should aim to make use of this condition:

(Real 1):   For each real number r, there is some equivalence class R of pairs of magnitudes (x, y) of the same magnitude-type such that $r = x{:}y$. That is, r is the measure of magnitude x in relation to magnitude y.

The equivalence class in question on pairs (x,y), (z,w) of magnitudes is generated by the Euclidean equivalence relation we noted back in Chapter 2:

$x{:}y = z{:}w$ iff for all integers m, n $(mx < ny$ iff $mz < nw)$.

It will be convenient to call a class of pairs of magnitudes generated by this equivalence relation a Euclidean class.

Any Applicationist who hopes to make use of (Real 1) in a philosophical account of the real numbers has to face an issue about magnitudes that are not in fact instantiated in the actual world. There are at least two options for someone working within a realistic ontology of magnitudes. Option One is to treat magnitudes like properties, which exist even if they are not actually instantiated. We can call this the Plenitude Option. I prefer this to the term 'Platonistic' because these magnitudes enter causal and scientific explanations, as argued back in Chapter 2, just as properties do too. The Plenitude Option accords with the view that there is also a natural correspondence between magnitudes and properties. What it is for something to have a certain length-property, for instance, is for it to have a certain length-magnitude.

Option Two is to say a magnitude does not exist if it does not have instances. We can call this the Instantiationist Option. This remains consistent with nevertheless still distinguishing magnitudes from magnitude-tropes. When actual, one magnitude may have multiple magnitude-tropes.

Under the Plenitude Option, the principle (Real 1) is plausibly true, and captures all the real numbers. Even if the whole actual material and mental universe is finite in all respects, under the Plenitude Option there is a nondenumerable range of uninstantiated magnitudes within the range of the magnitudes covered by the variables 'x' and 'y' in (Real 1).

If we adopt the Instantiationist Option, there is no a priori assurance that (Real 1) will capture all the reals, when its variables are restricted to the magnitudes that exist in the actual world. To capture all the reals, we need then to speak not just of Euclidean equivalence classes of pairs of actual magnitudes, but of Euclidean equivalence classes of possible pairs of magnitudes too. Every possible Euclidean equivalence class of pairs of magnitudes also determines a real number:

(Real 2):   Necessarily, if R is a Euclidean equivalence class of pairs of magnitudes, there exists some real number r such that r is the ratio of any pair in R.

There is an interesting contrast between the natural number case and the real number case that is relevant to the development of an Applicationist position about the real numbers. We can specify for the case of natural numbers the condition that all n-numbered concepts have in common. We specify that condition by giving the first-order-with-identity condition for there being n Fs, for each particular natural number n. But in the case of ratios, what would the condition be? We can give the condition that unifies everything in the equivalence class, the Euclidean condition on ratios displayed above. That, however, is the analogue of the existence of a one-to-one mapping between concepts in the natural number case. What we do not have for the real numbers is an analogue of the first-order-with-identity condition in the case of the natural numbers. The condition cannot be that there are natural numbers n, m such that the ratio is n/m, for that would imply that there are no irrational real numbers. We can classify kinds of abstract objects by whether there is a unifying condition beyond existence of the equivalence relation in question. We can call those cases in which there is such unifying condition *specifiable*.

The fact that the specifiability condition is not met has implications for the right way of carrying through the Applicationist programme. By themselves, the two conditions (Real 1) and (Real 2), even taken jointly, do not exclude the possibility that a different real number numbers two Euclidean classes in each of two possible worlds, even if, when considered as an equivalence relation that may hold across magnitudes in different worlds, pairs of possible magnitudes in the two classes meet the Euclidean condition across worlds. As Frege might have put it, it is no thanks to the condition (Real 1) and (Real 2) that there is exclusion of the possibility that there are two possible classes R1 and R2, both Euclidean equivalence classes, and yet associated with different real numbers, despite the fact that this cross-world condition holds for them:

For all pairs (x, y) in R1, and all pairs (z, u) in R2:
for all integers m, n (mx < ny iff mz < nu).

This is not a genuine possibility, but given that the real numbers do not meet the condition of specifiability, we cannot exclude it by giving a condition, not formulated in terms of the equivalence relation, that all such possible Euclidean classes R1 and R2 meet. Rather, we should simply say that the individuation of real numbers is such that the state of affairs just described is impossible. Euclidean classes R1 and R2 in different worlds that meet the cross-world condition most recently displayed above do correspond to the same real number. I call this requirement (Real 3).

The Applicational Individuationist should say that the real numbers are individuated by their conformity to the three principles (Real 1), (Real 2), and (Real 3), where (Real 1) is read in accordance with your preferred modal metaphysics of magnitudes (as covering possible magnitudes too if you do not accept the Plenitude position). There is nothing more to being a real number than being individuated by conformity to these three principles. The principles make essential reference to the role of real numbers as ratios of magnitudes.

This version of Applicational Individuationism also meets the requirement (2) of Uniformity, and the requirement (3) of Noncontingency mentioned above. No special or distinguished place is given in this account to any particular magnitudes in the account of the reals—not to distances on a real line, or to any magnitude involving arithmetic. That respects Uniformity. The account does not depend on, or vary, with which world is the actual world, and is not sensitive to which objects happen actually to exist. So the account respects a requirement of

Noncontingency, an intuitive requirement on any plausible account of the real numbers, or any other kind of number.

In the case of the natural numbers, we saw that once they have been individuated in terms of their application conditions, we can go on to explain talk of the number of natural numbers meeting a certain condition. Similarly, in the case of the real numbers, once individuated in terms of their application in measuring the ratio of magnitudes, we can go on to explain talk of the ratios of real numbers themselves. But the two-stage account of how this is possible is crucial if we are to respect the requirements of Applicational Individuationism. If we were to presume that the natural numbers were already individuated so that they were things concepts of which can be numbered, we would not be respecting Applicational Individuationism for the natural numbers. We would not have explained the nature of these natural numbers already presumed to fall under concepts. Similarly, were we to presume that the real numbers were already individuated so that they were things ratios between which could be measured by real numbers, we would not be respecting Applicational Individuationism for the real numbers. We would not have explained the nature of these real numbers already presumed to stand in ratio relations.

A concern about the immediate introduction of reals as cuts in the rationals, as originally developed by Dedekind, and employed also philosophically by Hale (2000), is that for these reasons that approach, considered as part of a philosophical elucidation of the nature of real numbers, is not a full-faith implementation of Applicational Individuationism. The real numbers when introduced that way have not been explained fundamentally in terms of their application in measuring ratios.

Applicational Individuationism needs also to explain the arithmetical operations on the reals; to elucidate the relation of the natural numbers to the reals, of which the natural numbers are normally conceived as a proper subset; and to provide a rationale for postulating negative real numbers. The present discussion is offered only as a sketch, but Applicational Individuationism has the materials for completing a more detailed picture.

Addition on the reals corresponds to non-mathematical operations on the magnitudes whose ratios they can be used to represent. Suppose the real number r_1 is the measure of a certain magnitude x of a certain type, given a particular unit for that type, and r_2 is the measure, with the same unit, of another magnitude y of that type. Suppose also that $\oplus$ is the non-mathematical operation on pairs of magnitudes of the given type in virtue of which the type is an extensive magnitude. Then if r_3 is the sum of r_1 and r_2, the measure of $x \oplus y$ will be r_3. The notion of addition of real numbers is constrained by that generalization. This is analogous to the way in which, for the Applicational Individuationist, addition on the natural numbers is constrained by the requirement that the sum of n and m be the number of things that are either F or G, in the case in which there are n Fs, there are m Gs, and nothing is both F and G. If we follow some of the psychological literature in classifying cardinal numerosity as a magnitude, this constraint on addition on the natural numbers is a special case of the addition constraint on the real numbers.

Certain real numbers r are such that, for any magnitude x that r measures, with a given unit magnitude y, there is a natural number n such that r = x:ny. Those reals can be identified with the positive natural numbers. The postulation of the negative reals can be justified by the principle that the reals are closed under the operation of subtraction. That closure principle could itself be founded in Applicational Individuationism, if we want the reals to be capable of measuring ratios of magnitudes that can themselves be negative.

The principle 'Individuation Precedes Representation' applies to the reals under the account given by the Applicational Individuationist. Minimal grasp of the real numbers, as such, requires a thinker to be willing to use them in measuring the ratios of magnitudes. The real numbers must also be conceived by the thinker as things that do not change between possible circumstances in measuring the same ratio. These are conditions on reference to the real numbers, as such, that are reflections of the principles (Real 1) through (Real 3). Those principles are principles of the metaphysics of the real numbers. On the Applicational Individuationist's account, they are prior in the order of philosophical explanation to the account of intentional contents and meanings concerning the real numbers.

These requirements of willingness to use the real numbers in measuring ratios of magnitudes concern the level of reference, of what is thought about. At the level of sense, the real numbers may be thought of collectively in many different ways. If one thinks of the reals as measuring magnitudes, the very existence of a magnitude that is the square root of 2 needs some initial justification, one of which is supplied by the Pythagorean Theorem about right-angled triangles in Euclidean geometry. The Pythagorean Theorem shows that there are magnitudes that stand in the ratio that is the square root of 2. If one thinks of the reals in terms of the existence of least upper bounds of sets of bounded rational numbers, the existence of $\sqrt{2}$ does not need to be justified by citing any non-mathematical magnitude. Those differences in justification relations are founded in differences of sense, of ways of thinking of the reals. There are obviously multiple legitimate ways of thinking of the real numbers. According to the Applicational Individuationist, some of those ways of thinking are more closely tied to what individuates the reals than other ways of thinking of them.

At this point in the discussion, we can step back and consider further both the affinities and the differences between the Applicational Individuationism proposed here and the neo-Fregean abstractionism of Wright and Hale. Back in the discussion of the natural numbers, I noted the asymmetry of individuation that is important to Applicational Individuationism, and this is an affinity with one of the points emphasized by neo-Fregean abstractionism. I emphasized that while the individuation of natural numbers presupposes that of concepts (and quantification and identity), the individuation of concepts does not in general presuppose the individuation of the natural numbers. A similar point holds for the real numbers. The individuation of the real numbers presupposes that of magnitudes; but, I have been arguing, the individuation of magnitudes does not in general presuppose the individuation of the real numbers.

It is important for the Applicational Individuationist that the property that collects together each equivalence class that corresponds to the relevant abstract object not be specified as one involving the abstract object in question. So, the condition met by all three-numbered concepts can be formulated without mention of the natural number 3. The condition met by all pairs of magnitudes of a given type that are measured by a given real number can be formulated using the Euclidean condition that does not quantify over real numbers. So the asymmetries of individuation that we noted play a crucial role in the Applicational Individuationist account of the real numbers too.

6. Carnap: Differences and Affinities

By the lights of Carnap's view, expressed in his famous essay 'Empiricism, Semantics, and Ontology' (1956), the preceding discussion of the individuation of natural and real numbers, and their relation to thought about them, is utterly misconceived. Carnap distinguished between internal questions, settled by the 'linguistic framework' for an area of discourse, and external questions, not so settled (206–15). Within the 'linguistic framework' for discourse about the natural numbers and real numbers Carnap clearly includes axioms for these numbers. These axioms entail such sentences as "there is an even number between 7 and 9" and "there is a number that is the positive square root of 2". So the internal question of the existence of numbers is trivially answered in the positive. The external question, however, the question of whether there are numbers, understood as something not settled within the linguistic framework, is not a genuine question at all. Of philosophers who believe that there is a genuine external question beyond the linguistic framework, Carnap writes, these philosophers have so far not given a formulation of their question in terms of the common scientific language. Therefore our judgment must be that they have not succeeded in giving to the external question and to the possible answers any cognitive content. Unless and until they supply a clear cognitive interpretation, we are justified in our suspicion that their question is a pseudo-question, that is, one disguised in the form of a theoretical question while in fact it is non-theoretical.   (209)

Carnap's position is not only a challenge for the special case of abstract objects. If there is a legitimate internal/external distinction, one with the consequences Carnap claims for it, then that is a distinction that arises for any area of thought and discourse whatsoever, as Carnap was very well aware. Correspondingly, if there is a reply to Carnap in any one domain, its general structure may be applicable in other areas too. That is in fact my own position.

Let us bracket the question of abstract objects for a while, and consider the case of the perception of and judgements about magnitudes, and the perception of observational properties, and judgements about those properties. What would Carnap say is the 'linguistic framework' for the language in which we express such judgements? Of internal questions such as "Is there a white piece of paper on my desk?", he writes, "These questions are to be answered by empirical investigations. Results of observations are evaluated according to certain rules as confirming or disconfirming evidence for possible answers" (1956: 207). So perceptual experiences ("observations") are mentioned in the linguistic framework. It is a legitimate question to ask, 'What is it to be capable of making such observations, to be capable of being in perceptual states that give reasons for making judgements about magnitudes and observable properties?'. Now this question is not an everyday question, nor is it one cast in the language of, or involving the presuppositions of, those branches the sciences that Carnap talks about (he does not, to the best of my knowledge, discuss developmental psychology in this connection). The question nevertheless seems intelligible; proposed answers to it are assessable by the method of considering proposals and alleged counterexamples, assessable by their explanatory power; and so forth. We do seem to have here a genuine question, open to rational assessment and resoluble if we are sufficiently resourceful. In the case of magnitudes, and our perception of them, I argued back in Chapter 2 that the answer to the constitutive question of what it is to enjoy such perceptual states involves a sensitivity to the magnitudes themselves, as possessed by material objects and events. This is a sensitivity to the same reality as is talked about by those employing the 'linguistic framework' itself. That seems to be at least part of the answer to a genuine question about the states mentioned in the framework itself, a genuine question that is not formulated in the vocabulary of the framework itself.

So, if by 'external question' we mean merely a question not answered by the linguistic framework as conceived by Carnap, the straightforward answer would be that there are such external questions. But these constitutive questions are not pseudo-questions; they are open to rational resolution, and they do have cognitive content. They just belong to a branch of science—a branch of knowledge—that Carnap does not seem to be acknowledging. This branch is the study of the constitutive. The study of the constitutive applies both at the level of the subject matter of thought and representation, and to the subject matter of ways of thinking and of representing. If the main claims of this book are correct, we need to draw on results about what is constitutive of a subject matter in giving a full account of what it is for a thinker to be employing one of Carnap's linguistic frameworks.

In the particular case of the perception of magnitudes, and thought about magnitudes, the magnitudes mentioned in the reality to which thinkers must be sensitive are the very same magnitudes to which thinkers are referring when they use the linguistic framework for ordinary talk and thought about magnitudes. It is not the case that it is one thing for the magnitudes mentioned in using the linguistic framework to exist, and something else for those magnitudes, to which thinkers must be sensitive to perceive magnitudes, to exist. They are the same magnitudes, and there is only one kind of existence of magnitudes in question here. 'Exists' is unambiguous, and here both in letter and in spirit we are in accordance with Quine's view (1960: 131, 242).

Now let us return to abstract objects. The point I have just been making is that the conditions for grasping contents about perceived magnitudes involve and require relations to a use-independent reality. Those relations are partially causal in the case of magnitudes of physical objects and events. But the idea of understanding involving and requiring certain relations to a use-independent reality can apply outside the cases involving causality. It applies, without a requirement of causal relations to a subject matter, in the case of thought about the natural and the real numbers under Applicational Individuationism. Under Applicational Individuationism, the constraints on the determination of reference mention the individuation of these numbers in terms of their application conditions. The constraints are committed to the existence of entities individuated by their application conditions in a way that goes beyond anything that is merely a matter of conceptual role or linguistic framework alone.

The Carnapian might reply to this, saying: "The use of 'Individuation Precedes Representation' in determining conditions for expressions/concepts to refer to natural or real numbers precisely specifies a conceptual role that by itself determines whether someone is referring to the natural numbers or to the reals. There is a requirement on conceptual role, or equivalently Carnapian linguistic framework, that is sufficient for reference to the natural numbers and to the real numbers. Doesn't that amount after all to an internalist view by Carnap's lights?" This reply, however, neglects the point that the conceptual role in question is determined by properties of the individuation of the numbers themselves, and their role in applications. That role does *not* concern thought, language, or representation. It is of crucial importance to remember that 'application' in Applicational Individuationism has nothing to do with some thinker applying the numbers to a concept or a ratio. 'Application' in the relevant sense has to do with the conditions for concepts (in the case of the natural numbers) or ratios (in the case of the real numbers) to be classified by a certain property involving the numbers themselves.

There is a partial parallel here with the logical constants that may be found helpful. It may look as if conceptual role or linguistic framework fully determines the meaning of the logical constants, and their contribution to truth-conditions, without mention of anything outside the role or framework. But in fact only those roles that correspond to genuine truth-functions determine genuine content that contributes to truth-conditions. We may not need an ontology of truth-values and functions on them to make this point, but we do need a notion of principles that determine the truth or falsity of complex contents from the truth or falsity of their constituent contents. So it is not only the conceptual role or linguistic framework, non-semantically described, that is relevant to the determination of genuine content, even in the case of the logical constants.

Despite these fundamental divergences from Carnap, I conclude by noting two important points of agreement between the Individuationism that I have been endorsing and another feature of Carnap's position in 'Empiricism, Semantics, and Ontology'. It concerns Carnap's principle of tolerance, stated in the last, and italicized, sentence of his essay: "*Let us be cautious in making assertions and critical in examining them, but tolerant in permitting linguistic forms*" (221). For Carnap, any linguistic framework is permissible, provided it has various desirable features—being "expedient, fruitful, conducive to the aim for which the language is intended" (214).

The first of the two points of agreement is that we can be tolerant of, and possibly welcome, any type of abstract object whose members are individuated in terms of their application conditions.

Second, not all abstract objects have such close connections with applications as the natural numbers and real numbers. Those kinds of abstract objects that are not individuated by application conditions are plausibly individuated by various principles to which they constitutively conform. In these cases, abstract objects of these types really are "known only by their laws", as Quine puts it (1969: 44). For these cases too, a form of the principle that Individuation Precedes Representation will also apply. It is just that in these cases, the constraints on representation flowing from individuation of the entities will concern only the laws, rather than principles involving applications. The second point of agreement with Carnap is then that, subject always to requirements of consistency, we can also be tolerant of, and in theoretically useful cases welcome, any ontology of abstract objects individuated by the principles governing them. Under the Individuationist approach, an ontology will be legitimate provided it has adequate principles that succeed in individuating an ontology. The constraint of consistency is required. But any ontology meeting the constraints on principles will be acceptable. No doubt some will be more "expedient, fruitful, conducive to the aim" than others, and which ontologies we actually employ will be determined in part by considerations that Carnap labelled as "practical". But any ontology meeting the requirements on individuating principles will be intelligible and in principle legitimate, whether useful or not. So this too is a form of a principle of tolerance. It shares one small part of its source with Carnap's own principle of tolerance, viz. the role of principles in determining an ontology.

6

Ontology and Intelligibility

1. The Task

In a diverse range of areas of philosophy, there are claims that intuitively involve a radical misconception of ways it makes sense to suppose that reality could be. The areas of philosophy of which this is true include certain treatments of space and time, of merely possible objects ('possibilia'), of fundamental physical properties, and of subjects of consciousness, amongst others. These misconceptions are radical in that they do not merely involve specifications that could not be fulfilled. Rather, we are inclined to say, the relevant misconceptions fail even to specify a genuine condition whose possibility or impossibility could be up for assessment. We are inclined to say these misconceptions draw distinctions where there could not be a difference, that they overstep the bounds of intelligible descriptions of the world. It is the nature of these misconceptions that I will be discussing. What is the rationale for classifying them as radical misconceptions? What can we learn from a plausible formulation of that rationale? Can we give an explanatory theory of why the boundaries of intelligibility lie where they do? I will be arguing that the approach to the relation between metaphysics and the theory of understanding outlined in the earlier chapters of this book is a resource that can be deployed to make some progress on these questions.

We are strongly inclined to say that the various problematic misconceptions all involve spurious concepts. If senses or concepts are individuated by their fundamental reference rules, there is just one basic way something can be a spurious concept, rather than a genuine concept. This is by the spurious concept not having a proper fundamental reference rule. If a proposed concept has such a fundamental reference rule, it is a genuine concept; and if not, not. At the level of language, a word may fail to express a genuine concept by vacillating between various different genuine concepts. In such cases, there are various genuine concepts in play, but it has not been settled which concept the word expresses. In the misconceptions with which we will be dealing, the spurious concepts involved suffer a more radical kind of defect. These are cases in which the kind of entity to which the proposed concept is said to refer, in its fundamental reference rule, is such that it is impossible to give any account of what it would be for a thinker to grasp that fundamental reference rule. Correspondingly, it is impossible to give an account of what it would be to understand a word alleged to express the proposed concept.

I will be arguing that a number of classically problematic ontologies should be classified as suffering from the defect just described. This classification gives a better account of why these ontologies are problematic than some other diagnoses that have been canvassed. I will be offering an account that unifies the problematic cases, and says what we need to avoid if we are to have a legitimate ontology. A correct conception of the relation between the theory of intentional content and meaning, on the one hand, and the metaphysics of the domain talked about, on the other, is crucial in addressing these issues.

These issues lie in the intersection of metaphysics, the theory of content, and the theory of knowledge. One of the tasks in addressing them properly is to provide an account that can be integrated with plausible theories of each of these areas, and of their interrelations. Several writers have considered issues in this broad intersection, including one of my previous selves (Peacocke 1988; Shamik Dasgupta 2015), and I will consider the relation of the proposals developed here to their positions. I begin with some examples.

2. Four Examples

Here are four examples in more detail of some problematic conceptions.

(1) There is the case of Newtonian absolute space. According to Newton's original conception, we should distinguish as genuinely distinct possibilities the case in which an object, or even the material universe as a whole, is stationary, from the case in which it is moving uniformly in absolute space. On the Newtonian conception, being in motion, or being stationary, with respect to absolute space does not supervene on facts about motion relative to other material objects and events. On Newton's view, absolute spatial properties and magnitudes can be adequately elucidated only in terms of a framework of place-times that does involves a notion of absolute identity of locations over time. The unacceptability of Newton's conception of absolute space is widely agreed, even if some core of his physical theory were correct. Such rejection of absolute space obviously raises the question, to which there is still no fully agreed answer, of the principle we should cite in explaining why it is unacceptable. Do we have only an epistemic defect here, or something deeper?

(2) The second example concerns a distinction drawn in some theories of nonactual objects, in particular theories of what I shall call strong possibilia. Under some cosmologies that were once seriously considered as candidates for truth, the steady-state theories of the universe, whose proponents included Fred Hoyle, it was postulated that hydrogen atoms spontaneously come into existence. Let us say that a theorist of *strong* possibilia is a theorist who distinguishes, even for a fixed location in space-time, between one possibile *a* coming into existence as a hydrogen atom at that location, rather than a distinct possibile *b* coming into existence there and then. Of a possible state of affairs in which a new hydrogen atom appears spontaneously at a given place-time, the advocate of strong possibilia says it is a substantive, genuine issue whether it is *a* rather than *b* coming into existence there and then. Strong possibilia are not individuated by their relations to actual objects; nor by their relations to possibilia so individuated; nor by any iteration of such a chain of individuating conditions. By contrast, weak possibilia are individuated in one of these ways. The theorist of weak possibilia says that there is only one possibile that could come into existence as a hydrogen atom at a given location in space-time. The theorist of weak possibilia is likely to say that this is so because possibilia are individuated by the conditions under which they would be actual. Strong possibilia are also widely rejected; but just as in the case of absolute space, the rejection is in need of a rationale. I do not know whether there are actual strong possibilists. It does not matter whether there are: what matters is what is wrong with such a position. If the position is wrong, we need an explanation of what is wrong with it.

(3) The third example concerns the quiddities which have in the past two decades reemerged as a topic in metaphysics (Langton 1998; Lewis 2007). To believe in quiddities is to hold that, for instance, two different properties could play the role that is assigned to the property of being an up quark rather than a down quark in fundamental physics. The suggestion is that there is some intrinsic property that plays this role; that a different property might have played it; and, on some quiddistic views, there is ignorance, perhaps even inexpressible ignorance, about which property plays this role. Quiddities are perhaps less widely rejected than the other metaphysical conceptions I will be discussing. They clearly raise some of the same issues. A rationale for a negative position on the intelligibility of quiddities is equally required.

(4) Another historical conception displaying the problematic features is that of Cartesian egos, or—if they are allowed to come into and to go out of existence—Cartesian-like egos. Under one conception of egos (not precisely Cartesian, but sharing in the Cartesian conception), one ego as the subject of a person's

experience may cease to exist, and be replaced by another, quite undetectably. It is supposed, under this conception, to be a substantive question whether there is one ego, or a series of egos, in an interval of the life of an otherwise normal conscious subject. And, just as in the case of absolute Newtonian space, the question must be legitimate whether the material universe as a whole, over the course of its entire history, is at one series of locations, or at another shifted 1 metre to the left, so there is a similar question about Cartesian egos. Under the Cartesian conception, it also seems to make sense to suppose that there is a genuinely different possible universe in which you and I have switched Cartesian egos throughout our existence. It should be no surprise that Leibniz, who objected so strongly to the intelligibility of the allegedly possible shift 1 metre to the left in the spatial case, objected to the intelligibility of the Cartesian switch as well, on which more below. Cartesian and Cartesian-like egos seem unintelligible. But, to say it for the last time, we need to have a reason, defensible in all its generality, for saying these things.

3. Moving Towards a Criterion: The Newtonian Case

If, perhaps *per impossibile*, fully Newtonian absolute space-time were actual, could we succeed in referring to and thinking about absolute locations? In an important paper that makes many other contributions, Tim Maudlin writes that we could:

For the substantivalist [that is, the Newtonian—CP], terms such as 'here' and 'now' can be used to drive linguistic pegs into the fabric of absolute space and time. Without such pegs, the static Leibnizian shift cannot even be formulated. The relationist will no doubt contest this interpretation of the indexicals: If no substantival spacetime points are available to pick out, such terminology must be explicated instead in terms of relations to particular physical bodies. But to object this to the substantivalist is a manifest petitio principii: If such points do exist, there is no reason that we cannot directly refer to them.   (1993: 191)

I disagree. Absolute locations are supposed to have a determinate identity over time under the Newtonian conception. I suggest that for the substantivalist who thinks she can use 'here' to refer to a Newtonian location, nothing about her linguistic practice or thought distinguishes the hypothesis that she refers to a particular absolute location from the hypothesis that she refers to what, in the Newtonian conception, is a location sliding over time through absolute space, but coinciding, at the moment of utterance of 'here', with one particular Newtonian absolute location. These sliding locations correspond to diagonals through 4D Newtonian space-time.

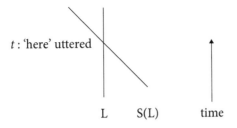

t : 'here' uttered

L   S(L)   time

For any given Newtonian absolute location, at any given time there are infinitely many such sliding locations that coincide, at that time, with that absolute location. For a given time t of utterance of 'here' at an alleged absolute location L, let S(L) be one such sliding location that coincides with L at t, as in the Diagram. I suggest that there can be, in principle, nothing in the Newtonian substantivalist's use of 'here' that could ground the interpretative claim that she is referring to L rather than S(L). Features of utterances concerning relative locations of objects at time t and relative locations of what under each interpretation are called 'places' at time t will not settle the matter. Such utterances will necessarily and as an a priori matter have the same truth-values under the rival interpretations, and will be answerable to the same kind of evidence.

Under such a hypothesis of sliding absolute locations as referents in absolute space, an utterance such as 'It was thus-and-so here yesterday' will be construed under the sliding hypothesis as a claim to the effect that the location on S(L) fixed as yesterday was thus-and-so yesterday. The rival interpretative hypothesis will of course be accompanied by the claim that the utterer believes the universe is stationary with respect to a frame of reference that treats anything on S(L) over time as stationary. Under the rival interpretation, the utterer also holds that an event of rain which the interpreter treats as occurring at L at some earlier time $t-1$ really occurred at S(L) at $t-1$. The frame of reference that the interpreter treats as stationary in absolute space is regarded as being in uniform motion by the interpretee under the rival interpretation. So phenomena of past-tense utterances will not distinguish the two hypotheses about the interpretation of the indexical utterances.

For clarity and simplicity of exposition, I have expounded the point for sliding locations that are straight lines in Newtonian absolute space, but, as David Albert and Shamik Dasgupta remarked to me, the same point could be made with bending or curved paths through absolute space.

The Newtonian substantivalist may want to say, "But I'm referring to *absolute locations*, not sliding ones!" This will not rule out the sliding interpretation.

Under the sliding interpretation, 'absolute location' in such utterances will be construed as location relative to what, if we accept Newtonian space, would be location relative to a particular frame of reference that is sliding in the allegedly true absolute space. The rival interpretation will make the interpretee's utterances of "I am referring to absolute locations" come out true.

The points just made about the inability of an utterance of 'here' to pick out an absolute location also apply equally to the mixed complex description 'my current absolute location'. Switching to that complex description is still consistent with a sliding location as the reference if there is nothing to distinguish whether by 'absolute' the thinker is referring to location relative to the alleged absolute space, or to a sliding frame relative to absolute space.

The point of the construal in terms of sliding locations is not to deny that if space were actually as Newton conceived it, any thinker at any given time would be at a determinate Newtonian absolute location. The thinker would be so located, under the Newtonian hypothesis. The issue I am raising is rather whether, under a Newtonian conception of space, the thinker would have any way of latching on to this alleged absolute location or, indeed, to the absolute frame of reference at all.

Are the points I am making self-refuting? Are we not considering what thinkers would be able to do if the universe were Newtonian, with absolute space? So do not the very terms of the argument presuppose that we must be able to think about the relation of absolute location in the first place? The argument I am offering is, however, meant to be a *reductio*. If talk about absolute space makes sense, then it does not make sense. Hence it does not make sense.

There is still a series of conceivable responses from a Maudlin-like position to these objections.

Can the objection to Maudlin's account of 'here' in Newtonian space be avoided by taking Newtonian place-times as referents for the relevant indexicals? Any utterance in Newtonian space-time will occur at a unique space-time location (modulo fuzzy boundaries), so will this modification not make the problem of non-unique paths through space-time disappear? But there is still a problem of an attribution of reference that goes beyond anything that could show up in judgemental practice. For there is equally a problem in distinguishing reference to Newtonian place-times, which are individuated in part by Newtonian places, from reference to the place-times of a neo-Newtonian space-time. In a neo-Newtonian description of space-time, there is no use of the notion of sameness of absolute location over time. For neo-Newtonian place-times, we can at most apply the notion of three nonsimultaneous place-times being inertial, that is being such that they constitute a physically possible path of a particle moving free of forces, moving inertially. An inertial path in neo-Newtonian space-time corresponds to multiple different paths in absolute Newtonian space-time, since an inertial path may be the path of a particle at rest in absolute Newtonian space, and equally may correspond to a path of uniform motion in absolute Newtonian space. (Intuitive expositions of neo-Newtonian space-time are given in Sklar (1976: 202–6) and Stein (1967: 174–200).) Now, even if space were truly Newtonian, a neo-Newtonian conception would still be definable for that universe, a conception that does not involve absolute identity of locations over time that floats free of everything else. There seems to be no account of what would make the Newtonian place-times, rather than the definable neo-Newtonian place-times, the references of a thinker's indexical 'here'.

An alternative response on behalf of Maudlin's position might say that for his proposed reference of the Newtonian indexical, it is distinctive that for "Yesterday, it was thus-and-so here" to be true is just for the Newtonian location that is zero in distance-magnitude from the Newtonian location at which 'here' is uttered to thus-and-so yesterday. This, the Newtonian may say, distinguishes his intended reference of 'here' from the multitude of alternate sliding references mentioned earlier. For any such distance-magnitude that is proposed for absolute distances across time, however, we can introduce, in Newtonian terms, a notion of distance*, for which a version of the sliding argument can then be developed. Absolute distance between places across different times is subject to versions of all the problems that arise for absolute locations.

Perhaps it will be replied that in a Newtonian world, thinkers do not need to refer to absolute locations indexically. They can rather think of them in purely general terms. Do they not need merely to think that there is some frame of reference such that location relative to that frame is absolute location, even if they do not have any other identification of what that frame is? The problem with this reply is that it is circular. The question we were asking is how thinkers could think about an absolute frame, as absolute, even if the world were Newtonian. This general answer, by using the notion of absoluteness itself in the general description thinkers are supposed to use in the offered solution, simply circularly presumes the problem is solved, rather than offering a solution to it.

Can this problem be met by adding a further level of generality, by using a definite description in the place occupied by the notion of absoluteness in the characterization? The question is what the descriptive material in the definite description could be. Is an absolute frame simply a frame that is not moving, *tout court*? This was Newton's own strategy—though with an added modal element—when he used the word "immovable" in his own characterization. Newton wrote of absolute space that "of its own nature without reference to anything external", it "always remains homogeneous and immovable" (Newton 1962: 6). The problem with this reply is that while we do have a legitimate notion of motion, of one thing relative to others, in the neo-Newtonian ontology, and even of one frame moving relative to another in that same ontology, these notions give us no clue as to what is meant by "not moving, *tout court*" in the offered explication. I doubt that there is any explication of "not moving, *tout court*" that does not require mention of absolute space; which takes us back to the original problem.

An entirely different response to the argument may come from someone who holds, like David Lewis, that natural properties and relations have a special place in interpretation, or who holds, in a Lewisian spirit, that there is some other 'reference-magnet' relation that determines the reference of a concept or an expression (Lewis 1983). So the response to the argument would be that absolute locations are natural reference-magnets in a Newtonian universe. They are more natural than locations that slide through absolute space. That, the objector will say, is why Maudlin is right to say that 'here' can refer to an absolute location in the Newtonian world.

I do not dispute the intuitive judgement about comparative naturalness of absolute and sliding locations in a Newtonian world, but I do question whether they have a role in semantic interpretation. It is, for instance, true that being a rabbit is a more natural property than being an undetached rabbit-part. But the reason for taking our discourse employing the word 'rabbit' to be about rabbits rather than undetached rabbit parts is, or should be, an explanatory one. As Evans argued (1975), attributing reference to rabbits has explanatory force, whereas attribution of reference to undetached rabbit parts involves attributing a sensitivity to distinctions that is not in fact present in those who understand the word 'rabbit'. I will not pursue the arguments for that point here—they, and many related issues, have gone through several cycles in the literature (Burge 2010: 216–23; Peacocke 2014b). More generally, when there are at least two referential interpretations that capture the relevant features of a thinker's judgements and assertions, and each interpretation involves distinctions that go beyond anything manifested actually or counterfactually in the thinker's judgements and assertions, then as Hartry Field argued in an analogous case, we should find a referential interpretation that captures only what is common to the two proposed referential interpretations (Field 1973). One way of doing this is to use a notion of partial reference, as Field recommends for pre-Einsteinian language using 'mass', a use that does not distinguish proper mass from relativistic mass. Another way is, in suitable cases, to identify some less fine-grained ontology. The less fine-grained ontology permits us to say, without excess attribution to the language users, that they are referring to entities recognized in that ontology. That was in effect the tactic I was employing in saying that in the supposed Newtonian universe, the indexical 'here' would have to be construed as referring to something at least no more fine-grained than neo-Newtonian locations.

In fact, however, when our concern is with distinctions that seem to go beyond what is intelligible, in the case of Newtonian physics it cannot really be a stable resting point to say that if our subjects were in a Newtonian universe, then their spatial vocabulary, including the indexicals, would refer to neo-Newtonian locations. Lawrence Sklar points out that even in the neo-Newtonian ontology, it is a hypothesis that makes sense that the entire material universe over the whole course of its history could have been located 1 metre to the north of its actual neo-Newtonian location (Sklar 1976: 203). To swallow that as an intelligible possibility while objecting to Newtonian absolute space certainly looks like a double standard.

There are two possible responses to this very reasonable reflection. A conservative response would be to suggest that, if the core of Newtonian physics were correct, then a proposition of neo-Newtonian physical theory is true only if it is true under all permutations of neo-Newtonian place-times onto themselves that meet three conditions: (1) they preserve those spatiotemporal relations between place-times that are recognized in neo-Newtonian theory; (2) they preserve the physical properties and relations attributed under the permutation; and (3) they preserve the three-place relation between nonsimultaneous neo-Newtonian place-times of being inertial. On this approach, an allegedly meaningful sentence of neo-Newtonian theory that is not true under all such permutations is not true outright. This would be essentially an application of Field's strategy of attributing partial reference-relations. This account of truth in neo-Newtonian physical theory rules out the truth of the hypothesis that everything in the whole material could have been 1 metre to the north. That hypothesis is not something that is true under all such permutations. Under this treatment of truth in neo-Newtonian physics, both Newtonian absolute locations and the alleged possibility of a shift throughout history of 1 metre to the north are treated on a par. They are not formulable in the theory as genuine hypotheses that could be true under this conception of truth.

I myself doubt that this conservative response is satisfactory. It is an unstable intermediate position. If the ontology of neo-Newtonian locations is objectionable, in still drawing distinctions where there is no difference, then it is problematic to use this ontology in the metalanguage. Yet it is still so used in the metalanguage in this supervaluationist approach. Here of course there is a sharp contrast with the case that Field discussed in his 1973 paper, since both proper mass and relativistic mass are genuine magnitudes in the more discriminating theory.

A more radical and stable response to the reflection is that the considerations of failure to determine a reference apply not only to Newtonian conceptions, but to neo-Newtonian conceptions as well. The *reductio* about sense applies equally to the neo-Newtonian conception too. I myself am inclined to the more radical response that would move one to a more thoroughly Leibnizian relational conception. For the purpose of the argument of this chapter, however, it does not matter which is correct. What matters is that there is a radical deficiency in the original Newtonian conception shown by the sliding argument and its extensions. It is a further question how far that deficiency applies to other conceptions too.

My position is that there is a lack of sense in talk of absolute rest and absolute location, rather than the weaker position that this is a case of a genuine sense that merely lacks a reference. When there is genuine sense that lacks a reference, there is a well-defined condition for something to be the reference; it is just that nothing meets that condition. My stance is rather that in the case of Newtonian absolute space, we have not even specified a condition that something must satisfy to be the reference.

Under a Fregean theory of sense, a sense is individuated by the fundamental condition for something to be the reference of the sense. A theory of understanding that respects that view of sense correspondingly holds: to understand an expression is to have some tacit knowledge, or some kind of grasp, of the fundamental condition for something to be its reference. Where there is no fundamental reference rule, there is no determination of what understanding could be. Hence there is no possibility of understanding, for there is nothing to understand.

We can contrast the case by considering the parallel issue of whether, if there were phlogiston, we would be able to refer to it. The answer seems to be unproblematically positive. Unlike the case of absolute space, if there were phlogiston, we would succeed in referring in saying or thinking 'the phlogiston released in the combustion of this log'. Loss of phlogiston would explain the reduction in mass of the log in combustion. 'Phlogiston' could have its reference fixed by such descriptions in a way in which, as we saw, talk about motion would fail to fix the reference of the term 'absolute location' even if there were absolute locations.[1]

---

[1] In fact the history of the use of 'phlogiston', and the reasons for rejection of phlogiston theories, are more interesting and subtle than in the oversimplifications we sometimes presume in philosophy. See Chang (2010).

It may be objected that the argument I am offering is making the same mistake as the one David Lewis (1984) rightly complained about in Hilary Putnam's 'Realism and Reason' (1977). Putnam argued that causal constraints could not fix interpretation of a language because the causal constraints would be reinterpreted, and come out as true, under the interpretations that he, Putnam, was considering. Lewis convincingly complained, concerning any proposed constraint C that avoids Putnam's argument,

The constraint is *not* that an intended interpretation must somehow make our account of C come out true. The constraint is that an intended interpretation must conform to C itself.   (1984: 225)

Lewis particularly emphasized the point in relation to causal constraints on interpretation.

The argument I have given respects Lewis's well-taken point when it is applied to the term 'absolute'. In the metalanguage in which I have been discussing the interpretation of the discourse of an inhabitant of a Newtonian universe, I have not been reconstruing 'absolute'. I have rather taken the predicate as prima facie meaningful for granted without reconstrual, in the course of developing an argument by *reductio*. My objection in the argument was only that the inhabitant of the Newtonian universe was unable, by her use of it, to fix a genuinely Newtonian reference for the term.

The argument I have offered also entirely respects Lewis's point if one wants to consider causal notions as contributing to the determination of reference. Suppose some snow at absolute location L at time t causes a person's utterance of "It's snowing here" at t. There is no attempt at reconstrual of causal relations under the sliding interpretation. If it is snowing at t at L, it will be snowing at the location on S(L) at t, for it is the same snow at the same absolute place-time. Causal relations, insofar as we can make sense of them in a Newtonian universe, are preserved under the sliding interpretation and its ancillary hypotheses. There is no question of reinterpreting 'causes' or 'causally explains'. The causal inertness of absolute space and absolute time are crucial to the point.

Suppose someone is inclined to say that an earlier state of affairs causes a later one in the Newtonian universe if the latter is explained by Newton's laws from the former. If the interpretee holds that thesis about causation, she will not need to disagree on claims about causation under the rival interpretive hypothesis and its ancillary claims. Such claims about causation will be preserved under the sliding hypothesis and its ancillary hypotheses, since Newton's laws are invariant under uniform motion.

The sliding argument I have offered is open-ended. If someone can come up with a good constraint on eligible reference that is met by absolute locations, and which the sliding interpretations violate, then the sliding interpretation of a speaker's utterances, and their variants, must be rejected. I have been trying to make it plausible that there is no such constraint. In any case, the form of the sliding argument does not violate Lewis's point against Putnam. I have not been trying to reconstrue constraints, but rather to take them at face value, and to argue that they do not rule out the sliding interpretation in a Newtonian universe.

I have two ancillary observations on the sliding argument.

(1) The argument developed in this section is an example of what Quine once called "indeterminacy in second intension" (1970). In the present case, a physical indeterminacy about what absolute location to assign to events induces a corresponding indeterminacy of reference and intentional content in the interpretation of discourse and thought apparently about such events. It is worth quoting Quine's argument in full:

> Now let us turn to the radical translation of a radically foreign physicist's theory. As always in radical translation, the starting point is the equating of observation sentences of the two languages by an inductive equating of stimulus meanings. In order afterwards to construe the foreigner's theoretical sentences we have to project analytical hypotheses, whose ultimate justification is substantially just that the implied observation sentences match up. But now the same old empirical slack, the old indeterminacy between physical theories, recurs in second intension. Insofar as the truth of a physical theory is underdetermined by observables, the translation of the foreigner's physical theory is underdetermined by translation of his observation sentences. If our physical theory can vary though all possible observations be fixed, then our translation of his physical theory can vary though our translations of all possible observation reports on his part be fixed. Our translation of his observation sentences no more fixes our translation of his physical theory than our own possible observations fix our own physical theory.   (1970: 179–80)

Quine makes two claims here, one unconditional and the other conditional. The unconditional claim is that:

> The class of true observation sentences underdetermines physical theory.

The conditional claim is that:

> If there is underdetermination of physical theory, there is underdetermination of translation of the sentences of a foreign physicist.

The parallel with the sliding argument runs as follows. There is the unconditional claim that:

> Truths about the spatiotemporal relational properties and about neo-Newtonian properties of objects and events underdetermine absolute locations.

And there is the conditional claim:

> If there is underdetermination of absolute locations by relational properties and by neo-Newtonian locations, then there is underdetermination of the content of thought and language about absolute locations.

The argument for the conditional claim in the case of absolute space is structurally parallel to Quine's argument for his conditional claim. I do not accept that Quine has formulated the notion of a possible observation in the right way; I correspondingly doubt his claim of underdetermination, but that is not presently relevant. The two conditional claims seem to me correct, and to be supportable by parallel arguments.

(2) The second ancillary observation is that it seems to me that Newton himself may have held that the condition of understanding I am insisting on here is a genuine one. Newton thought, though falsely, that the condition on understanding could be met. Newton held, to quote him directly, "The causes by which true and relative motion are distinguished, one from the other, are the forces impressed upon bodies to generate motion" (1962: 10). In an extraordinarily striking passage, he described his very goal in writing the *Principia* in these terms: "But how we are to obtain the true motions from their causes, effects, and apparent differences, and the converse, shall be explained more at large in the following treatise. For to this end it was that I composed it" (1962: 12). If Newton had been right in all his beliefs, there certainly would not have been a problem, in his own case, of saying what it is for him to be thinking about absolute motion or rest. For him, the absolute magnitudes were related, by law, to detectable forces, and his judgements could be causally sensitive to forces themselves. But the point that only neo-Newtonian space is required for Newtonian physics completely undermines any attempt to explain concepts of absolute space in terms of its lawful relation to forces.

4. A General Diagnosis: Excess Dimensions

This all suggests a diagnosis of what is wrong with the ontology of absolute space. I will argue that the diagnosis extends to the other three examples too. I call it the *excess dimension* diagnosis:

> An ontology is illegitimate if it attributes to entities of whatever sort features involved in their nature, as conceived in the ontology, but which are of such a kind that there is actually no saying—there is no account possible—of what it would be to be thinking of one rather than another of these entities, or more generally, to be thinking of entities of that sort rather than some other.

In the case of Newtonian locations, the excess dimension is their identity over time as conceived by Newton. The argument that this is an excess dimension is the argument given in Section 3.

If the possession of an excess dimension is a sufficient condition for the illegitimacy of an ontology, the application of this principle applies also to the thought and language of advocates of such an ontology. The true Newtonian may think that she means something by 'absolute space' when she advocates her position. But under this diagnosis, she is under an illusion that she is succeeding in referring to something.

It is important to distinguish two varieties of excess dimension, which we can label *intraworld* and *crossworld*. Cases of an intraworld excess dimension are cases in which the problematic ontology allows a description of a given world (including the actual world) of such a kind that it is impossible to give any account of what is involved in thinking about one rather than another entity of the sort allowed by the problematic ontology, even though both are elements of the world. The argument of Section 3 about sliding locations, if sound, establishes it to be a case of intraworld excess dimension in the Newtonian ontology. The argument is intended to show that there is no account of what it is to be thinking of the alleged absolute locations, rather than sliding locations in absolute space, all in a given world.

Cases of a crossworld excess dimension are those in which a problematic ontology draws distinctions between possible worlds, distinctions drawn using its ontology, of such a kind that it is impossible to give an account of what it is to be thinking that one rather than another of these allegedly distinct worlds is actual. The Newtonian ontology also plausibly has a crossworld excess dimension. The Leibnizian challenge that under the Newtonian ontology, there are possible worlds in which the whole material universe could have been located 1 metre away from its actual location, throughout history, and they could have been actual, can plausibly be developed into a complaint about a crossworld excess dimension. I will return to that issue; if the point is correct, then the Newtonian ontology involves both intraworld and crossworld excess dimensions. First I want to consider further the intraworld excess dimension diagnosis as applied to the Newtonian case.

As I said a few paragraphs back, it is plausible that what makes something a genuine concept is that it is individuated by a genuine condition for something to be its reference. In Chapter 1 I endorsed a generalization of Evans's view, the generalization to the effect that any concept is individuated by the relation a thinker must have to something in order for it to be the reference of the concept. The arguments above about absolute space are intended to show that there is no stating the relation a thinker must have to absolute space to be thinking about it. If these views about concepts and sense are correct, then when there is an excess dimension in an ontology, we have not merely a failure of reference, we have further a conceptual deficiency, a failure of sense or concept. If there is no condition for something to be the reference of a proposed concept, the proposed concept does not exist. A genuine concept can be contradictory, of course, but that is a case in which there is a genuine condition for being the reference of the concept, a condition that cannot be met. Under the excess dimension diagnosis, the deficiency of the alleged concept of absolute space is more radical. No condition has been given for something to be the reference of the concept.

Newton and his supporters on absolute space had propositional attitudes that we do ordinarily characterize as believing that absolute space was thus-and-so. The legitimacy of these attributions does not mean there must be such a genuine concept. These attributions can be regimented thus: Newton believed there was such a thing as absolute space, with such-and-such properties, and conforming to so-and-so laws. On the proper development of the present position, these believed properties do not fix a condition for something to be the reference of terms for absolute space. Newton believed that there was a notion of location that goes beyond both relative location and neo-Newtonian location, but there is no such notion. The situation is analogous to someone who believes that the spurious connective devised by Arthur Prior, the famous *tonk*, is genuinely meaningful (Prior 1960). That person may believe various things about the operator *tonk*, but those beliefs will not determine a condition for something to be the reference of *tonk*. No coherent condition has been specified for something to be the reference of *tonk*, and the fact that someone mistakenly believes that it is meaningful in no way determines such a condition.

There are three distinctive features of the excess dimension diagnosis of what is unacceptable about the metaphysics of Newtonian absolute space.

(i) The excess dimension argument highlights the impossibility of a thinker latching in the actual world on to absolute space, even if there were such a thing. The argument specializes to thinkers and concepts a highly general consideration that applies to anything in the universe that is supposed to stand in a certain relation to absolute locations. The highly general consideration is that there is no saying what it is for some object, event, or experimental apparatus to stand in one, rather than another, relation to the alleged absolute locations. In this sense, although the argument given focuses on considerations about concepts, because we want to think and talk meaningfully, it is a special case of an argument that one could develop in much greater generality. The entirely general argument would mention the absence of constitutive conditions for an object, event, or apparatus to stand in one rather than another relation to absolute space. The thinker and her concepts are just one example of an object and her properties that are alleged to stand in one rather than another relation to absolute space.

(ii) In discussions of what is wrong with a conception of absolute space, the issue sometimes arises of whether hypotheses about absolute space, and laws of motion stated in relation to absolute space, can be explanatory of truths about absolute locations. The later absolute location of an object might, it is suggested, be explained by the force exerted on it at some earlier location, together with its mass. This idea fails if the excess dimension diagnosis is correct. There is no content concerning absolute locations to be grasped; hence there are no truths about absolute locations that might, otherwise, be candidates for explanation.

(iii) In a paper 'The Limits of Intelligibility' some decades ago, I argued that the concept of absolute space fails what I called the Discrimination Principle (1988). That is, the concept of absolute space fails the requirement that there has to exist some account of what it is for a thinker to be employing that alleged concept rather than some variant concept equally admitted by the proponent of absolute space, such as location in a frame in uniform motion with respect to that alleged absolute frame. My treatment in that earlier work was, like the excess dimension diagnosis, a non-verificationist approach to these issues. So the question arises: what is the relation of the excess dimension account to the failure of the Discrimination Principle for the proposed Newtonian concepts? The issue could be discussed at length, but a simple, plausible hypothesis is that the Discrimination Principle fails for these Newtonian contents precisely because the excess dimension diagnosis applies. If there is no saying what relation to the level of reference a thinker would have to stand in to be thinking of Newtonian absolute space, and if concepts are individuated by such relations, then it follows that there is no saying what it is to be employing the alleged Newtonian concept rather than some other variant alleged concept. The excess dimension diagnosis can be seen as an explanatory elaboration of why the Discrimination Principle fails in the Newtonian case.[2]

---

[2] Would the same arguments that apply against the intelligibility of Newtonian absolute locations apply against the notion of distance at a given time in a Newtonian universe? And if so, would the arguments when pressed through uniformly in all cases leave us with no materials for Newtonian laws, as usually formulated, to explain at all? These important questions would take us too far off our main track; here I just note that this does indeed seem to be a genuine issue. It is a real question how

5. Wider Applications of the Diagnosis

How does the excess dimension diagnosis apply to the other examples? I suggest that the other cases are examples in which the problematic ontology exhibits a crossworld excess dimension. The structural problem in crossworld cases is that though there is some property or relation that thinkers can refer to in the actual world, it is an illusion to think that what is referred to in the actual world is of such a kind that we can make sense of the range of possibilities for that property or relation that the problematic ontologies advocate. So, for instance, in the Newtonian case we have already argued that use of the term 'absolute', and conditions involving it, will allow thinkers at most to latch on in thought to an inertial frame, and not to absolute locations. That will not give the resources needed to make sense of the idea of absolute locations with respect to which the material universe could have been differently located throughout time. I suggest that a similar structural diagnosis of crossworld excess dimensions applies in the three other examples with which we started.

We can take the case of strong possibilia first. In what relation could a thinker stand in order to be thinking about strong possibilia? Since strong possibilia are not actual, there is no plausibility in the view that we can think of them indexically or demonstratively. The nonactual is rather thought about by definite descriptions that involve modal materials. We can think about the unique possible object that would exist if such-and-such conditions were met. This is fine for the believer in weak possibilia; but the distinctive thesis of strong possibilism is that more than one possibile meets the 'such-and-such' condition. So these descriptions cannot be used to think of particular possibilia under the strong possibilist view.

We can also talk about what a thinker would say has come into existence if, for example, a hydrogen atom suddenly came into existence at a particular place-time. But both the weak and the strong possibilist will say that a possibile is made actual in such an event. There is no distinguishing, under the strong possibilist's view, which of the more than one it is.

Can a move to a general characterization of the domain of strong possibilia help here? The strong possibilist may speak of the domain of nonactual things that would exist if certain possible conditions were to hold, or certain possibly possible conditions were to hold, or...and so forth. But the weak possibilist also believes in such a domain. These general characterizations will not succeed in

to formulate the core of Newtonian physics once we remove from it all properties and relations to which the present considerations apply.

isolating the domain of strong possibilia, as opposed to the domain of weak possibilia that also meet the condition that they would exist if certain possible conditions were to hold, or certain possibly possible conditions were to hold, etc.

In the case of possibilities for actual objects, we have a positive account of what it is for a possibility to concern, say, Napoleon rather than Wellington. The thinker has actual relations to Napoleon that he does not have to Wellington, and that makes it intelligible that our thinker is entertaining a possibility concerning one person rather than the other. But there is no such corresponding relation to mere *possibilia*. For the friend of strong possibilia, there is no saying what it is for him to be entertaining the counterfactual that *a* has come into existence and not *b*, as opposed to *b* coming into existence and not *a*. For the believer in weak possibilia, the distinction between *a* and *b* is a distinction without a difference, since for him possibilia are individuated by the conditions under which they would exist. There is no such excess dimension in the ontology of weak possibilia. There is only one *possibile* that could come into existence as a spontaneously existing hydrogen atom at a given place-time.

Similarly, there is no excess dimension for weak *possibilia* individuated by their relations to actual material particulars. Suppose that in the actual world there are two sperm cells *c* and *d* neither of which actually unites with egg cell *e*. In a nonactual possible world, *c* unites with *e*, let us say. This union produces a person who exists in that world, but who does not actually exist. But that world also has a rather different history from the world in which the other sperm *d* unites with *e* instead. In the latter, *c* continues with a history of its own, likely very short. In the former, *d* continues with a distinct spatiotemporal history of its own, also likely short. We can make sense of the thinker being sensitive to the counterfactuals that distinguish these two distinct worlds.

The problem faced by the strong possibilist in saying how a thinker can employ some concept or other to think of the distinctive ontology he proposes is structurally analogous to that faced by the theorist of absolute space. Just as there are, if the Newtonian conception of absolute space is correct, many different absolute locations that can correspond with a neo-Newtonian location, so there are multiple strong possibilia corresponding to a weak possibile. In each case, our conceptual resources allow us at most to latch on to the weaker entities, which do not have excess dimensions. But those resources, it seems, cannot take us as far as identifying the entities with additional dimensions to their identity, whether the identification is singular or more general. The friend of strong possibilia distinguishes between two worlds that differ only in which strong possibile springs into actual existence. No account seems to be possible of what it is for a thinker to be representing one, rather than the other, of these two worlds. In short, while the believer in strong possibilia may think she believes in entities of which it is an open question which of two different entities has sprung into existence, in fact there is nothing to distinguish her from someone who is quantifying only over weak possibilia, and has the false belief that there are two possibilia which could have become actual. There is no saying what it is really to be thinking about strong possibilia, as opposed to making that mistake about the range of legitimate possibilia. So a supposed ontology of strong possibilia is an ontology with a crossworld excess dimension.

There is an interesting parallel here with the diagnosis of spurious cases that I offered back in Peacocke (1988). Cases of intraworld excess dimensions are cases that are vulnerable to what in the earlier work I called 'switching' arguments, arguments that show that there is no distinction between the thinker employing one alleged concept rather than another, when concepts employ the problematic ontology. Cases of crossworld excess dimensions are cases that are vulnerable to 'reduced-content' arguments, to the effect that there is no distinction between employing one of the problematic concepts legitimized within the problematic ontology, and simply making a mistake with a false belief about a legitimate ontology. This is further evidence that the excess dimension diagnosis is explanatory of the Discrimination Principle I endorsed in the earlier work.

Now we can turn to the third case, that of quiddities. A full discussion of this case would require a different book, and here I will just outline a position on the issue. The believer in quiddities says that there are intrinsic properties that realize the roles picked out by the Ramsification of a scientific theory—even a basic physical theory—and says that other intrinsic properties could have played these roles. The friend of quiddities believes in a level of properties individuated more finely than the role specified in a theory, even a fundamental theory. On this conception, the quiddities can in other possible circumstances float free of the roles they occupy in the actual world. This is one extreme position, which we can label *free-floating quiddism*. At one opposite extreme from free-floating quiddism is the view we can label the *role-exhaustive position*. The role-exhaustive position, as its name implies, holds that there is no more to the identity of a property mentioned in a fundamental physical theory than is given in its role in that fundamental physical theory. I myself think that neither of these extreme positions is correct. I consider free-floating quiddism first.

Just as Newtonian absolute space was motivated, incorrectly, by the bucket-experiment and thought-experiments involving globes connected by a spring, so there is an argument motivating free-floating quiddism. The argument is that something, even a property, cannot have only relational properties, and must have an intrinsic nature as well. Inertial mass is sometimes thought of as an intrinsic property, whereas the force exerted by an object is thought of as one of its relational properties. But it is not clear that there is really any intelligible conception of mass as something independently of a property that is involved in the exertion of force. The Ramsification of a physical theory involving mass and force will give mass a role that relates it to what is in fact force, but the idea that inertial mass must have some further intrinsic nature seems to me problematic.

One reason it seems problematic is that the other clear cases in which we have a property that has an allegedly intrinsic characterization are cases in which the role is given in a nonfundamental theory, and so there is a more basic level at which the property playing the role can be individuated. There are no conceptual or philosophical difficulties in the idea that there is an intrinsic characterization of the property of being an antibody to a certain bacterium. The intrinsic characterization of the antibody will be given at the level of molecular chemistry. But this is a model which in the nature of the case is not available at the scientifically fundamental level.

In the nonfundamental case, there can also be explanations of why the intrinsic property has the role it does. A good biochemistry will explain why an antibody with a certain molecular structure is an antibody for a bacterium, chemically described. But how could there be an explanation of how a quiddity has the relational properties possessed by mass? Again, it is in the nature of the case that this is problematic, since we are already at the fundamental level, and there is no level below it on whose explanatory resources we might draw in offering such a scientific explanation of how it is that the quiddity plays the role in question.

From the standpoint of this critique, it is an illusion that there is a range of quiddities of the sort envisaged in free-floating quiddism. The only properties available to play the roles determined by a fundamental physical theory are those already mentioned in the fundamental physical theory. The believer in free-floating quiddism thinks that the notion *intrinsic realizer* has application beyond its legitimate boundaries, just as the believer in absolute space has a corresponding illusion about the range of cases in which the notion *same location* has application. In each case, there is not even a condition for something to be the intended reference of the problematic terms. Any attempt to draw up such a condition will use notions of realization or sameness of location that, legitimately applied, will not reach as far as the intended ontology. In short, the excess dimension of quiddities is one that attempts to extend the notion of intrinsic realizer beyond its legitimate scope when applied to the terms of nonfundamental theories.

The case is not precisely structurally parallel with the case of strong possibilia. In the case of legitimate possibilia whose actualization would be continuant particulars, it is plausible that for each of them, there is an individuating condition, of a sort that rules out strong possibilia. But it is less plausible that a role in true fundamental physical theory fully individuates physical properties and magnitudes, at least if this is taken to imply that the property or magnitude must have that role in any world in which it is instantiated. It is not at all plausible that if the fundamental laws were somewhat different, there would be no such thing as mass, or distance, or time. Certainly magnitude-types such as distance and duration (both relative to a frame of reference) seem to have a transworld identity, and so too do some specific magnitudes. It is plausible that the notions of straight lines, and right angles, make sense across universes with different geometries and correspondingly different laws. If this is so, what makes it possible is a subject for further investigation in metaphysics and the philosophy of science. But it remains in common between quiddities and the other problematic examples that they possess an excess dimension. The friend of quiddities will distinguish two worlds which are governed by the same laws, and assign the same fundamental physical magnitudes at all place-times, but which allegedly have different quiddities playing the roles of the fundamental physical magnitudes.

For the fourth of our initial examples, that of Cartesian egos, the argument that this ontology has excess dimensions is essentially one found in Kant, in some of his discussions of the Paralogisms in the *Critique of Pure Reason*. If Cartesian egos can cease to exist, and one can be replaced by another, yet still be associated with the same continuing subject of experience, then we can ask what it is to be thinking of distinct egos, that pass their memories on to their successors, in a given subject or person, as opposed to there being only one, or fewer egos over time associated with a given subject of experience. There seems to be no account of what it is to be thinking of one particular continuing Cartesian ego, with an identity over time, as associated with a particular person, as opposed to a series of Cartesian egos associated with the same person, and which pass on their memories to one another, just as Kant said (1998: footnote spanning A363–A364). All that thinkers can be sensitive to in their judgements, either from the first-person or third-person standpoint, is identity of the subject of consciousness. That genuine identity is founded in the identity of something else. Views vary on the nature of that something else. According to Peter Strawson, the role of the body is ultimately fundamental in the identity of subject over time (1966: 163–9). On neo-Humean views, the identity to which thinkers are sensitive is that of a constructed entity, built from psychological continuity and other matters not involving an unreduced subject of consciousness (Parfit 1986). My own view, as stated in Chapter 4, is that the identity of subject involves the identity of integrating apparatus over time (Peacocke 2014a). Under each of these views of the metaphysics of subjects, there is, in the ontology of neo-Cartesian egos, an excess dimension of identity and distinctness over time beyond what is involved in genuine identity of subjects over time.

Even if, perhaps *per impossibile*, there were Cartesian egos, it seems impossible for there to be an account of how thinkers could latch on to the relation 'the subject of consciousness s has ego e_1 at time t_1 and has ego e_2 at time t_2'. One continuing ordinary subject of consciousness may, under the problematic conception, be associated with one or multiple egos over time. This one-many problem in the domain of subjects of consciousness corresponds, in the theory of excess dimensions, to the many different locations, according to the theorist of absolute Newtonian space, that the material universe could have had in absolute space. In both cases we have a crossworld excess dimension. There is no saying what it is for our neo-Cartesian to be exercising the alleged concept of an ego, as opposed to being radically mistaken about the range of genuine possibilities for a more defensible notion of a subject of experience. Similarly, there is no saying what it is for the Newtonian to be exercising the alleged concept of absolute location, as opposed to being radically mistaken about the range of possibilities for a more defensible notion of location. As in the other cases of crossworld excess dimensions, this a reduced-content objection, rather than a switching treatment of the kind applied in the cases of intraworld excess dimensions.

There is a further illusion of the powers of indexicality that is parallel in the case of absolute space and Cartesian egos. Just as Maudlin argued that in a Newtonian universe, thinkers can use 'here' to refer to absolute locations, so the Cartesian may attempt to argue that, if there really are Cartesian egos, each thinking of 'I' refers to one of them. The illusions are structurally similar. There should not be any dispute with the rule that any use in thinking of the pure indexical 'here' refers to the location at which it is thought (modulo vagueness of the extent of the location to which reference is made). Similarly, any use in thinking of 'I' refers to the agent who is doing the thinking. The parallel continues in the fact that in each case, no perception of the place or any perception of the subject is required for these pure indexicals to succeed in referring. But the nature of the entities so referred to in each case is a further question. If no thinker is capable of being sensitive to the alleged absolute identity of places over time, or to the alleged identity or distinctness of Cartesian egos over time, then it follows that in uses of 'here' and 'I', such Newtonian and Cartesian entities cannot be the references of uses of these indexicals.

There is also a crossworld excess dimension of Cartesian-like egos if their association with persons or subjects of consciousness is supposed to be contingent. Leibniz replied to someone who said he wished to be King of China that all the interlocutor wanted was that he should not exist and that there be a King in China (Leibniz 1918: 58, end of §34; and in a letter to Molanus, Leibniz 1989: 243; see also Williams 1973: 42–3). We can take it that Leibniz's interlocutor was not just talking about the conceptually unproblematic possibility of usurping the position of the current King of China in a coup d'état (the interlocutor probably was not envisaging the vexed practicalities of a coup). Leibniz might have been influenced by more than one of his doctrines in making his remark, but he was at least insisting that without a transfer of memories, what was wished for would amount to no more than precisely what Leibniz said. Now a distinction between two worlds which differ only in respect of which Cartesian egos are assigned to Leibniz's interlocutor and to the King of China is a distinction to which no thinker could be sensitive. The alleged distinction involves an ontology that has an excess dimension. Considered as a remark against Cartesian egos, Leibniz's remark is not only compelling, but it also generalizes to cover instances of the more general position that he also deployed in his arguments against Newtonian absolute space. If someone suggested that two subjects of consciousness could have had different Cartesian egos throughout the whole of their existences, the arguments that one would marshal against the intelligibility of this alleged possibility would be substantially parallel to those Leibniz himself used against the idea that the entire material universe could have been 1 metre to the left in space throughout its whole history.

6. Understanding, Knowledge, and the Explanation of Limits

Some contents are true but unknowably so. If some of these contents were such that there is no saying what the reference-relation is for one or more of their components, the preceding arguments would lose their force. For then absolute space, quiddities, and the rest would be in no worse state than any other concept that features in some true but unknowable contents.

My position, however, is that this is far from being so. There are plausible accounts of what is involved in understanding some unknowable but referentially determinate contents. These plausible accounts draw on theories of what fixes the reference of the relevant concept or concepts in the true-but-unknowable examples. They do so in ways that sharply distinguish the case of genuine but unknowable contents from alleged contents concerning the four problematic ontologies we listed at the outset.

The most relevant model of grasp of unverifiable contents for present purposes is one that gives a crucial role to the grasp of an identity relation in elaborating the nature of understanding in the unverifiable examples. A plausible fundamental reference rule for the observational concept *square* is that an arbitrary thing falls under the concept if and only if it is the same shape that things are presented as being in perceptual experiences of objects as square (Peacocke 2008: chs. 1, 5). Since shape is evidently relative to a frame of reference, a stricter formulation would make this relativization to frames explicit, but I will ignore it as not important for the present point. This fundamental reference rule individuates the concept, makes it the concept it is. In talking of a perceptual experience as presenting an object as square, we are talking about its nonconceptual representational content, so there is no circularity in the condition. For present purposes, however, for those who agree with McDowell that perception has only a conceptual content, the point about identity-involving explanations of concepts can still get a grip. The rule uses the identity relation *is the same shape as*. In grasping the concept *square*, one has tacit knowledge of this fundamental reference rule.

In this fundamental reference rule, the relation *is the same shape as* cantilevers from local, perceptible instances of squareness to potentially inaccessible cases. On this account of the nature of the concept *square*, it is unproblematic that a predication involving the concept can feature in a content that can be unknowably true. Objects outside our light cone can have the same shape as things are presented as being in our perceptual experiences of things as square. The content that exactly a million years ago, there were four boulders here forming the corners of a square may be true but currently unknowable. Contents about the squareness of things outside our light cone will be unknowable by us at any time. Such contents have determinate truth-conditions because the concept *square* has determinate reference in inaccessible cases too, because its reference is determined by a relation of identity of shape to local, perceptually accessible cases.

This is neither a purely evidential, nor a consequence-based, account of the concept. It may take intellectual effort to work out what would be evidence that some object, not currently encountered, is square. It may take intellectual effort to work out what would be the consequences of some object, not currently encountered, being square. Under this approach, such evidence and consequences are not primitively written into the identity of the concept.

This model of understanding is not going to carry us all the way to justifying the claim that alleged concepts of absolute location, or of Cartesian egos, have determinate reference-conditions. In those problematic cases, there are no local cases in which our judgements are genuinely sensitive to identity of absolute location, or to identity of Cartesian ego. The conception of absolute location, and of Cartesian egos, makes them always and in all cases not something to which a thinker's judgements may be sensitive. We cannot even get a grasp on local, accessible cases, let alone raise the question of some extension to the inaccessible.

The truth-conditional approach to meaning and intentional content just outlined is entirely consistent with the excess dimension explanation of what is wrong, at a first pass, with the problematic ontologies. I draw the conclusion that the excess dimension diagnosis I have offered of the problematic cases does not involve any commitment to verificationist, evidentialist, or consequence-based treatments of meaning and intentional content. The materials used in the sub-stantive elaboration of the truth-conditional account will not carry a commit-ment to making sense of the excess dimension cases. On the contrary, I would argue that the truth-conditional accounts exploit materials, in particular reliance on the locally accessible cases, that in the nature of the case are unavailable in the ontologies with excess dimensions. The particular way this substantive truth-conditional account is developed shows that not merely is it consistent with the excess dimension diagnosis; rather, the very form of the substantive account itself explains why, when there are excess dimensions in an ontology, there can be no genuine reference-relations for its elements. The excess dimensions make impossible the kind of local sensitivity of judgements that would be required for reference to elements of the alleged ontology.

Because these accounts of understanding of verification-transcendent but nevertheless genuine contents exist, it seems to me that the argument from excess dimensions is not simply an example of indeterminacy of meaning or indeter-minacy of translation that is also found in cases of concepts with which we have no problem. I believe it is a determinate matter what the fundamental reference rule is for our familiar expressions. A full development of the position for which I am arguing would, I acknowledge, need to be accompanied by a response to the Quinean arguments that there is no saying even in quite ordinary cases what the reference-relation is for 'gavagai', or for our own 'rabbit'. There are several arguments in the literature against Quine's claim of indeterminacy.[3]

On the conception I advocate, an account of understanding is prior in the order of philosophical explanation to the conditions of possible knowledge of a particular intentional content. Whether there is a genuine content that is know-able depends on at least three things. It depends on the existence of an understanding-condition for the content; it depends on the way the world is;

---

[3] For one style of reply to Quine, see Evans (1975), and for another, see Burge (2010: 211–64). I conjecture that all scientific theories should have their ontology constrained by the kind of principles Evans formulated.

and it depends on our position in the world relative to the subject matter of the content. There is, by contrast, a kind of radical unknowability, which it is reasonable to describe as unacceptable unknowability, in the case of the problematic ontologies in the four examples at the start of this chapter. On the account I have proposed, the reason there is no genuine content to be known, or believed, or hoped for involving these alleged ontologies is that there is no understanding-condition for the alleged concepts involving these proposed ontologies.

In short, the account I have been developing distinguishes two species of unknowability. There is the species instances of which involve genuine contents for which there are understanding-conditions, and which, given their nature and the character of the universe, and our position in it, we cannot know. There is another species of unknowability which involves no genuine content at all, the case in which there is no content to be known.

The unknowability of contents concerning absolute locations was repeatedly emphasized by Leibniz in his critique of Newton. "I answer, motion does not indeed depend upon being observed, but it does depend upon being possible to be observed. There is no motion when there is no change that can be observed. And when there is no change that can be observed, there is no change at all" (1969: 705).[4] But for Leibniz, this objectionable unobservability was a consequence of a violation of a more fundamental principle, mentioned in his very next sentence: the violation of the principle of sufficient reason involved in the "supposition of a real, absolute space". In more recent philosophical literature on Newtonian absolute space, its troubles are often initially characterized as undetectability. In a relatively recent critical survey, Oliver Pooley described Newtonian absolute space as an "epistemological embarrassment" (2013: 530). On the present approach, we can agree with these points about undetectability: but we do need the additional point that distinguishes the case from other kinds of legitimate unverifiability to justify the claim that they are also an embarrassment. The legitimate cases of undetectability are no embarrassment at all. It would rather be an embarrassment to have a theory that does not recognize them as legitimate cases of unknowability.

Given that we can distinguish between cases of radical unknowability and acceptable unknowability, the question arises of whether there is a rival approach to the one offered here, an approach that successfully characterizes the radical cases as unacceptable, and does so without presupposing an explanatory priority of the theory of understanding over the conditions of knowability. There are at

---

[4] In the same work, Leibniz also mentions unobservability (1969: 700) and unknowability (707).

least two forms of such a rival view that might be taken by such a theory that does not prioritize the theory of understanding.

One form of view would aim simply to characterize the unacceptable kind of unknowability without drawing on the theory of understanding at all. The view would then endorse the norm that the unknowability so characterized is unacceptable. It would in turn be a question for further consideration whether that norm is fundamental, or whether it can be derived from others. So on this view, the initial characterization of the norm would not involve notions drawn from the theory of understanding. It would also be open to such a view to hold that we should draw conclusions about whether there is anything to understand from the presence of the unacceptable kind of unknowability. So the question is: what characterization of unacceptable unknowability might this first form of view offer?

One suggestion would be that a content involves the unacceptable kind of unknowability if the content is not built up from knowable concepts of properties, relations, and operators. This is certainly a characterization that does not mention the theory of understanding, and indeed claims involving concepts of absolute space are always unknowable. But the characterization also seems to be too strong. Are the acceptable contents concerning what is going on outside our light cone defined in terms of knowable properties, relations, and operators? Small, local instances of distance and temporal magnitudes do not take us beyond the knowable. But if we use numerical notions such as 10^{30} in characterizing distance and temporal magnitudes, such notions will take us from the knowable to the unknowable. We understand them, but not on the basis of our possibly knowing what was or will be happening vast magnitudes of time or distance away, beyond what light signals can tell us. It is not true that only contents defined in terms of, or built up out of, small and local distance and temporal magnitudes are acceptable.

Maybe the defender of this first form would reply that it is sufficient if the concept of properties and relations are knowable in some local, accessible cases. That condition is indeed met by genuine contents about what is going on outside our light cone, but not by contents about absolute location. However, it seems to me that relying on this point is to give priority in the philosophical explanation to the theory of understanding after all. On a plausible theory of these concepts of properties and relations, it is our ability to know their instantiations in local cases that is a crucial component of a theory of understanding that fixes determinate references for the concepts in the inaccessible cases. As noted, a plausible theory appeals to a thinker's grasp of a sameness relation applicable both in the local and the inaccessible cases. We need the theory of understanding to explain why knowability in the local cases contributes to understanding in the non-local cases. Without that, the relevance of the existence of local, knowable cases to the understanding of non-local cases remains unexplained.

A second form of rival view would not dispute the intertwining of the theory of understanding with the distinction between acceptable and unacceptable instances of unknowability. Rather, this second form of rival view denies the strict priority of the theory of understanding, and asserts that neither is prior to the other. The suggestion is that the substantive theory of content can be developed equally well either in terms of conditions for knowledge, or in terms of conditions for understanding (grasp). The idea is that these are equally legitimate ways of characterizing the same object, the individuation of particular intentional contents.

This no-priority view has its attractions in certain limited, very basic cases, but it still has to say how it is going to get over the hurdle of capturing the acceptable unknowable contents, such as those about the distant past, or events outside our light cone. Is it going to talk about the situation of possible knowers who are situated so that they can know what we cannot know? We do understand such talk, in some cases, but it is plausible that we do so only because of our prior understanding of the existence of the place-times at which they might be located, and our conception of the properties and relations that can be instantiated there. We can make sense of what such distantly located subjects could know only because we can make sense of certain conditions holding, or not holding, at those distant locations. The priority of understanding over the possibility of knowledge seems to continue to hold.

An important new approach to characterizing radical unknowability without mentioning the theory of concept possession and understanding is developed in the proposals by Shamik Dasgupta in his paper 'Inexpressible Ignorance' (2015). If the universe were Newtonian, Dasgupta argues, we would have inexpressible ignorance of our absolute location. This inexpressible ignorance is a kind of alienation, and "avoiding alienation is an overlooked epistemic value" (442). In that paper, Dasgupta agrees with Maudlin that a subject in a Newtonian universe could use 'here' to refer to an absolute location; but since there is evidently a sense in which this subject still remains ignorant of which absolute location this is, the subject's ignorance is inexpressible.

What I have argued in Section 3 of this chapter places me in disagreement with Dasgupta about Maudlin's claim, but that does not matter for present purposes. Since I have argued that reference to absolute locations in absolute space is not possible at all, I think that even less is expressible by a subject in Newtonian space than Dasgupta does.

It seems clear that any case of an ontology with an excess dimension, in the sense discussed above, will be a case of inexpressible ignorance in Dasgupta's sense. If there is an excess dimension in an ontology, a thinker cannot latch on to that dimension in thought and language at all, and so her ignorance of matters concerning it will be inexpressible. There is some confirming evidence for this point in the fact that in the cases of strong possibilia and of Cartesian egos, we equally have inexpressible ignorance. There is inexpressible ignorance of which Cartesian egos are associated with which people, when egos are conceived in such a way that the assignment of egos to persons can switch around without anything else changing. Similarly there is inexpressible ignorance of which of several strong possibilia have come into existence when some new object comes into existence. There is also inexpressible ignorance in the case of quiddities, as Dasgupta himself argues (2015: 448–9).

Is the converse also true? That is, does it also hold that any case of inexpressible ignorance ('II') is a case in which we have a metaphysics with an excess dimension ('ED')? Is it true that II→ED?

At first glance, it may seem that approximate spatial reduplication gives a counterexample to II→ED. Suppose that the layout of things and events in space roughly repeats itself qualitatively in space, with tiny qualitative differences between the approximately duplicated regions. Can there not be ignorance of which region is the one in which you're currently located, and is it not obvious that your knowledge 'I'm in *this* one' does not remove the ignorance in question?

This is in fact no counterexample, and we have to distinguish. If these are meant to be regions of Newtonian absolute space, with approximately repeating qualitative contents, so that absolute location is not settled by any relational facts, then this is, by the arguments earlier in this chapter, still a case of excess dimensions. So it is then no counterexample to II→ED, since ED holds for the case.

If, by contrast, space is conceived relationally (as the reference to tiny qualitative differences suggests), then relational differences between the thinker's actual current region and others will fully determine which region of the universe the thinker currently inhabits. There will, on the relational view of space, be no failure of the relational facts to determine which region is the one the thinker currently inhabits. So any ignorance the thinker has about his location will after all be expressible, by characterizing the thinker's ignorance of the distinctive relations in which his actual region stands. This case too then is not a counterexample to II→ED, because under this construal of the case, II fails.

One lesson from this example is the importance of not confusing which metaphysical possibilities are genuine, which is the issue here, with epistemic possibilities, which are not the fundamental issue here (though of course the metaphysical has consequences for the epistemic). Certain kinds of ignorance, epistemic possibilities that are left open, can occur in a Leibnizian universe in which the thinker does not have full knowledge of which relations individuate the thinker's current region. But this ignorance, unlike that of Newtonian absolute location, can be expressed, and can in principle be overcome.

I conjecture that it is in fact also the case that II→ED. The intuitive consideration in support argues the point by contraposition. If there were no excess dimensions, there would be no difficulty of principle in thinking about the entities or properties in question, so any ignorance about the subject matter could hardly be inexpressible. There would be contents and meanings available to express what it is that is not known.

If it is indeed the case that II⟷ED, so that the excess dimension and inexpressible ignorance approaches classify all the examples the same way, the question arises: which approach, if either, is more fundamental? Or are they both a consequence of something more fundamental?

It may be tempting to say that the excess dimension approach is more fundamental, because failures of expressibility must trace back to the failure of conditions for the possession of genuine concepts. But the failure of conditions for genuine concept possession arguably traces back in turn to the failure of facts about the excess dimensions in a proposed ontology to be explanatory of anything at all outside the realm of the excess dimensions. The impossibility of saying what it is for a thinker to stand in a relation to one rather than another absolute location, or to one rather than another strong possibile, and the rest, all seem to be special cases of the impossibility of saying what it is for anything at all to stand in a given relation to one rather than another of the problematic entities.

Similarly, it is plausible that if an ontology that is in question were to have explanatory powers in domains outside that ontology, a thinker could use those relations in expressing some aspects of her ignorance about the ontology in question. The thinker could express her ignorance of such-and-such facts about the entities that explain the phenomena outside the domain of the ontology in question. So if there were some such explanatory powers, there would not be inexpressible ignorance. I conjecture that the explanatory redundancy of the problematic ontologies underlies both ED and II.

If some conception of the metaphysics of a domain leads to insoluble problems about the possibility of possessing concepts of that domain, those problems must have their source in some defect or defects in that conception of the metaphysics of the domain, defects in the metaphysics that are specifiable independently of features of thinkers and concept possession. A corresponding principle is equally plausible in relation to epistemic defects, such as inexpressible ignorance. If some conception of the metaphysics of a domain leads to insoluble problems in the epistemology of that domain, problems that ought to be soluble, then those epistemological problems must have their source in some defect or defects in that conception of the metaphysics of that domain, defects specifiable independently of the relations of elements of that domain to thinkers.

The problematic ontologies explain nothing that cannot equally be explained without them. Absolute space, contrary to what Newton himself thought, is not needed to explain anything that could not be equally explained using a version of Newtonian laws in a Leibnizian universe. Cartesian egos cannot explain anything that cannot equally be explained by construing the first person as referring to a subject whose identity over time is grounded in the identity of something else (a human body, or brain, or physical integrating apparatus), and explained by the various experiential and representational capacities those entities can sustain. Legitimate ontologies of either the spatiotemporal world, or the mental world, must not be explanatorily redundant.

Grasp of the concept of some newly proposed entity or range of entities must either involve some kind of grasp of its theoretical role, or some explanation by the entity or entities of the mental states of the thinker, such as her perceptual states. My position has been that there is no genuine explanatory role of absolute space, or of the other problematic ontologies. Nor do these entities enter the explanation of perceptual or other states that might be involved in grasp of concepts or notions of these alleged entities.

The absence of a genuine explanatory role is crucial. In discourse that purports to be about absolute space, we do not, to say it one more time, have merely a case of sense without reference: for this is not a case of a specifiable explanatory role that is not in fact satisfied by anything. Rather, because there is no explanatory role of absolute space in Newton's theory at all, there is not even a sense-fixing role at all that will pick out absolute space. There are genuine explanatory roles in Newtonian theory, but they will pick out something less stringent than absolute space and time.

Here then again there is a contrast with other cases in which we seemingly have sense without reference. If there were a phlogiston-like substance, or if there were unicorn-like creatures, we could refer to it or them respectively. But if the core of Newton's theory were true, we would still not have a way of thinking of absolute space, as opposed to neo-Newtonian space, to something more radically relationally individuated. For while the role attributed to phlogiston is something that might be fulfilled by something in some possible universe, and while there might be a species with unicorn-like features, there is no specification given to us of what absolute space would explain. Unlike phlogiston, absolute space is noncontingently explanatorily redundant. The metaphysical defect does correspondingly generate conceptual defects.

There have been interesting investigations of what notions are genuinely meaningful in various scientific theories. The work of McKinsey and Suppes (1955) elucidating meaningfulness in classical mechanics by reference to certain kinds of Galilean invariances is one example of this. I suggest that such investigations, when successful, give substantive, domain-specific instantiations of the conditions for some property, magnitude, or relation to be genuinely explanatory, in the domain and theory in question. Such investigations elaborate the intrinsic connection between the metaphysical notion of explanatory significance, on the one hand, and meaningfulness or genuine conceptual content, on the other, as it is exhibited in the particular domain and theory in question.

When the impossibility of a good account of concepts of an alleged domain can be traced back to defects in the proposed metaphysics for that domain, we have another illustration of the explanatory priority, in the order of philosophical explanation, of metaphysics over the theory of meaning and intentional content. I have emphasized the thesis that if there is no possibility of giving a condition for being the reference of an alleged concept, it cannot be a genuine concept at all. But that thesis, linking conditions for reference and the existence of a concept, is in itself neutral on the question of the explanatory priority of the metaphysics of the domain the concept is about. Indeed a thesis linking reference-conditions and concepts or sense was in fact accepted by Dummett, who explicitly, and at length, rejects any explanatory priority for metaphysics.[5] By itself, the link between reference-conditions and concepts is compatible with a priority of concepts over metaphysics, and is equally compatible with a no-priority thesis. But when we have an explanation from the nature of the distinction between good and bad metaphysics for various proposed domains of why there cannot be good fundamental reference-conditions for certain proposed concepts, we have thereby an example of the philosophical explanatory priority of metaphysics over the theory of intentional content. In such cases, conceptual deficiencies are traceable back to, and are explained by, defects in a proposed metaphysics. Taken as a whole, the arguments of this chapter can be taken as a further part of the case for an explanatory priority of metaphysics over the theory of meaning and intentional content.

---

[5] For his views on reference-conditions as individuating sense, see Dummett (1981).

Kant said in several famous passages that the limits of intelligibility are given by the bounds of possible experience (for instance, Kant 1998: A498, B524–5). My position is that the limits of intelligibility are set not by application of the notion of possible experience, but by the range of legitimate possession-conditions or understanding-conditions, conditions that are not in fact tied in every case to the possibility of experience of a genuine content's holding. What is wrong with absolute space, strong possibilia, and the rest is not just that they involve commitments to unknowability, or to outrunning possible experience, but rather that there is in the first instance no possible understanding-condition or possession-condition for concepts of them, where understanding-conditions or possession-conditions are required to determine a reference-condition. The boundaries of legitimate understanding-conditions will certainly accommodate language and thought about what is outside our light cone, but they will not include absolute space, strong possibilia, quiddities, and Cartesian egos.[6] If the arguments I have been presenting are sound, the range of legitimate understanding-conditions is explained by the range of legitimate reference-relations, and ultimately by the legitimate metaphysics for any domain that is in question. The idea that the human mind can somehow latch on to physical properties that have no explanatory powers in the physical world involves an exceptionalism about the minds that inhabit that same physical world. It seems impossible to justify the exceptionalism. Our efforts are better directed to understanding our distinctive relations to what in the world does have a genuine metaphysics. The limits of understanding are explained by the limits of a metaphysics of a domain, and not conversely.

---

[6] This is also, incidentally, another example in which any updated, revised form of Kant's position in metaphysics, epistemology, and the theory of understanding would need to draw on a substantive theory of the nature of Fregean senses, and their constitutive relations to the level of genuine reference.

7

Conclusion

Avenues for Further Development

There are several broad areas on which the conclusions of this book bear, and which suggest both tasks for further development and some distinctive challenges. I mention five.

(1) The correct account of the relation between concepts of a domain and the metaphysics of the domain bears in various ways on the issues about the acquisition of those concepts. In the spirit of Chomsky's discussion of a language-acquisition device, we can formulate the issues by speaking of a concept-acquisition device (Chomsky 1965: ch. 1, §6).

Consider concepts of a domain for which the metaphysics-first view is correct, and in which there is causal interaction between the domain of objects and properties on the one hand, and the device on the other. Once the device has acquired those concepts, it will be in a state that involves a certain complex causal sensitivity to those objects and properties. By contrast, in noncausal metaphysics-first cases, as in the treatment in Chapter 5 of numbers, the sensitivity in the acquired state will be a sensitivity to the holding of the principles that individuate the ontology. In both cases, however, the concept-acquisition device will have to have some procedure for selecting, from a body of data of positive and possibly negative instances (analogous to Chomsky's 'primary linguistic data'), certain properties as the ones to which it needs to be sensitive if the concept is to be mastered. This selection procedure will need to involve a sensitivity to certain higher-order properties $\{P_1, \ldots P_n\}$ of the properties of the instances. The instantiation by positive instances of the target concept of first-order properties which in turn have higher-order properties $\{P_1, \ldots P_n\}$ will favour the selection of those first-order properties as what is required for instantiation of the target concept. We need a much better general philosophical understanding of this process, and how it could operate. The higher-order properties $\{P_1, \ldots P_n\}$ obviously cannot involve concepts of the domain, on pain of presupposing what was to be explained, viz. acquisition of those concepts. The higher-order properties $\{P_1, \ldots P_n\}$ of first-order properties may be innate in the psychological structures of the concept-learner; they may be species-specific; and their playing this role will likely be a result of natural selection mechanisms, even if the first-order properties do not involve psychology at all. The first-order properties in question may not involve concepts in the family to be acquired, but they may involve other concepts. The consideration of what is involved in a good theory of a concept-acquisition device needs to involve a constant back-and-forth between the demands of a good empirical theory of the contingent features of the device, the constraints imposed by the nature of the concept to be acquired, and its relations to the metaphysics of the domain to which the concept refers.

(2) Reflection on concept-acquisition also highlights what is independently clear: the need for a much better philosophical understanding in detail of the no-priority cases in the sense of Chapter 1. There must equally be an account of concept-acquisition in the no-priority cases. In the no-priority cases, there can be no question of an explanation solely in terms of sensitivity to properties whose nature is explanatorily independent of the concepts whose acquisition is in question, because the properties picked out in the domain are precisely not so independent in the no-priority cases. A more detailed account of the character of various kinds of no-priority cases, and of concept-acquisition devices that would allow us to attain the concepts for which the no-priority classification is correct, is needed.

(3) In Chapter 5, I developed an account under the rubric 'Individuation Precedes Representation' solely for the cases of natural numbers and real numbers. Accounts according to which Individuation Precedes Representation may be available for other domains too. It is tempting to develop them for normative cases, both for the normative properties of concepts, and for moral and political thought. The general model would be one in which we individuate some property or relation, such as that of a fair distribution or arrangement, or the conditions for a correct application of a concept, and then develop a theory of how a thinker can represent these properties and relations by grasping these conditions of individuation. As in the case of numbers, this can be done without requiring causal contact with a normative realm. There are opportunities for explaining how certain systems of representation, related to the individuating conditions, may be selected for both at the individual level and the social level. A territory opens up in which there is a middle route between mind-dependent views on the one hand, and on the other, extreme forms of Platonism about values that leave it

problematic how minds could ever grasp values at all. The treatment of numbers in Chapter 5 also steered between these extremes.

(4) There is the task of elucidating the relations between the conclusions of this book and what in earlier work I called the Integration Challenge; the challenge of properly integrating our accounts of the metaphysics and the epistemology of a domain (Peacocke 1999). In effect, we have here a second integration challenge, raised by the position for which I have been arguing in this book. (a) The metaphysics of a domain is involved in an account of grasping concepts of that domain. (b) Grasping concepts of a domain involves appreciating that certain states and propositions give good reasons for making judgements about that domain involving those concepts. If both (a) and (b) are true, then we ought to be able to offer an explanation of how the involvement of metaphysics in an account of grasping concepts contributes to the status of certain states and propositions as giving good reasons for making judgements about that domain using those concepts. This is the second Integration Challenge that we ought to address. We will not have a full philosophical understanding of the nexus of interrelations between metaphysics, epistemology, and concept possession—either in general or in particular domains—until we have addressed this second Integration Challenge. If the arguments of this book are roughly in the right direction, a good conception of the relations between the metaphysics of a domain and contents concerning the domain should function as a structuring principle in all these investigations.

(5) It is a highly plausible principle, with its origins in central Europe, that any mental relation to an object must be a relation to that object under some mode of presentation or other. So if any mode of presentation involves the metaphysics of a domain, as the arguments of this book suggest, then any mental state that relates a mind to an object will involve the metaphysics of that domain. Mental states with content, whether specified de re, de dicto, or any combination thereof, ineluctably involve the world and its nature.

Bibliography

Anscombe, G. E. M. (1969) 'Causality and Extensionality', *Journal of Philosophy* 66(6): 152–9

Bardon, A. (2013) *A Brief History of the Philosophy of Time*. New York: Oxford University Press

Block, N. (1990) 'Inverted Earth', *Philosophical Perspectives* 4: 53–79

Block, N. (2016) 'The Anna Karenina Principle and Skepticism about Unconscious Perception', *Philosophy and Phenomenological Research* 93: 452–9

Brandom, R. (1994) *Making It Explicit: Reasoning, Representing, and Discursive Commitment*. Cambridge, MA: Harvard University Press

Brandom, R. (2000) *Articulating Reasons: An Introduction to Inferentialism* Cambridge, MA: Harvard University Press

Brandom, R. (2009) *Reason in Philosophy: Animating Ideas*. Cambridge, MA: Harvard University Press

Brewer, B. (1992) 'Self-Location and Agency', *Mind* 101: 17–34

Burge, T. (1979) 'Individualism and the Mental', *Midwest Studies in Philosophy* 4: 73–121

Burge, T. (2003) 'Perceptual Entitlement', *Philosophy and Phenomenological Research* 67(3): 503–48

Burge, T. (2005) 'Frege and the Hierarchy' and 'Postscript to "Frege and the Hierarchy"', in his *Truth, Thought, Reason: Essays on Frege*. Oxford: Oxford University Press

Burge, T. (2010) *Origins of Objectivity*. Oxford: Oxford University Press

Carey, S. (2009) *The Origin of Concepts*. New York: Oxford University Press

Carnap, R. (1956) *Meaning and Necessity: A Study in Semantics and Modal Logic*. Chicago, IL: University of Chicago Press

Chalmers, D. (2002) 'Does Conceivability Entail Possibility?', in *Conceivability and Possibility*, ed. T. Gendler and J. Hawthorne. Oxford: Oxford University Press

Chalmers, D. (2011) 'Propositions and Attitude Ascriptions: A Fregean Account', *Noûs* 45: 595–639

Chalmers, D. (2012) *Constructing the World*. Oxford: Oxford University Press

Chang, H. (2010) 'The Hidden History of Phlogiston: How Philosophical Failure Can Generate Historiographical Refinement', *HYLE: International Journal for Philosophy of Chemistry* 16: 47–79

Chisholm, R. (1979) 'Brentano's Analysis of the Consciousness of Time', *Midwest Studies in Philosophy* 4: 3–16

Chomsky, N. (1965) *Aspects of the Theory of Syntax*. Cambridge, MA: MIT Press

Cohen, J., Hansel, C., and Sylvester, J. (1953) 'A New Phenomenon in Time Judgment', *Nature* 4385: 901

Copeland, J. (1978) 'Communication Systems of Fireflies', *American Scientist* 66: 340–6

Dasgupta, S. (2015) 'Inexpressible Ignorance', *Philosophical Review* 124: 441–80

Davies, M. (1981) Meaning, Quantification, Necessity: Themes in Philosophical Logic. London: Routledge and Kegan Paul

Davidson, D. (2001a) 'The Second Person', in his *Subjective, Intersubjective, Objective*. Oxford: Oxford University Press

Davidson, D. (2001b) 'Three Varieties of Knowledge', in his *Subjective, Intersubjective, Objective*. Oxford: Oxford University Press

Dedekind, R. (1963) *Essays on the Theory of Numbers*, tr. W. Berman. New York: Dover

Devitt, M. (2010) *Putting Metaphysics First: Essays on Metaphysics and Epistemology*. Oxford: Oxford University Press

Dowker, F. (2010) 'An Invitation to Causal Sets', http://pirsa.org/10100038. Accessed 14 May 2017

Dummett, M. (1973) *Frege: Philosophy of Language*. London: Duckworth

Dummett, M. (1981) *The Interpretation of Frege's Philosophy*. Cambridge, MA: Harvard University Press

Dummett, M. (1991) *The Logical Basis of Metaphysics*. Cambridge, MA: Harvard University Press

Eilan, N. (2016) 'You Me and the World', *Analysis* 76: 311–24

Euclid. (1956) *The Thirteen Books of the Elements*, Vol. 2 (Books III–IX), tr. T. Heath, second edition. Dover: New York

Evans, G. (1975) 'Identity and Predication', *Journal of Philosophy* 72: 343–63

Evans, G. (1982) *The Varieties of Reference*. Oxford: Oxford University Press

Evans, G. (1985) 'Understanding Demonstratives', in his *Collected Papers*. Oxford: Oxford University Press

Field, H. (1973) 'Theory Change and the Indeterminacy of Reference', *Journal of Philosophy* 70: 462–81

Fine, K. (1995) 'The Logic of Essence', *Journal of Philosophical Logic* 24: 241–73

Fine, K. (2002) *The Limits of Abstraction*. Oxford: Oxford University Press

Firestone, C. and Scholl, B. (2016) 'Cognition Does Not Affect Perception: Evaluating the Evidence for "Top-Down" Effects', *Behavioral and Brain Sciences* 39: 1–19

Fodor, J. (1974) 'Special Sciences (Or: The Disunity of Science as a Working Hypothesis)', *Synthese* 28: 97–115

Frege, G. (1967) *Grundgesetze der Arithmetik*. Hildesheim: Olms

Frege, G. (2013) *The Basic Laws of Arithmetic*, tr. and ed. P. Ebert, M. Rossberg, and C. Wright. Oxford: Oxford University Press

Gallese, V. (2005) '"Being Like Me": Self-Other Identity, Mirror Neurons, and Empathy', in *Perspectives on Imitation: From Neuroscience to Social Science, Volume 1: Mechanisms of Imitation and Imitation in Animals*, ed. S. Hurley and N. Chater. Cambridge, MA: MIT Press

Gallistel, C. (1990) *The Organization of Learning*. Cambridge, MA: MIT Press

Gibbard, A. (1990) *Wise Choices, Apt Feelings: A Theory of Normative Judgment*. Oxford: Oxford University Press

Goodman, N. (1968) *Languages of Art*. Indianapolis, IN: Bobbs-Merrill

Habermas, J. (1992) *Postmetaphysical Thinking: Philosophical Essays*, tr. W. Hohengarten. Oxford: Polity Press

Hale, B. (2000) 'Reals by Abstraction', *Philosophia Mathematica* 8: 100–23

Hale, B. and Wright, C. (2009) 'The Metaontology of Abstraction', in *Metametaphysics: New Essays on the Foundations of Ontology*, ed. D. Chalmers, D. Manley, and R. Wasserman. Oxford: Oxford University Press

Harman, G. (1982) 'Conceptual Role Semantics', *Notre Dame Journal of Formal Logic* 23: 242–56

Harman, G. (1999) '(Nonsolipsistic) Conceptual Role Semantics', in his *Reasoning, Meaning, and Mind*. Oxford: Oxford University Press

Haugeland, J. (1998) 'Analog and Analog', in his *Having Thought: Essays in the Metaphysics of Mind*. Cambridge, MA: Harvard University Press

Hilbert, D. (1971) *Foundations of Geometry*. La Salle, IL: Open Court

Hodes, H. (1990) 'Where Do the Natural Numbers Come From?', *Synthese* 84: 347–407

Hölder, O. (1901) 'Die Axiome der Quantität und die Lehre vom Mas', *Bericht. Sächsisch Akademie der Wissenschaften., Math-Physik Klasse* 53: 1–64

Hornsby, J. (1980) *Actions*. London: Routledge Kegan Paul

Hume, D. (2000) *A Treatise of Human Nature*, ed. D. Norton and M. Norton. Oxford: Oxford University Press

Hurley, S. (1998) *Consciousness in Action*. Cambridge, MA: Harvard University Press

Iacoboni, M. (2008) *Mirroring People: The New Science of How We Connect with Others*. New York: Farrar, Straus, and Giroux

Ismael, J. (2011) 'Temporal Experience', in *The Oxford Handbook of Philosophy of Time*, ed. C. Callender. Oxford: Oxford University Press

Jackson, A. (1960) *Analog Computation*. New York: McGraw-Hill

James, W. (1910) *The Principles of Psychology*. New York: Holt

Johnston, M. (2017) 'The Personite Problem: Should Practical Reason be Tabled?', *Noûs* 51: 617–44

Kant, I. (1998) *Critique of Pure Reason*, tr. and ed. P. Guyer and A. Wood. Cambridge: Cambridge University Press

Kaplan, D. (1989) 'Demonstratives', in *Themes from Kaplan*, ed. J. Almog, J. Perry, and H. Wettstein. New York: Oxford University Press

Katz, M. (2008) 'Analog and Digital Representation', *Minds and Machines* 18: 403–8

Kelly, S. (2005) 'The Puzzle of Temporal Experience', in *Cognition and Neuroscience*, ed. A. Brook and K. Akins. Cambridge: Cambridge University Press

Kitcher, Philip (1978) 'The Plight of the Platonist', *Noûs* 12: 119–36

Kosslyn, S. (1994) *Image and Brain: The Resolution of the Imagery Debate*. Cambridge, MA: MIT Press

Kosslyn, S., Ball, T., and Reiser, B. (1978) 'Visual Images Preserve Metric Spatial Information: Evidence from Studies of Image Scanning', *Journal of Experimental Psychology: Human Perception and Performance* 4(1): 47–60

Kripke, S. (1980) *Naming and Necessity*. Cambridge, MA: Harvard University Press

Kripke, S. (2011) 'The First Person', in his *Philosophical Troubles Vol. 1*. New York: Oxford University Press

Kuhn, T. (1996) *The Structure of Scientific Revolutions*, third edn. Chicago, IL: Chicago University Press

Langton, R. (1998) *Kantian Humility: Our Ignorance of Things in Themselves*. New York: Oxford University Press

Lee, G. (2014) 'Temporal Experience and the Structure of Temporal Experience', *Philosophers' Imprint* 14(3): 1–21

Lee, G. (2017) 'Making Sense of Subjective Time', in *The Routledge Handbook of Philosophy of Temporal Experience*, ed. I. Phillips. Abingdon and New York: Routledge

Leibniz, G. (1918) *Discourse on Metaphysics*, tr. G. Montgomery. Chicago, IL: Open Court

Leibniz, G. (1969) *Philosophical Papers and Letters*, ed. L. Loemker. Dordrecht: Reidel

Leibniz, G. (1989) *Philosophical Essays*, tr. R. Ariew and D. Garber. Indianapolis, IN: Hackett

Leslie, S.-J. and Johnston, M. (forthcoming) 'Essence and Accident: Against Limited Variety'

Lewis, D. (1971) 'Analog and Digital', *Noûs* 5(3): 321–7

Lewis, D. (1983) 'New Work for a Theory of Universals', *Australasian Journal of Philosophy* 61: 343–77

Lewis, D. (1984) 'Putnam's Paradox', *Australasian Journal of Philosophy* 62: 221–36

Lewis, D. (1986) *On the Plurality of Worlds*. Oxford: Blackwell

Lewis, D. (2007) 'Ramseyan Humility', in *Conceptual Analysis and Philosophical Naturalism*, ed. D. Braddon-Mitchell and R. Nola. Cambridge, MA: MIT Press

Linnebo, Ø. (2012) 'Metaontological Minimalism', *Philosophy Compass* 7: 139–51

Lloyd Morgan, C. (1904) *An Introduction to Comparative Psychology*, second edn. New York: Charles Scribner's Sons

Lupyan, G. (2016) 'Not Even Wrong: The "It's Just X" Fallacy', *Behavioral and Brain Sciences* 39: 40–31

Maley, C. (2011) 'Analog and Digital, Continuous and Discrete', *Philosophical Studies* 155: 117–31

Marcel, A. (2003) 'The Sense of Agency: Awareness and Ownership of Action', in *Agency and Self-Awareness*, ed. J. Roessler and N. Eilan. Oxford: Oxford University Press

Maudlin, T. (1993) 'Buckets of Water and Waves of Space', *Philosophy of Science* 60: 183–203

McDowell, J. (1994) *Mind and World*. Cambridge, MA: Harvard University Press

McKinsey, J. and Suppes, P. (1955) 'On the Notion of Invariance in Classical Mechanics', *British Journal for the Philosophy of Science* 5: 290–302

Mead, G. H. (1967) *Mind, Self, and Society: From the Standpoint of a Social Behaviorist*, ed. C. Morris. Chicago, IL: Chicago University Press

Meltzoff, A. (2007) 'The "Like Me" Framework for Recognizing and Becoming an Intentional Agent', *Acta Psychologica* 124: 26–43

Morales, J. (forthcoming) Doctoral Thesis, Columbia University

Mudrik, L., Breska, A., Lamy, D., and Deouell, L. (2011) 'Integration Without Awareness: Expanding the Limits of Unconscious Processing', *Psychological Science* 22: 764–70

Mundy, B. (1987) 'The Metaphysics of Quantity', *Philosophical Studies* 51: 29–54

Nagel, T. (1974) 'What Is it Like to Be a Bat?', *Philosophical Review* 83: 435–50

Neander, K. (2016) 'Peacocke on Primitive Self-Representation', *Analysis* 76: 324–34

Newton, I. (1962) *Mathematical Principles of Natural Philosophy*, tr. A. Motte and F. Cajori. Berkeley, CA: University of California Press

O'Brien, L. (2007) *Self-Knowing Agents*. Oxford: Oxford University Press

Parfit, D. (1986) *Reasons and Persons*. Oxford: Oxford University Press

Parsons, C. (1990) 'The Structuralist View of Mathematical Objects', *Synthese* 84: 303–46

Peacocke, C. (1981) 'Demonstrative Thought and Psychological Explanation', *Synthese* 49: 187–217

Peacocke, C. (1983) *Sense and Content: Experience, Thought, and Their Relations*. Oxford: Oxford University Press

Peacocke, C. (1985) 'Imagination, Possibility and Experience', in *Essays on Berkeley*, ed. J. Foster and H. Robinson. Oxford: Oxford University Press

Peacocke, C. (1988) 'The Limits of Intelligibility: A Post-Verificationist Proposal', *Philosophical Review* 97: 463–96

Peacocke, C. (1989) 'What Are Concepts?', *Midwest Studies in Philosophy* 14: 1–28

Peacocke, C. (1992) *A Study of Concepts*. Cambridge, MA: MIT Press

Peacocke, C. (1993) 'Externalist Explanation', *Proceedings of the Aristotelian Society* 67: 203–30

Peacocke, C. (1996) 'Entitlement, Self-Knowledge and Conceptual Redeployment', *Proceedings of the Aristotelian Society* 96: 117–58

Peacocke, C. (1998) 'The Philosophy of Language', in *Philosophy 2: Further Through the Subject*, ed. A. Grayling. Oxford: Oxford University Press

Peacocke, C. (1999) *Being Known*. Oxford: Oxford University Press

Peacocke, C. (2001) 'Does Perception Have a Nonconceptual Content?', *Journal of Philosophy* 98: 239–64

Peacocke, C. (2002) 'Principles for Possibilia', *Noûs* 36: 486–508

Peacocke, C. (2004) *The Realm of Reason*. Oxford: Oxford University Press

Peacocke, C. (2007) 'Mental Action and Self-Awareness I', in *Contemporary Debates in the Philosophy of Mind*, ed. J. Cohen and B. McLaughlin. Malden, MA: Blackwell

Peacocke, C. (2008) *Truly Understood*. Oxford: Oxford University Press

Peacocke, C. (2009) 'Frege's Hierarchy: A Puzzle', in *The Philosophy of David Kaplan*, ed. J. Almog and P. Leonardi. Oxford: Oxford University Press

Peacocke, C. (2014a) *The Mirror of the World: Subjects, Consciousness, and Self-Consciousness*. Oxford: Oxford University Press

Peacocke, C. (2014b) 'Perception, Biology, Action, and Knowledge', *Philosophy and Phenomenological Research* 88: 477–84

Peacocke, C. (2015) 'Magnitudes: Metaphysics, Explanation, and Perception', in *Mind, Language and Action: Proceedings of the 36th International Wittgenstein Symposium*, ed. D. Moyal-Sharrock, V. Munz, and A. Coliva. Berlin: de Gruyter

Peacocke, C. (2017a) 'Temporal Perception, Magnitudes, and Phenomenal Externalism', in *The Routledge Handbook of Philosophy of Temporal Experience*, ed. I. Phillips. Abingdon, Oxon: Routledge

Peacocke, C. (2017b) 'Philosophical Reflections on the First Person, the Body, and Agency', in *The Subject's Matter: Self-Consciousness and the Body*, ed. F. de Vignemont and A. Alsmith. Cambridge, MA: MIT Press

Peacocke, C. (2018) 'Epistemology, the Constitutive, and the Principle-Based Account of Modality', in *The Routledge Handbook of Modality*, ed. O. Bueno and S. Shalkowski. Abingdon, Oxon and New York: Routledge

Peacocke, C. (forthcoming) 'How Is Logical Inference Possible?', in *Judgement*, ed. B. Ball and C. Schuringa. London: Routledge

Perry, J. (1979) 'The Problem of the Essential Indexical', *Noûs* 13: 3–21

Perry, J. (2002a) 'The Self, Self-Knowledge, and Self-Notions', in his *Identity, Personal Identity, and the Self*. Indianapolis, IN: Hackett

Perry, J. (2002b) *Identity, Personal Identity, and the Self*. Indianapolis, IN: Hackett

Phillips, I. (2013a) 'Perceiving the Passing of Time', *Proceedings of the Aristotelian Society* 113: 225–52

Phillips, I. (2013b) 'Hearing and Hallucinating Silence', in *Hallucination: Philosophy and Psychology*, ed. F. Macpherson and D. Platchias. Cambridge, MA: MIT Press

Phillips, I. (2014) 'Breaking the Silence: Motion Silencing and Experience of Change', *Philosophical Studies* 168: 693–707

Phillips, I. (2016) 'Consciousness and Criterion: On Block's Case for Unconscious Seeing', *Philosophy and Phenomenological Research* 93: 419–51

Piccinini, G. (2015) *Physical Computation: A Mechanistic Account*. Oxford: Oxford University Press

Pooley, O. (2103) 'Substantivalist and Relationist Approaches to Spacetime', in *The Oxford Handbook of Philosophy of Physics*, ed. R. Batterman. Oxford: Oxford University Press

Prior, A. (1960) 'The Runabout Inference-Ticket', *Analysis* 21: 38–9

Putnam, H. (1973) 'Meaning and Reference', *The Journal of Philosophy* 70: 699–711

Putnam, H. (1975) 'On Properties', in his *Philosophical Papers Volume I: Mathematics, Matter, and Method*. Cambridge: Cambridge University Press

Putnam, H. (1977) 'Realism and Reason', *Proceedings of the American Philosophical Association* 50: 483–98

Quine, W. (1960) *Word and Object*. Cambridge, MA: MIT Press

Quine, W. (1969) *Ontological Relativity and Other Essays*. New York: Columbia University Press

Quine, W. (1970) 'On the Reasons for Indeterminacy of Translation', *Journal of Philosophy* 67: 178–83

Recanati, F. (2012) *Mental Files*. Oxford: Oxford University Press

Reichenbach, H. (1938) *Experience and Prediction: An Analysis of the Foundations and the Structure of Knowledge*. Chicago, IL: University of Chicago Press

Renner, M. (1960) 'Contribution of the Honey Bee to the Study of Time-Sense and Astronomical Orientation', *Cold Spring Harbor Symposium on Quantitative Biology* 25: 361–7

Roca-Royes, S. (2010) 'Modal Epistemology, Modal Concepts and the Integration Challenge', *Dialectica* 64: 335–61

Rock, I. (1973) *Orientation and Form*. New York: Academic Press

Rosen, G. (2002) 'Peacocke on Modality', *Philosophy and Phenomenological Research* 64: 641–8

Sartre, J.-P. (1992) *Being and Nothingness: A Phenomenological Essay on Ontology*, tr. H. Barnes. New York: Washington Square Press

Sartre, J.-P. (2004) *The Transcendence of the Ego: A Sketch for a Phenomenological Description*, tr. S. Richmond. Abingdon, Oxon: Routledge

Schellenberg, S. (2016) '*De Se* Content and *De Hinc* Content', *Analysis* 76: 334–45

Schiffer, S. (2003) *The Things We Mean*. Oxford: Oxford University Press

Schlesinger, G. (1994) 'The Stream of Time', in *The New Theory of Time*, ed. L. Nathan Oaklander and Quentin Smith. New Haven, CT: Yale University Press

Scott, D. (1967) *A General Theory of Magnitudes*, Mimeo, circulated at the University of Oxford, Mathematical Institute

Shepard, R. and Chipman, S. (1970) 'Second-Order Isomorphism of Internal Representations: Shapes of States', *Cognitive Psychology* 1: 1–17

Shepard, R. and Metzler, J. (1971) 'Mental Rotation of Three-Dimensional Objects', *Science* 171: 701–3

Shoemaker, S. (1984a) 'Embodiment and Behavior', in his *Identity, Cause, and Mind: Philosophical Essays*. Cambridge: Cambridge University Press

Shoemaker, S. (1984b) 'Self-Reference and Self-Awareness', in his *Identity, Cause, and Mind: Philosophical Essays*. Cambridge: Cambridge University Press

Shoemaker, S. (1984c) 'Causality and Properties', in his *Identity, Cause and Mind: Philosophical Essays*. Cambridge: Cambridge University Press

Sklar, L. (1976) *Space, Time, and Spacetime*. Berkeley and Los Angeles, CA: University of California Press

Spearman, C. (1904) 'General Intelligence, Objectively Determined and Measured', *American Journal of Psychology* 15: 201–92

Spering, M., Pomplun, M., and Carrasco, M. (2011) 'Tracking Without Perceiving: A Dissociation Between Eye Movements and Motion Perception', *Psychological Science* 22: 216–25

Stein, H. (1967) 'Newtonian Space-Time', *Texas Quarterly* 10: 174–200

Strawson, P. (1966) *The Bounds of Sense*. London: Methuen

Suchow, J. and Alvarez, G. (2011) 'Motion Silences Awareness of Visual Change', *Current Biology* 21: 140–3

Suppes, P. (1951) 'A Set of Independent Axioms for Extensive Quantities', *Portugaliae Mathematica* 10: 163–72

Suppes, P. and Zinnes, J. (1963) 'Basic Measurement Theory', in *Handbook of Mathematical Psychology, Volume 1*, ed. R. Duncan Luce, Robert R. Bush, and Eugene Galanter. New York: Wiley

Thompson, B. (2010) 'The Spatial Content of Experience', *Philosophy and Phenomenological Research* 81: 146–94

Vaidya, A. (2015) 'The Epistemology of Modality', in *The Stanford Encyclopedia of Philosophy*, ed. E. Zalta, https://plato.stanford.edu/entries/modality-epistemology. Accessed 28 December 2016

Walsh, V. (2003) 'A Theory of Magnitude: Common Cortical Metrics of Time, Space and Quantity', *Trends in Cognitive Science* 7(11): 483–8

Watzl, S. (2013) 'Silencing the Experience of Change', *Philosophical Studies* 165: 1009–32

Wiggins, D. (2001) *Sameness and Substance Renewed*. Cambridge: Cambridge University Press

Williams, B. (1973) *Problems of the Self*. Cambridge: Cambridge University Press

Williams, B. (1978) *Descartes: The Project of Pure Enquiry*. Harmondsworth: Penguin

Williams, D. (1951) 'The Myth of Passage', *The Journal of Philosophy* 48: 457–72

Wright, C. (1983) *Frege's Conception of Natural Numbers as Objects*. Aberdeen: Aberdeen University Press

Wright, C. (1987) 'Reply to Strawson', in his *Realism, Meaning, and Truth*. Oxford: Blackwell

Wright, C. (1996) 'Human Nature?', *European Journal of Philosophy* 4(2): 235–53

Wynn, K. (1990) 'Children's Understanding of Counting', *Cognition* 36: 155–93

Wynn, K. (1992) 'Children's Acquisition of the Number Words and the Counting System', *Cognitive Psychology* 24: 220–51

Yablo, S. (2008) 'Is Conceivability a Guide to Possibility?', in his *Thoughts: Papers on Mind, Meaning, and Modality*. Oxford: Oxford University Press

Young, H. and Freedman, R. (2004) *University Physics with Modern Physics, 11th Edition*. San Francisco, CA: Pearson Addison Wesley

Index

absolute space and time 28–9, 172, 174–83, 185–9, 194–5, 198–9, 201, 203
absolutism about magnitudes 43–4
abstract objects 32, 166–70
acquisition of concepts 204–5
action 31–2, 47, 67–8, 81–3, 91–4, 101–2, 108–9, 114, 122–7, 136–8
agency-involving account of the first person 122–9
Albert, D. 175
analogue mental process 54–9
anarchic hand 136–7
Anscombe, G. E. M. 17, 45
anthropocentrism about properties 37
anti-individualism in the theory of meaning and content 15
Applicationist Individuationism 140–4, 151, 153–4, 156–66, 168–9
arithmetical operations on natural numbers 144–5
asymmetry of individuation 149, 166
attention in perception 79

Ball, T. 54
Block, N. 84–5, 109–12
Brandom, R. 7–8, 35
Brentano, F. 104–5
Breska, A. 111
Burge, T. 12–13, 15, 23–4, 85, 87–8, 109, 178–9

Carey, S. 58, 135–6
Carnap, R. 36–7, 166–70
Carrasco, M. 111
Cartesian egos 173–4, 191–5, 199, 201, 203
causal explanation 12–14, 16–17, 21, 31, 41–7, 72–3
causal sensitivity 16, 21–2, 31–2, 74, 85, 87–8, 90–1
Chalmers, D. 74, 82–5, 141–2
Chipman, S. 57
Chisholm, R. 104–5
Chomsky, N. 204–5
Cohen, J. 87
concepts 4–6, 10–11, 16–18, 20, 23, 26, 33–4, 184–5, 206
conceptual role theories of meaning 35–6
constancy in perception 85–90
constitutive 4

continuity, not required for analogue computation 53
Copeland, J. 90
core cognition 58
crossworld excess dimension 184, 187, 189, 192–3

Dasgupta, S. 172, 175, 198–200
Davidson, D. 17, 21–5, 27
Dedekind, R. 156–61, 164
demonstratives 54, 59–61, 67–8
Deouell, L. 111
Descartes, R. 112–13
Devitt, M. 29–30
Discrimination Principle (Peacocke) 186–7
domain 4–7
Dowker, F. 53
Dummett, M. 2, 5, 7–10, 12–13, 15, 25–6, 29–30, 36, 202

entitlement 18–19
epistemology 2, 27–9, 33–4, 153, 200–1, 206
Euclid 45
Evans, G. 10–11, 134, 178–9, 184–5
excess dimension 183–93, 195, 199–200
experience as of change 97–100
explanatory priority 1–2, 5, 9
explanatory role 201–2
expressivism 6
extensions 43
extensive magnitudes 40–1, 47
externalist explanation 23–4, 67–8

fictional characters 20–1
fictionalism about natural numbers 142–3
Field, H. 178–80
Fine, K. 107, 149–53
Firestone, C. 70–1
first person 119–20, 192
Fodor, J. 52
frame of reference and magnitudes 42, 72–3
Freedman, R. 83–4
Frege, G. 7–8, 10–11, 40, 148–9, 151–2, 156–7
fundamental reference rule 194–5

Galileo 19
Gallese, V. 136–7
Gallistel, C. 88–9
generalized analogue magnitude representation system 58–9